"Fathers should be neither seen nor heard. That is the only proper basis for family life."

Oscar Wilde
"An Ideal Husband," Act III

From Here To Paternity

An intimate look at a father's day

JAY TEITEL

VIKING

VIKING
Published by the Penguin Group
Penguin Books Canada Ltd, 10 Alcorn Avenue, Toronto, Ontario, Canada M4V 3B2
Penguin Books Ltd, 27 Wrights Lane, London W8 5TZ, England
Viking Penguin, a division of Penguin Books USA Inc., 375 Hudson Street, New York, New York 10014, U.S.A.
Penguin Books Australia Ltd, Ringwood, Victoria, Australia
Penguin Books (NZ) Ltd, 182-190 Wairau Road, Auckland 10, New Zealand

Penguin Books Ltd, Registered Offices:
Harmondsworth, Middlesex, England

First published 1993

1 3 5 7 9 10 8 6 4 2

Printed and bound in Canada on acid free paper ♾

Canadian Cataloguing in Publication Data

Teitel, Jay, 1949–
From here to paternity

ISBN 0-670-84748-8

1. Fathers. 2. Father and child. I. Title

HQ756.T44 1993 306.874'2 C93-093515-2

For K. and S., for Z and E.R.
Initials don't tell half the story.

ACKNOWLEDGMENTS

It's tricky enough to write about your own family indirectly; to write about them without artifice is to play with fire. So that the reader doesn't feel singed along with yours truly, I'd like to affirm that the book that follows appears with the foreknowledge and endorsement of the immediate family members who appear in it — my wife, my two daughters and my son. It also appears with a couple of conditions: one, I had to agree to change their names (although as my older daughter pointed out, this cuts down on the "star" possibilities); and two, I had to promise to help them get *their* books published when they write them to correct all the mistakes I've made in this one. The former condition has already been fulfilled; the names have been changed to protect the innocent — them — and the guilty — me. Whatever versions of our shared reality they might come up with in the future I can only look forward to — I think.

That said, I have to restate the obvious: without, first and foremost, the love, support and good sportsmanship of my wife and my children, this book would not have been possible. I thank them for everything they've given me.

I'd also like to thank Meg Masters, for her unflagging patience and enthusiasm in editing this book, and Jan Whitford, for her grace and perseverance in convincing people, me included, that if an hour can hold infinity, a day can hold a book.

Finally I'd like to thank my own parents, in particular, noting the subject, my father. "The fundamental defect of fathers," wrote Bertrand Russell, "is that they want their children to be a credit to them." My father, bucking the crowd, always wanted his children to be a credit to themselves; anything we were was enough for him. I hope he enjoys this.

Jay Teitel
January 1993
Toronto, Canada

CONTENTS

1

Wake Up
Return from the Living Dead

"Tell me the story of when I was born, and you saved my life."
Ben Teitel, aged 5, 6, 7 & 8

7:00 a.m.

In the morning children are clear as blown glass; parents are zombies.

It has nothing to do with simple fatigue. If it were just simple fatigue how can I explain the fact that since I've had children I can sleep fourteen hours from a Friday night to a Saturday morning and still wake up feeling wrapped in gauze — or at least in one of the judo holds my son Ben's been working on lately? Judo would probably be merciful — it only binds the body. Lately my tiredness mummifies my syntax. It gropes for meaning the way a hand looks for an aspirin. Monosyllables abound. My wife's favourite word on waking up these days is "Wow," or sometimes "God." Mine is usually "Hi" (whether or not there's anyone else in the room). Sometimes I throw in a gesture my father used to make and that I would have been amazed to realize would one day belong to me, too. Call it the "father's salute." To execute the "father's salute" you start to raise a cupped palm to your forehead, as though you're planning to shield your eyes from blinding sunlight, and stop halfway there. Because of course there is no sun. "No wonder kids grow up crazy," Kurt Vonnegut has a character say in his novel *Cat's Cradle*. "A cat's cradle is nothing but a bunch of X's between somebody's hands, and . . . No damn cat, and no damn cradle." Waking up for me is like this now, all response without stimuli. Who am I talking to? What am I ducking from? No one knows.

By contrast, kids wake up instantaneously. Wake a child, especially a small child, and click, his mind is simply "on," with a clarity that goes leagues beyond cuteness. Children know exactly who they are when you wake them up, and exactly what their place in the universe is; it's not a great feat for them to rise completing a sentence they started the night before. The smartest things my children have said they've said in the sixty seconds after opening their eyes. The other day, for instance, I walked into my baby daughter Rosie's room when she was fast asleep on her back in her crib. She lifted her lids perfectly smoothly, as though she'd been expecting me — as though her ten hours of slumber had been an eyeblink — and said: "What's doing?"

What's doing. Two and a half years old, and a quip already on her lip. Hearing may be the most common form of hallucination, but I heard her say the words. By noon they'd be gone, fallen away like a pre-natal tooth, but in the morning they were accessible to her, glinting up from some corner of her deep structure like Chomskyite gold. I looked down at her like a rube and thought about a theory I'd read about once: the doctrine of Relative Psychic Distance. If when we sleep we return to the place we originally came from — the place before birth and maybe after death — then children have less far to go to get there, and a shorter distance to travel on the way back. So they arrive home faster, and it hurts less. It's like falling on a ski hill; the shorter you are the better.

Children are blown glass; parents are zombies. This is the cliché for parental waking-up. Like most parental clichés, it's perfectly accurate — and also a million miles from the truth.

On this particular morning, for instance, when I swim into consciousness, I'm staring at a rectangle of yellow light and listening to the sound of falling water. My wife is taking her shower. The yellow rectangle is the bathroom doorway, at least the doorway to the outer half of the bathroom, which actually has no door to close it. We've been meaning to add a door for six years now — ever since we moved to this house — but we never got around to it. Paula — my wife — could of course turn off the outer light fixture, a bank of Hollywood bulbs, when she takes her shower, but she never does. I'm not sure whether this is because she resents the fact that since we've been married I've gotten to sleep at least a half an hour longer than she has, or more likely the fact that at 6:00 in the morning I do not figure largely in her universe. Either way, the yellow rectangle is as much part of my waking now as the humid hint of perfume that wafts into the bedroom with the light, sexy and self-sufficient and as indifferent as my wife herself to my zombified status. It is routine.

This *is* our morning routine, so established now for the past four years that I've forgotten there's anything out of the ordinary about it: At 6:00 a.m., or a little earlier, my wife, an elementary-school vice-principal, rises with the alarm clock, showers and dresses for school. At 6:30 I get up, and wearing the same sweatpants and a T-shirt and possibly socks I've slept in if I've stayed up late, I go downstairs to make breakfast for her and my two older children, my son Ben, aged 8, and my daughter Jennifer, 12. In the meantime, Paula wakes up the two kids and tries not to let them go back to sleep. At 7:00, ideally, everybody comes down for breakfast, at which point I make lunches for the three of them. At 7:30, unless Ben's lost half his homework or Jenny's fallen into a fugue state in front of the mirror, the three of them leave for school — the same school — Paula to be a vice-principal, the kids, handily, to learn. I sit down and read the sports section and the comics and the front page in that order, and eat whatever's left on the table. Then I go upstairs and get Rosie, the baby with the gift of gab, who's usually awake by now. I take her out of her crib, change her, dress her, help her brush her teeth, give her her vitamins and comb her hair. Then I take her downstairs, feed her and watch a combination of "Phil Donahue" and "Sesame Street" with her (depending on who has the remote control). By this time it's 9:30, and our baby-sitter, Lucy, arrives to take over. I hand Rosie to her, and go down to my office in our basement to work.

Even this close to the bi-millennium, I admit, it is not a typical father's routine. For a long time, in fact, I was under the impression that I was also not a typical father. But of all the human conditions, atypicality may be the shallowest. The other day, pulling the car into the garage ("docking," Jenny calls it), I asked Rosie, who was sitting in the car-seat behind me, a "life-style" question, probably to hear her be smart. "Rosie," I said, "what does a mother do in the morning?" "She goes to work," said Rosie. "And what does a father do?" "He stays home," she said, "and takes care of a girl."

It was the "a" *in* "a girl" that struck home deepest, the indefinite article. "The" girl, or "his" girl could have made her description specific to me, but "a" girl generalized it to the planet. This was the way Rosie saw the world. Mothers went to work; Fathers stayed home to take care of "a" girl. But in spite of fifteen years as a "liberated" husband and twelve as a father, I don't think I had ever really believed in the accuracy of Rosie's vision. My notion of fatherhood was locked up not in what I lived, it turned out, but what I remembered. I had always been under the impression that I *was* a conventional father: provider, hunter, stoic. My view of myself as a father derived as much from a murky archetype of fatherhood, with its rigid and creaking set of paternal commandments, as it did from the specific oddness of my fatherly life. If I wasn't Everyfather, I thought I was. And in fact I was Everyfather in at least one sense — how I felt when Rosie said what she did in the car. For every father, hearing his child describe his function in life is like catching a glimpse of himself in the mirror before he has time to recompose his face.

On this particular morning, mind you, I'm not thinking about any of this when I fold myself to a sitting position. I am thinking one simple, relentless thought.

I have to get up. I have to get up. I have to get up.

I'm a father. I get up.

It's early spring, so the hallway, when I find my way through our bedroom door, is already filling up with milky, undifferentiated light, like the light God created on the first day. Our upstairs hall is a perfect perimeter square, with the bedrooms arranged symmetrically around it. The first room I pass is the baby's; her door is cracked ajar six inches, and after squinting through to see if she's sleeping with a deck of cards again (her new bedtime companion along with a teddy bear), I close it so my son won't wake her up when he starts speaking in his normal voice. Next I pass the unstained pine louvre doors of the linen closet (which I've been planning to stain since we moved in); then Jennifer's room, where I knock twice and call her name, but don't open the door, mainly because I'm still wearing short-sleeves and she sleeps with her windows wide open, like someone in an exorcism movie. At Ben's room, I do go in, partly to turn off his humidifier and flip up his blind, and partly to check out how he's sleeping. His unconscious poses are family-famous — one morning I found him on his back with his right hand raised straight up in the air, levitating, as though he was trying to answer a question in math class.

Today he's in his standard jaunty-corpse mode, hands flat on the Ninja Turtle quilt beside him, one knee up, tenting out its folds. From the tattersall blue wallpaper above the bed, the armoured turtles Michelangelo,

Leonardo and Rafael look down at him, along with the Blue Jays' Joe Carter, and higher up a phalanx of team pennants harking from professional sports he will not play. In the blue gloom he is the coolest chunky man alive, my son, a paragon of thick grace. If I stuck a cigar in his mouth it wouldn't look out of place. I offer up my usual morning prayer for him, asking God not to let him become a dentist, then I throw his underwear in the hamper and go downstairs to get breakfast ready.

This house we live in — maybe because we watched it being built — has a hushed, woody feel to it in the morning, as though someone's been doing secret carpentry work overnight. Downstairs I retrace the night-time ritual of the Unknown Father, undoing all the actions I linked together last night, turning off the porch lights, unlocking the front door, opening the wooden shutters in the living-room and the venetian blinds in the kitchen. (This is *true* typicality. Why is it so hard to track down a single two-parent family where the wife is the last person upstairs at night, and the first person downstairs in the morning?) Last I go back to the front door to get the papers. Outside the sky's off-white has brightened to a cool but not cold blue, more like an August morning than one at the beginning of October. On the sidewalkless crescent a neighbour, a recent Russian immigrant, is walking her dachshund, the neighbour — not the dog — wearing a khaki trench-coat. Her choice of pet and coat has always seemed strange to me, considering her place of origin. My sweatpants and the fact that I'm around all day are obviously just as suspicious to her. She nods coolly as she goes by, as though I'm a sloppy KGB agent, and carries on up the street. I take the papers back inside to the kitchen, and start to unthaw bagels.

Generations of women have known this secret; now I know it, too — that making breakfast before your mind is fully conscious can be a gift. For ten heavy-lidded minutes there is nothing to concentrate on but the sound of your own shuffling and the dumb details of the meal: counting the number of strokes of a serrated bread-knife you can safely dig into a bagel before you have to flip your hand-hold and drag the blade out, gauging the index-finger pressure it takes to guide a paring-knife the length of the membrane of one grapefruit section, choreographing the steps you need after half a body-rotation to reach the refrigerator and take out the milk.

I'm just putting out the grapefruits — thinking that when I clean up I can slam-dunk the rinds in the garbage on the same trip back from the table that I use to reshelve the cereal, and so enhance the fluid efficiency of the meal cleanup — when I hear my wife reach my older daughter's room in the upstairs hall, on the way to get her up. I picture her briefly leaning into the chill in her pantyhose and slip. The conversation that drifts down the stairs starts so typically that at first I only listen to it with half my mind, the way you would a radio program in another room.

"Jennifer, you don't have time to read your script. Listen to me.... Jennifer, don't tell me you're tired, you're reading; a person who's reading can get up.... Jenny," Paula says, "it's time to get *up*." This time my older daughter does answer, her voice low, but perfectly clear. "If it's time for me to get up," my daughter says, "it's time for you to get out of here." There's a brief pause, and then I hear the sound of footsteps. Then the door slams.

In a famous scene in Ford Madox Ford's novel *The Good Soldier*, Leonora, the wife of the helpless philanderer Captain Ashburnham, exclaims in anguish to the narrator, who's already baffled: "Don't you know that I'm an Irish Catholic?" The trick in the book is that the narrator, a kind of middle-aged male Victorian Gracie Allen, doesn't see it at all, and neither do we. The emotion in Leonora's tone so outweighs what she's actually said that it's loopy. There's a hidden code in the word "Catholic." What Leonora is actually saying is that she's doomed to live with her husband forever *because,* as a Catholic, she believes divorce is a mortal sin. This is her permanent lot.

My daughter's lot is more ambiguous, but her comment could be the same. In other houses — maybe even in our house at a later (hopefully distant) date — what she's just said might not be that noteworthy; in other houses it might pass for another piece of run-of-the-day pre-teen churlishness. But here, today, it's a kind of miracle. Not once in her dozen years of life has Jennifer been this blatantly rude to either Paula or me. It's not that she's a Pollyanna — moods are to Jennifer lately what breath is to life — but up till now her moods have all been directed inward, the kind of brooding time-outs that let her put up a sign on her bedroom door when she was six that read: "Jennifer Teitel: Failure." Till today her crankiness almost always ended up torturing herself more than anyone else. And like a lot of pre-adolescent girls, at the core of her there was always a swoon of goofy surrender; if you surprised her doing something — acting out a scene from *Les Misérables* or playing with her Barbies when she was pushing twelve, say — her first look up at you would always be younger than her years, humble and a bit lost, with a blush and maybe a self-diverted guffaw built into it.

But the voice that's just come out of her was low-down and calculated and more — seasoned. It's totally unexpected — so much that I'm almost more impressed than surprised.

I feel a restless grief for the day that might have been.

Paula comes through the kitchen door first, buttoning her blouse, the look of disbelief still on her face. "Did you hear that? I'm sorry, we have to do something about that."

"Who slammed the door?" The key is to keep the questions neutral.

"She did."

"What's bugging her?" This seems safe, too.

"You're asking me? All I know is she's been treating me horribly lately. This is open season on Mom time."

"It hasn't been that bad."

"Oh, no? You don't notice, because you don't get the fallout. Welcome to the brave new world." She takes a bite of her bagel. "We've got to figure something out. There has to be a consequence, something serious. And she better be ready on time, too, I'm not waiting for her." She takes another bite. "Maybe you should go talk to her."

I don't want to go; the entropy of the morning, the coziness of my sweatpants, the delusion, as my wife's grandfather used to phrase it, that I can "stay out of it," say don't go. But my wife is looking at me the way Margaret

Anderson used to look at Jim on "Father Knows Best." I go up the stairs and into my daughter's room.

She's sitting on her bed with her legs crossed and her hands in her lap, staring out the window. Ordinarily, she's too sweet-looking a kid to look dictatorial, but her stare lately, the stare of wounded twelve-year-old girls everywhere, is true.

"You want to talk about anything Jenn?"

This gets no response; she just improves her posture a bit.

"What you said just now was nuts," I say. "You can't say things like that. It's not acceptable." "Acceptable" sounds pretty stilted to me on the way out, but she doesn't seem to notice. "If there's something bothering you, you should say something. Otherwise the only conclusion anyone can draw is you're just a basically rotten human being." This elicits a full body shift, as if she's trying to get rid of the dimension we're sharing and move into another one.

"Okay, I give up. But you can't be late. If Mummy has to leave without you there's going to be some major repercussions." She doesn't answer. "Hey," I say. "Jennifer Bernhardt." For a moment I think I get her mouth to lift a bit at the corners, but she covers it neatly by putting the back of her hand to her eyes, in a kind of Camille swoon. When she takes the hand away, her eyes are welling with tears. This is the point when my wife might mention our daughter's acting lessons, but I'm a way softer touch. I'm convinced she has a problem now; I just have no idea what it is. If I hazarded a guess, it would probably be too grandiose by half. What's always surprised me about the critical secrets of women is not how mysterious but how familiar they turn out to be. *Don't you see, I'm an Irish Catholic.*

"This is bullshit, Jenny," I try, nothing else having worked. This does elicit a response. She gets up, picks up her school pack, walks swiftly out of her room, and goes down the stairs and bangs out the screen door. A second later I hear the car door slam.

Paula's waiting for me when I get back to the kitchen. Ben is down too by now, eating breakfast with his shirt off.

"Dad, you have to sign my form for Fantasy Farms."

"Did she tell you anything?"

"No," I say, "but I'm sure something's bothering her."

"Of course something's bothering her. I know exactly what's bothering her."

"Dad —"

"What?"

"You wouldn't understand." She picks up her purse. "But I'm getting pretty tired of it, though. And your attitude, too." Now I think I see the beginning of tears in *her* eyes — or is it her contact lens.

"Dad —"

"What attitude?"

"That attitude."

"Ben, why do you have your shirt off?"

"My rash is really bad, Dad. I'm delaying putting it on."

"When's the last time you had a bath?" Paula says to him. "Don't tell me. Ben, get *dressed,* we're late. So what are we going to do?" she says on the way to the door.

"I was thinking about it. She can miss skating."

"Perfect." She opens the door, hauling Ben with her.

"But you can't back down."

"We'll have to pay her coach, though."

"I don't care. Swear you'll follow through."

"I will follow through."

"Here." She rummages in a bag and hands me a sheet of paper. "Those are the questions to ask the doctor about Rosie today. You forgot about her appointment, didn't you?"

"I didn't forget."

"You can't forget. And no skating."

"No skating."

"Swear."

"I *swear*."

"All right. Bye."

"Bye."

There's a little pause, enough for one of us to say something — but we're not sure whether we're having a fight or not. Now my wife hustles my son, still pulling on his shirt, down the front steps, and pushes him into the back seat. Jennifer's already in the front, staring wounded out the windshield straight ahead. Karen sits down beside her, glances back at me, looking suddenly like a teenager herself — and then, with a tenderness so pronounced I can feel it through the car window, reaches out and brushes the hair away from our oldest daughter's eyes. The car backs up onto the crescent, and then shifts into drive, and pulls away too fast beyond the frame of the screen door.

And this is where the second coincidence of the morning — and the day — occurs.

It doesn't happen right away. First I have to go upstairs to get the baby. She's already awake when I open the door, sitting up in the nightgown she thinks makes her look like Dorothy in *The Wizard of Oz*, and talking to herself. "Why did the witch put poison in the poppies?" she asks me when I come in, which happens to be the last thing she asked me the night before. She's asked the same question at least twenty times a day since we rented *The Wizard of Oz* for her two weeks ago; she seems to be as interested in the cadence of the question as in the answer. I give her my stock answer, take her out of the crib, change her, do a short toothbrushing lesson, give her vitamins and brush her hair ("Is it a monkey? No. Is it a lion? No. It's a girl!") and lead her (carrying is now out) downstairs to give her breakfast, an Eggo and a mixture of various cereals, no milk, small spoon. She takes the opportunity to ask it one more time with her mouth full: "Dad, why did the witch put poison in the poppies?" I tell her why, and slide the paper in front of me before she can ask again.

It's on the front page — a small Associated Press article in the lower right-hand corner, hemmed in by a story about a Blue Jay pitcher's elbow injury, complete with anatomical drawing, and a report about a Texas oil-fire expert who's been hired to put out fires in Kuwait, still burning as a result of the Gulf War. It's the kind of story you can imagine coming in across the wire with the latest sighting of Elvis.

GRIEVING DAD'S HEART-TUGGER

RALEIGH, N.C.
Heart-transplant surgery would have meant missing his son's funeral, so Ed Reid passed on

> the chance to have his diseased heart replaced with his son's. The heart of 23-year-old Eric Reid, who died Friday of head injuries suffered in a fall from a golf cart, went to someone else.
>
> "It would have been a good heart for me, but I just didn't feel like my family and I could deal with it at that particular time," Reid said.
>
> Reid, 47, said he is on a waiting list for a transplant and believes another donor heart will be available soon.

I read the story over again. Then I put the baby in my lap, and read it again. Then I pick her up — even though she likes to move everywhere herself now — and carry her into the den and turn on the TV. On "Sesame Street" Grover is playing his classic waiter character, tormenting the blue-faced businessman customer. Today the customer wants a cheese sandwich, with a pickle *beside* it. *Beside* is the key. Grover keeps bringing out the pickle on top of the sandwich, or under it, or in it. "Hey, Charlie, gimme a double Cheddar with a side of dill!" he yells. When he finally gets it right, the customer's bus is there and he's gone, and Grover does his standard backwards collapse, complete with huge sound effects.

I flip to "Phil Donahue," overruling Rosie's yelp of protest. On Phil there are parents and children too, but this isn't as coincidental as it might seem. If you deleted families and Louis Farrakahn from the universe, Phil would have no show. Today Phil has on sons of abusive mothers who married, can this be, their cousins? Playing horsie by herself, Rosie balances her narrow torso on my shin like a slender gyroscope, as a woman with a goitre sits beside the son she abused and says, Phil, I never liked him. No, I never did.

And as she does, I'm thinking about two things: my older daughter's silence, and the story in the paper. The first is like a dim ghost of disaster, chastening in its mildness. The second, if it's true — why do these things always happen in the South? — is indescribable. Its permutations of pain are as crazy as they are incredible. It's like a hieroglyph of agony. Where do you start in a story like that? At the golf cart? What kind of decision is that to have to make? Suppose you could attend the funeral, would you take your son's heart then? Could a parent possibly take the heart of a dead child at all? And who talks like the Raleigh father, Ed Reid? "I didn't feel like it was the best thing for my family at that particular time?" Rosie slides up and puts her arms around my neck, laying her almost weightless body on my chest. It's no hoax, I think. People do talk like that. At times of disaster human beings can be direct and dignified enough to break your heart. I can't imagine what it must be like to be the father in the story.

And yet I can't imagine anything else. Once I might have been able to. Twelve years ago, for instance, I would have felt the crazy horror of the story, but I wouldn't have felt the underside of the horror. I wouldn't have known how strangely rational it was, how a funeral could be as significant as a new heart, how Ed Reid acted, according to a particular set of rules, in a logical and possibly heroic way. But now my options are limited. I'm seeing this moment through a specialized lens, the way I've seen the bulk of this short day so far. Its angle of refraction is only subtly different from the lens I used before I had children, but worlds apart. The question is its origin.

Women know, they say, when they start to become parents; their bodies tell them. ("It's called pregnancy," my wife tells me, with not much humour.) But men only know it's happened. Even then, the "it" is elusive. Of all the truly irrevocable actions a man can take in his life — suicide, murder, mutilation — the only creative one, becoming a father, is also the most temporally mysterious. Yet at some point in the lives of all men who become fathers an all-or-none lever is pulled, and the world will not be the same again. We can't wake up the same way, or regard the day the same way, or read the paper the same way, ever again. And while I have the time, in the lazy sun, with the day's labour postponed for twenty minutes, with the baby on my lap and Phil Donahue barking intimate questions at people who are dying to answer them, I try to remember exactly when my moment was.

Jennifer Ruth Teitel was born at 4:45 on a winter afternoon in 1979, in a room full of light. The sun was setting as she was born, in the centre of the large rectangular window on the south wall of the delivery room, giving the space the feel of an aquarium at dawn. The presiding obstetrician, a bit of a joker, paused with the baby out only to its waist, like a kayaker. "Last bets on the sex," he said. Then he pulled the slick little body all the way clear, and it was a girl.

She was two weeks early. My wife and I had gone out to eat the night before at a Greek restaurant where you had to visit the kitchen to order your food, and after we got home I went upstairs to my office to build shelves, and Paula went to sleep. A half-hour later she came up and, lying down on the floor, said she had indigestion from the "fucking" food and my "fucking" hammering. It actually didn't occur to either of us that she might be in labour. When her water broke five minutes later, we made up for it by becoming geniuses of cliché. "I'm not ready," said Paula. "I'm changing my mind." They had told us at our Childbirth Ed class to bring a tennis ball for back massages. I brought a can, and felt useless.

From a historical perspective this uselessness should not have been. Uselessness at birth was my father's birthright, not mine. My father became a father in one sentence, the paternal verdict of his generation: "Congratulations, you're a father." In his case it was delivered by a nurse in a waiting-room decorated with phalanxes of rubber plants, like a Greek restaurant, in a small Jewish hospital in downtown Toronto in the spring of 1947. News of my father's paternity, and the paternity of the fathers of his generation, arrived *as* news, from a kind of front. People disappeared through a door, mysterious things happened on the other side of the door; then people reappeared, and they were fathers. It was taken for granted, in that era of hygienic postwar innocence, that my father and his peers would miss their big metaphysical moment. To hear my father talk about it later, he *wanted* to miss it; he was worried that he would faint. Forty years after the fact, the only thing my father would remember from his waiting-room experience, besides the rubber plants, was a joke a fellow sailor had told him, about a ship's captain who refused to give a swabby leave to be with his about-to-give-birth wife. "You might have been essential for the laying of the keel,

Seaman Blake," the captain said in the punch-line, "but you're extra baggage at the launching."

"Human fatherhood is a social invention," Margaret Mead wrote, the year I was born. "Paternity may be a legal fiction," James Joyce had written three decades earlier in *Ulysses.* My father would have understood them both. Twenty-six years old, blessed with a natural modesty to go along with his times', he knew which of nature's messy mysteries was his province and which wasn't. Uselessness in the waiting-room he accepted as part of Malraux's dictum: it was man's fate.

But four decades after that, shivering behind the cold steering wheel of a car on the way to a larger hospital, I should have felt differently. Two years before I was born, in 1947 (unbeknownst to my father and the vast majority of his contemporaries) an American doctor named Robert A. Bradley — who would become internationally known as the "Father of Fathers" — was doing experiments in natural childbirth-coaching with out-of-wedlock young mothers at Porter Memorial Hospital in Denver, Colorado, when he noticed a confusing trend. His out-of-wedlock mothers tended to be much better patients than his married mothers were, even when all the other variables were constant. His conclusion was simple: the married women missed their husbands; the unmarried ones had no partners to miss, and so were more willing to put up with the obstetrician. His solution was to invite fathers not only into the labour room but also into what he called the "no-man's land" of the delivery room, where the "great white father of authority, the doctor, reigned supreme." The innovation was hugely controversial in the medical community — a college student in Arcata, California, actually had to chain himself to his wife in the early 60s to prevent hospital officials from banning him from the delivery room — but the tide was turning. By the mid-60s a law had been passed in the U.S. Congress guaranteeing a father's right to attend the birth of a child if the mother consented. By 1973 twenty-seven percent of all births in North America included a father in the delivery room. By 1983 the figure had climbed to seventy-nine percent.

I was one of them, an entrenched member of the baby-boom generation of fathers-to-be who had been caught up in Robert A. Bradley's wave. "Integrated" birth, in fact, was one of the clarion calls of my generation. Ours was the generation that had supposedly rejected the old male/female trade agreement on birth-responsibilities — pain for one party, cluelessness for the other — in favour of a shared parenting that involved the father from the outset. My wife had bought the beyond-Spock bible of our generation — Burton White's *The First Three Years of Life* — and I had actually read part of it. And, most important, where my father had dropped my mother off at her Lamaze classes after the birth of their children, Paula and I had dutifully signed up together for the new-parents country club of the times — another of busy Dr. Bradley's legacies — Childbirth Ed.

My memory of the class is as clear as of the birth. It took place in the upstairs day-care room of a community centre due for demolition; the lighting was poor, and the big corduroy pillows we relaxed on had a smell that was half milk, half apple-juice. Sitting back with my legs splayed, I watched our instructor, a rail thin woman who had four kids and was now training for the triatholon, insert a doll's head into a fibreglass pelvic girdle with a deftness that was weirdly sexy. The whole place was bathed in a general gravid eros. Every Wednesday night I surrendered to it, kneeling beside my wife with my hands on her belly, like someone getting ready to play the piano. I learned about breathing stages, and transition; I had my ice-chips, and my focal point (a little fox on a red golfing shirt). I was ready, not to rumble, but to facilitate.

But occasionally I would look up and meet the gaze of the guy beside me or across the room, and in the little unguarded grin that passed between us, that moment of locker-room sheepishness, I could tell that in spite of the breathing and massaging and coaching, he was thinking the same thing I was.

We were all useless.

At the hospital my uselessness increased. There were two pieces of furniture in the labour room, a chipped blond coffee table and a framed picture of the Matterhorn over the bed. I felt less functional than both. To make things worse, the more useless I felt, the more beautiful my wife got. Beautiful and suspicious. "Where are you going?" she kept asking me every time I moved a foot, as though I was a felon being arraigned. But I had to go. Outside of make-work projects like timing her contractions and giving her ice-chips, my one crucial job was to get the anaesthetist when the pain became too strong and she decided she needed her epidural. The maternity ward we were at, though, in a downtown teaching hospital, was long on interns and short on angels of mercy. In the hallway, surreally bright with yellow light, I left message after message with the nurses for the anaesthetist, but I couldn't track him down. When he finally showed up, a blasé young Chinese guy with a thousand pens in his chest pocket, Paula had already done most of the worst work, and was very close to delivering. The anaesthetist compensated by throwing me out of the room while he hooked up the epidural. "Where are you going?" Paula asked me, nostrils flaring. "To the bathroom," I said. For the life of me I couldn't figure out why she wanted me around. I went into the men's washroom, and cried.

Cried is not totally honest: I sobbed, in a way I had been too embarrassed to since I was in the third grade. I'm not sure to this day exactly why I cried; I only know that for a moment I felt less completely useless than completely helpless. If there is such a thing as crying which is "honestly" theatrical — genuine enough but aimed at the audience of the crier himself — this was probably it. Half of me was weeping, while the other half was watching me weep, and listening interestedly to the same phrase coming out of my mouth over and over again while I did — "She's so brave," "She's so brave." At some point or other I probably wondered if this piece of self-indulgence was *the* moment for me, if maybe by evoking the corny child in me I was saying goodbye to immaturity forever and being born again as an adult and father. But if anyone was being born in my high-octane mind then it wasn't me, but my wife; she was emerging as a brand new person capable of a heroism I hadn't guessed at. She was moving beyond practical sexiness to practical grandeur. She was doing my work for me, and although, if I was going to be totally honest, I was glad she was doing it and not me, the least I could do was to mark it. My crying, probably melodramatic, definitely irrelevant, was something like applause.

The delivery room I remember mainly for its colour. *Technicolour* actually. I had no idea that the hue of organic things could be so red and so blue, or so vivid in general. The colours were so bright they seemed unreal; the parts they coloured were so symmetrical they might have been manufactured goods. Instead of a medical landscape I had the feeling I'd stumbled into an extraterrestrial one. My father's fear, fainting, turned out to be a non-issue. Standing at Paula's head like the original fifth wheel, I was wary of looking in the big concave mirror at her feet, but I couldn't help it. I was in my "greens" now; with the help of a nurse I'd donned them over my street clothes. The hat and mask weren't bad, but the huge booties made me feel as though I was wearing my shoes in bed, like a kid dressing up, but clumsy at it, and doubly illegitimate. Not only was I impersonating an adult, but Ben Casey, too. Bending to help raise Paula's shoulders as she pushed, the thin fresh green of my tunic rustled against hers in a foreign contact; these, I thought, were the clothes of the new world. I had the feeling her thoughts weren't as poetic.

The delivery room was as crowded as a bus station now, and in the welter of interns and residents Paula had shifted her suspicion to the obstetrician. At one point he mentioned that since nothing much was happening, he was just going to step outside for "a sec." "No, you're not," my wife said. Whatever mysteries were left were obviously no big mystery to her. A moment later the head crowned, white and vegetal, like something from a horror movie parody, and a second later our daughter was out halfway, her fists raised like Jack Johnson and her mouth wide open as Lucy getting ready to yell "Blockhead!" at Charlie Brown. The doctor made his deathless joke, the interns laughed dutifully, and then she was all out, joined to her mother by an umbilical cord that looked like a meaty, beautiful red and blue telephone cord. "Are her digits all there?" said Paula. It was a cliché, but it wasn't a cliché — it felt as dewy as the doctor's lousy joke. "Everything's there," I heard myself say. The would-be comedian clamped and cut the cord, and the baby was carried like a brisket to the little stainless-steel grocer's counter set up at the foot of the bed, weighed, suctioned, silver-nitrated, injected, wrapped in a blanket, and brought to me. Her weight in my arms was half cloth, a narrow living wire inside flannel. My wife's hand was on my arm. "Let me see," she said, inaugurating without knowing it the anthem we would repeat ad infinitum into the future. And now we were three.

And nothing had changed.

How can I explain this? How can any father, without having it come out as the baldest cliché in the world? Maybe this way: Change usually involves a noticeable component, something detectable added or subtracted: a skin shed, a decision made. But when my daughter Jennifer was born that winter afternoon, although something had definitely happened, nothing had changed. What happened to me at that moment was more like a seamless migration from one body to another equally familiar one. The second she was there, it was as though she'd always been there. As impossible as it had been to imagine what it would be like to have a child, it was immediately impossible to imagine what it would be like not to have one. The feelings I was feeling were large, but the transition was mist. It was as though someone had slipped me a mickey in the delivery room, and I had woken up a millisecond later behind a stranger's eyes — except that this stranger was no stranger at all.

"Everything old is new again," the line goes in the song describing romantic love. "Everything new is old again," describes birth better. Fatherhood in its first flush revised the past as well as the future. It was pure sci-fi.

My son's birth three and half years later didn't do much to fill in the blanks. Not happy with Henny Youngman as her obstetrician and the entire Eighth Army assisting, Paula had switched doctors and hospitals by now, opting for a female obstetrician and a hospital with "Women" positioned prominently in its name. The total population in the delivery room this time was six — five women and one man: me. It may have been a coincidence, but things seemed to run a lot smoother and with less fanfare than they had the first time. Even the pretence of my functionality was gone. When the moment came to push and I reached down for Paula's shoulders, a wiry little grey-haired nurse slipped in front of me, folded my wife up from the waist, and told her just to "get the job done, dear." The only thing left for me to do was the play-by-play. Paula's glasses were fogging up in the summer humidity, and she needed someone to tell her what was going on. "What's *happening*?" she kept asking me, as opposed to "Where are you going?" So now I got to use the narrative skill I had honed on my friend Larry Ginsler's driveway playing ball-hockey thirty years before. I was still commentating when my wife "saved the baby's life." At least she saved his life in her version of events, the version she never tired of telling and the one my son, as fascinated by details of his birth as any kid, would demand to hear on a weekly basis when he got older. In both versions the doctor's first words were "Oh, look. A boy baby. A beautiful *boy* baby. And so peaceful." "He's taking a nap," laughed one of the nurses. "What do they mean a nap?" Paula yanked my arm. "What's happening?" "He is," I said. "He looks like he's sleeping." "What do you mean sleeping?" she asked, hauling herself up on an elbow and squinting at the end of the table. "He's not sleeping. He's blue. Why is he blue?" "Oh," replied the doctor with unruffled equanimity, "he just spent some extra down time in the birth canal. Could I get some oxygen here?" Paula's version differed: in her version the doctor gasped, like Dr Zorba, "You're right! Oxy-*gen*!" Whichever version was true, oxygen was administered, and the beautiful boy baby was saved — and into his mother for a life.

I felt no different. Without any apparent ripples in the cosmic dust, the universe now included a son as permanently, backwards and forwards in time, as it did a daughter. "Two" is different, people had told me. "One is just playing around. When you have two you'll really feel like a father." But if anything, at the time I felt less like a father. It was the beginning of June, and the hospital abutted the University of Toronto, where I'd gone to school. Leaving the building after visiting, I walked through knots of undergraduates coming from the St Michael's college library, the girls smelling of perfume, the boys doing little jittery dance-steps to show off on the sidewalk. I was thirty-three years old, but in my heart I felt like one of them. I was a student, but with secret bonuses: a profession of sorts, and two kids. On Yonge Street I bought Jenny a little silk kimono and Paula a comb for her hair, gifts I knew would be either unfunctional or grown out of too quickly. I didn't know what to buy the baby, a boy, without it ending up feeling hackneyed. A baseball glove? A uniform? Sport that I was, I compromised by buying him nothing at all.

And all things being equal, I would probably have stayed in the dark when our second daughter, and last child, was born five and half years later. By this time we'd moved to the suburbs — where I'd sworn I'd never set foot again after growing up there — and my office had moved from a third-floor loft to an extra bedroom which we'd agreed would be taken over by the incoming baby. The change was lucky, because the pregnancy turned out to be Paula's worse. Of the several things she became allergic to, I was one. I ended up buying a futon, setting it up in my office and sleeping there for most of the winter, while she opened the windows in our bedroom during blizzards, and suffered. "This one will kill me," she told me on days when I could get close to her. "She's the one."

She went into labour on a night in May, feeling relatively healthy, if fed up. With the local hospital no more than five minutes from the house we put on James Taylor tapes and drove around the back roads, listening to "Handy Man" and waiting for her contractions to become legitimate. The obstetrics wing of the hospital, a pre-fab extension that was half-underground like a basement apartment, was virtually empty on this particular night, adding to the general summer-camp casualness in the air. For her doctor this time Paula had chosen a young female GP, a petite, serene woman with spectacularly beautiful wide-set green eyes, like a cat who had swallowed something valuable. The doctor got us set up in the labour room and, because the baby was a few days late, attached a wire lead to the baby's scalp to monitor its heartbeat. With my third child, I finally had a job: I watched the digital heart-rate read-out, going up and down like an elevator, always coming reassuringly back to the average of a hundred and twenty beats that the nurse told me was optimal. The only change took place just after the anaesthetist came in with the epidural. At that point the digits on the machine bounced down to fifty and stayed there for longer than usual, it seemed to me. I pointed it out to the nurse, trying to be polite, but she was already moving to Paula.

"You have to move a bit, mom," she said, pulling my wife a bit roughly in her haste onto her other flank. "Get the doctor," she said to the younger nurse with her.

"What's wrong?" Paula said, not as tactful as me in her terror.

"Your baby's not happy. We just have to find a position it likes more."

Your baby's not happy. This, then, I thought, in a kind of haze, was the folksy little euphemism the medical profession used when something horrible was about to happen. Things were happening at a strange speed, too slow and too fast at once. The doctor came in and looked at the monitor while the nurses got Paula to sit up; it was still beeping around forty beats a minute. No longer serene, she said something about calling the obstetrician.

Someone else said he was on his way already. "What's *wrong*?" Paula asked. "It's all right," the doctor said, not bothering with consistency any more, "we have to get the baby out faster than we thought." She asked the nurse again if the obstetrician had arrived yet, and when the nurse said no she said there was no time to wait, they had to go *now*.

Salman Rushdie, writing about *The Wizard of Oz* two years later, would claim that the final, most terrible rite of passage people go through is the passage from being children to being parents, when we all "become magicians without magic, exposed conjurers, with only our simple humanity to get us through. We are the humbugs now." If he was right, then this was the moment I became a parent. I followed the bed out into the hallway with everyone else, mechanically wondering if I was allowed to be here, then realizing that I had obviously been forgotten anyway. I wasn't wearing a tunic, but there was no one to help; fumbling, repeating a mantra I couldn't identify, I lagged behind to do it, tying the robe behind me and putting on a mask. By the time I reached the delivery room the anaesthetist had joined the entourage for moral support, and a nurse was on the phone at the foot of the bed. In the unreal movie in front of me all the running jokes of the two previous births were resurfacing with a grim kind of vengeance, turning our deficits democratic: I was as blind as my wife had ever been, and she was as helpless as me. "Are you going to do a Caesarian?" Paula asked, sounding very young. "We'll have to wait for the obstetrician," the cat-eyed doctor said, even younger. The nurse hung up and said he still wasn't there. "I can't wait," the doctor said, and reached behind her for the forceps. They were shaped like a clubby pair of large children's shovels, two separate pewter shovels not joined in the middle like the tongs of my imagination, and twice as long as I had expected. Later I would find out that they were mid-forceps, and the doctor hadn't used them since medical school. Now, though, she inserted them, and said, "I've got her." Her — she used the pronoun. She pulled; there was a sound like a ripping ripple and Paula made a noise deep in her throat that I'd never heard anyone make before. The baby's head appeared; her eyes were closed, and the umbilical cord was wrapped tight several times around her neck like an elegant snake, strangling her. Without bothering to unravel it, the doctor clamped the cord where it was, cut it, and pulled the baby the rest of the way out. And now for the first time, as they carried her swiftly to the table to undo what I knew could not be undone, I saw her face clearly.

Of all the things I had ever thought death might be, beautiful was not one of them. At least not in the aesthetic sense, not in a way divorced from sentiment or faith. Because she was beautiful, our daughter, when she entered the world, far more purely beautiful than I remembered her brother or sister being. She was blue and waxen and flawless, like a sculpture. Her colour in particular was novel: a deep saturated blue, not precisely cold but still intimidating in its perfection. *She* was intimidating in her beauty. She was something to bow down to. Except for the fact that her eyes were closed, I would realize later, she resembled more than anything the floating baby in the final scene of the movie *2001: A Space Odyssey*.

But her eyes were closed, and she was dead. Ironically I had never seen a dead body before, but I knew at that moment that the corpse of my daughter was the first, in spite of what the clinical definitions said. Her first Apgar score, an index to denote basic life signs, was two out of ten, where five was considered borderline. Her second, taken four minutes later, was still two. At some point in the confusion a pediatrician, summoned while I was oblivious, had entered the room; a big gruff man with a beard visible beneath his mask, he deftly suctioned the baby, feeding the flimsy plastic tubing into her mouth with bulky fingers, picking her arms up and letting go to see if she had muscle tone, saying, "Come on, baby, come on, baby," like a gentle baseball catcher to a pitcher with control problems. (From Paula's vantage point, all she could see, she would tell me later, were the two little arms flopping back lifeless when the big man released them.) The obstetrician on call had arrived as well, too late — he was watching the GP finish up at Paula's end, reassuring her the way he might a high-strung colt: "You did the right thing, you did very well, everything was perfect." Reassurance was the order of the moment. Beside me Paula dug her fingernails into my palm and asked, "Is she all right?" really meaning "What's going to happen to us?" And I said, "Hold on. She'll be fine," meaning I didn't know. The disbelief I was feeling now was already moving towards the apprehension of change — I was imagining the conversations I would have with people, the arrangements to be made, the way our lives would be marked now by tragedy where before they had been unblemished records of unappreciated luck.

But still I couldn't really believe any of it. This was the unique thing about my fatalism; it still did not belong to me. Dead my baby was, but her death was the property of someone, or something else. So that when her cry came, a weak excuse of a cry, I felt more vindicated than surprised. Colour flushed beneath the blue, so gradual it was painful. Her crying got louder. "That sounds better," said the cat-eyed doctor into her mask. Who could map the complex river of her relief? Oxygen mottled our child's perfect skin splotchy red now, like a fitful sunrise. Irony had the last laugh. Where death had been exquisite, life was homely.

In the recovery room afterward, when they let us hold her for a while before taking her to the incubator just for precautions, I told Paula, "She's a fighter. She's tough. That's why she's here." But it was a protocol cliché, jury-rigged for the moment. I said it to avoid evoking wonder. In fact I had never had the feeling, in the interval between my daughter's lifeless entrance into the world and her first cry, that she was fighting for life. I never thought she was fighting for anything. I got the feeling instead that she had retreated somewhere, deep into herself maybe, to make a decision. She was looking back at the door through which she had come, the door into death or the place before birth, where that supernatural beauty lay, and she was weighing its relative merits. And when she decided to return she had brought not only herself, but me, too. If she hadn't come back to life, a piece of me would have stayed unborn. I would have had to live with the absence of it leaving me unbalanced, like an amputee feeling a phantom limb. I wouldn't have been made heavy by grief, but lightened by the lack of myself.

Sometimes, at the tops of mountains, houses are assembled in sections, carried piecemeal up the dangerous grade. But houses like this are always hard to finish. So one man attends the birth of a daughter, in all his uselessness, the same way two years later a man in Raleigh, just as futile, will attend the funeral of his son. There is no single moment after all when we become fathers; we shed no skin, make no decision. We are constructed instead by craftsmen of infinite cunning. Mothers create children. But children build fathers, from pieces they find in space.

2

The Picture on the Desk

"I just happen to have one in my wallet . . ."
Paula Friedman, 1979

"The parent who could see his boy as he really is would shake his head and say, Willie is no good: I'll sell him."
Stephen Leacock

9:30 a.m.

At 9:30 Rosie's babysitter, Lucy, lets herself in the front door. I try to be doing a reasonable simulation of life by the time I meet her with the baby in the hallway, but her expression tells me not to bother. Good-natured and ruthlessly punctual, Lucy looks impossibly refreshed for a Tuesday morning; she takes Rosie out of my arms and immediately starts laughing. After two and half years of these regular morning transfers, I'm still not sure where this laughter comes from, whether it's because she thinks I'm funny or pitiable. For a long time I was convinced it was the logistics of my job, the fact that instead of heading out the door like a "legitimate" father after I give her the baby, I slink down to the basement to sit at a keyboard. The few times I tried to sound her out, though, she made some vague, polite proclamation no one could argue with, ending it with "isn't it?" — her postscript to any sentence she wants to be noncommittal.

Then one lunchtime, about a month ago, with no prompting whatsoever, she looked over at me with Rosie's tiny spoon in her hand for a long count, and said: "I didn't see any fathers like you before in the Philippines, isn't it?"

Towards Rosie, though, Lucy displays no ambivalence whatsoever, which is a good thing. When she takes the baby today, my daughter immediately starts grilling her with her question about the Wicked Witch and the poison in the poppies. I head downstairs thinking that at least she identifies with Dorothy. During my older daughter's Wizard of Oz phase she wanted to be Auntie Em. Paula had become seriously concerned. Auntie Em? Who wanted to be Auntie Em? What turned Jennifer on, it turned out, was the way Em yodelled "Dor-*thy*?" when she was trying to find her niece during the twister, making the pitch rise into falsetto on the "thy." For six months we listened to loony wails of "Dor-*thy*?" drifting from behind our daughter's door. It was enough to turn anybody off Kansas.

About eight years after Jenny did her farmer's wife impersonation in her room, Salman Rushdie emerged from four years of hiding from the Ayatollah Khomeini and his psychopathic fundamentalist cronies, and wrote an essay in *The New Yorker* about *The Wizard of Oz*. The movie had apparently represented a kind of magic for him when he was growing up in India, and his essay was basically an attempt to understand why. One of his central theories was the theme of adult abandonment — the idea that all children are eventually betrayed by adults who make promises to them, both tacit and bald-faced, and then end up being impotent to save them. The Wizard himself was an obvious target, but Rushdie picked Auntie Em and her performance in the twister scene as the clincher. The fact that Auntie Em lets Uncle Henry persuade her to go into the storm cellar without knowing if Dorothy is safe, Rushdie claimed, just proved her basic unreliability, and the shakiness of the grown-up world in general.

I was happy to see Rushdie writing again, but in my opinion his observation just proved that Em was Dorothy's aunt and not her parent.

My office is tucked into a corner of the basement, hemmed in by the furnace room behind me and the playroom on the right. It contains an enlarged overhead window, a desk without drawers, an electronic piano keyboard, a fax machine, a computer, a guitar, about a thousand books, and a fireplace. The broadloom, a nice piece of beige wool Berber, would ordinarily work with the fireplace and the pot lights to give the impression of comfort, even luxury, but the components do not quite fit in the space, which is, to put it mildly, *snug*. When I was originally kicked downstairs, the plans were for the creation of something a lot more expansive, but somehow things "happened," and the playroom grew, while my space dwindled.

In fact, my space, like my time, has been eaten away in increments since my first child was born. When we were first married I rented a room overlooking a park across town from our apartment, where I went to write every day. The room wasn't perfect — there was an eighteen-year-old couple with a loud baby in the next flat — but it was the minimum, I told Paula, and non-negotiable. (What I didn't tell her about was my plan one day to have a huge single room designed by Buckminster Fuller, a kind of writing arena, the Nobel Dome.) The rented room lasted until Paula got pregnant and we decided to gamble on buying a house, which had a mortgage that ate up my room's rent and then some, but which did have a large third-floor loft, which became my office. The loft survived the birth of my first daughter, but not of my son, who evicted Paula and me from our bedroom and forced us to subdivide the third floor into a bedroom *and* an office, the latter just big enough to fit my desk into if I took off the legs. (A cousin of my father's, freshly arrived from Moscow, told me my office was "cozy" — from a Russian not a good sign.) When we moved to the suburbs — for more space — I commandeered an official room again, one of the upstairs bedrooms, not on its own floor, granted, but at least not in a basement. "Forget the basement," I told my wife. "not even a walk-out. I'll kill myself first." Then Rosie was born, and we found out how much opening the attic would cost. I ended up in the basement, at the far end of the house, working in a spot smaller and more remote than anything Bucky Fuller had ever worked on. Meanwhile, the people I'd gone to high-school with were increasing both their living space and their work space every couple of years. They were moving up and out; I was moving down and in. I was geographically regressing.

But I was also working at home. I'm not sure when this became the status quo, I only know, as it was with the birth of my children, that one day I woke up and it was a given. Not surprisingly my wife thought it was a terrific idea — on the other end of a reversed traditional home-work tandem she could now go to work and feel totally relaxed because her husband was at home. I wasn't so sanguine. In fact the distractions I grew to know too well at home were a whole degree more invasive than anything I'd known at a school library or in a rented room. It had very little to do with the specifics you could see in gender-switch movies: the washing machine overflowing on Bob Hope, or the baby peeing on Jerry Lewis. *Home* was the distraction itself. A house has a rhythm of its own, I was finding out; you fall out of lockstep with it at your peril. And because the preoccupations of a house are the unglamorous stuff of life — food, mess, maintenance — you can end up at the end of a day working at home owing a psychic debt of agitation and guilt that is unlike anything you'll ever know on a factory floor or an office. Women have known this for centuries. Working at home is a pain in the ass. The only redeeming feature is a paradoxical one: *peace*.

If you could bisect the average parent's brain at 11:30 in the morning or 3:30 in the afternoon — at any time for that matter — you would see in your cross-section slice a kind of dim photograph, behind the preoccupations of the work day, the parent attached by gauzy tendrils to his mate and to each of his children, and to home. The thickness of the strands might vary according to the family, but the strands are always there. Women admit it readily; men have more trouble with it. Ulysses came home at the end of the Trojan war because he couldn't get it out of his mind, but he left to find Helen again before he learned what its fatal attraction really was. In fact home when you have children, whether the children are actually there or at school or hitch-hiking to Alaska, is the safe centre of the photograph. Even for people who can leave home without, apparently, a second thought, a sacrifice of security is made. The trick is that you have to experience the benefits of both sides of the deal to know what you're giving up when you choose just one. Again women know. (The allure of "home-peace" kept them at home historically at least as much as the fist of any "patriarchy.") Men like Ulysses have never really *been* at home — so they've never known how hard it is to leave.

But I'd had a taste of it, and for some reason it wouldn't let me go. Gradually my writerly demand for a separate space started to seem childish even to me, and gradually I realized that as sentimental as the feeling might have been it was easier for me to work when one of my progeny was within ear-shot. As opposed to having to totally block out the outside world, now it helped if I could be aware of its feathery presence. Every other week, true, I would go crazy at the distractions, and swear I was going to move out and rent an attic somewhere. But Paula didn't believe it, and neither did I. On paper I wasn't in love with the kind of father I was becoming, not blithe and independent like Ulysses, but glacial and grounded like Jabba the Hut. In reality I couldn't deny the signs: the hearth, not for everyone, was starting to suit me. At home, I was at home.

Staying home, I get to look at this photograph, too. I'm thirty years old, sitting in front of an old Underwood Five typewriter as heavy as a Chevy pick-up, and between me and the keys, slung in a papoose, is my one-month-old daughter. I type around her compact bulk, my nose in her scalp, holding my breath to avoid waking her, letting it out when I have to in controlled exhalations like a scuba diver. The photo is a hoax, a set-up; no one can work like this. I staged it at the time to convince myself. But it's definitely nice to look at and pretend.

What flicks on today is no Underwood Five but a computer screen, the "treatment" for a movie script filling it: Working title — "Lady Einstein."

> "Lady Einstein": Romantic Comedy. Charlotte Dubois, a female real-estate agent from the deep South, turns out to have been working, in her spare time, on a scientific theory that may be the greatest discovery since Albert Einstein's General Theory of Relativity. Quarantined for security reasons by the U.S. Army for a week in one of the homes of the suburban New Jersey subdivision she's representing — she transforms the lives of the host family, a feisty twelve-year-old boy, Joey Wise, and his cynical journalist (single) father, Seymour. While the army scientists pore over her material, trying to decide if Charlotte is Einstein or a deranged phony who's been plagiarizing other physicists, Joey falls in love with the agent, and Seymour becomes convinced she's trying to

steal his son from him, as well as dupe the world. Seymour is sure she's a fraud; Joey, a pint-sized Harry Hope, is praying she's for real. Winona, their Filipino housekeeper, thinks Charlotte can cure her indigestion with psychic surgery. In the end, everyone's right . . .

It's a living.

ACT ONE — SCENE 1 — LADY EINSTEIN

EXTERIOR, ROOF, DAY
Medium shot of two carpenters on the roof of a suburban home under construction, trying to check level with a plumb line. They bicker, the plumb falls . . .

THE CAMERA tightens on the plumb as it hits the second floor subflooring, rolls along a crack, bounces crazily down a newly installed flight of circular stairs, rolls in and out of two-by-fours with a mind of its own, out the front door, down the porch steps, and into a bucket of cement . . .

A FEMALE HAND, LONG FINGERNAILS, MANY RINGS, extracts it . . .

FIRST CARPENTER
(an Italian accent)
Cheesie Christ.

Cheesie Christ? I pick up the phone, and call my wife.

She sounds shy and harried when she answers, the way she usually does when I call her at work, as though I'm asking her out on a date but there's another man in the room. I pretend to be calling to remind her that we're going to a movie tonight, so she can't be late. She promises, and reminds me again about Rosie's doctor's appointment.

"I'll *remember,* don't worry. What happened with Jenny? Did she say anything in the car?"

"One thing. Two. Your daughter said, and I quote: 'Do me a favour. Don't come into my class today. There's this way of talking you have.' "

"Did she say, 'Do me a favour'? Or did she say, 'Do me a favour, Mom'?"

"What's the difference?"

"One's completely rude, and the other is just a foray into rudeness."

"I don't care about her forays."

"She's basically a great kid, you know."

"She's a wonderful kid. But this isn't about how wonderful she is. Hang on." She calls something to someone in the other office. "I have to go. I just want to know what we're planning to do."

"That's what I wanted to talk to you about. This doctor appointment with Rosie is going to totally screw up my day, especially if I have to try to work at home when her friend Jessica comes over to play after her nap. I figured if I take Jenny skating I at least have an excuse to take my stuff to the rink and get something done while I wait."

"I don't get it; you want to drive somewhere?"

"It's better than trying to work with those two outside my office."

"So throw them outside."

"Then what do we have a playroom for?"

"Look, what do you want me to say? We should let her get away with it just because it's inconvenient?"

"I don't know. It just seems that her crises always end up being inconvenient for me. She swears at you, I end up paying for it." She doesn't say anything. "By the way, you didn't happen to read the front page of the *Star* this morning, did you? A story about this father refusing a transplant —?"

"What are we talking about here? Just promise me you won't take her to skating before you talk to me, okay? And remember Rosie's appointment."

She hangs up. I look at the screen.

Ahhhhh!

EXTERIOR, FRONT STEPS, DAY
THE WOMAN holding the cement-encrusted plumb is wearing a tight flowered dress and heels approaching stiletto-height. He big sunglasses are propped up on her forehead. She's beautiful in a friendly, spectacular way. She could do anything in her dress, we get the feeling, from turning tricks to calling hogs. This is CHARLOTTE MILLER.

CHARLOTTE
You-all might need this, no, boys?

FIRST CARPENTER
(indicating drawer he's working on)

Carlotta, this drawer, she makes no sense. It's cock-eyed. This blueprint, she's a for a lunatic.

CHARLOTTE

That's a laundry room up there, Benito, not a cocktail bar. A woman needs space to bend over doin' laundry. We spread as the years go by.

FIRST CARPENTER

Cheesie Christ.

The phone rings, on its own this time. It turns out to be my sister-in-law. A photographer by trade, she wants to know what running shoes she should buy for her one-year-old son. As a quasi-jock who's married into a family of non-athletic in-laws, I get questions like this from time to time. I promise to do a little research, then before she can hang up, partly to avoid going back to the screen, I tell her the story of the Raleigh father.

"Yikes," she says when I'm finished, "what a story."

"So what do you think? He did the right thing, right?"

"I don't know," she says. "Maybe I don't agree. No. It would have been meaningful for him to have the heart. Him more than anyone else, I mean. A piece of his son would be still alive."

"A memento?"

"Well, I don't know if I'd use that word."

"A wallet photo," I say. "Instead of 'Take a look at my son, some face, eh?', you say, 'Take a feel of my son. Some beat, eh?' "

"Shut up," she says. "You know what I mean. Phone me about the running shoes."

Maybe she has a point, I think, after she hangs up. If a woman in Washington can have a baby so that that baby can grow up and donate her bone marrow to her older sister who's stricken with cancer, what's wrong with a son donating a heart to a father?

I've reached that point in the morning when I've completely run out of avoidance strategies. I have no one left to call, and it's not even eleven yet. There may be no alternative to actually working.

And that's when I look over to the other side of the desk and see the picture of my son looking back at me.

It's actually one of four pictures of my family, all eight-by-ten colour blow-ups, two on each side of a red-hulled Panasonic Auto-Stop pencil sharpener. All four were taken in the front yard of a farm where we went apple-picking on a Thanksgiving weekend a couple of years ago. In it my son is lying on his stomach in a pile of leaves, facing the camera with one cheek propped up on his hand. The leaves are muted brown, the trees behind him a wall of green, his ski-jacket burgundy. My son is just my son. There's a serenity about his face, a knowledge of his pluses and his minuses that I will never have, not as long as I live. Look how young he looks, I think — it was, what, three years ago, so he was must have been five and change at the time — but look how much like himself he looks at the same time. His expression says, "I know you're out there looking at me. It's okay, I can hack it." His face is filled with a kind of sleepy fondness for himself and the universe, plus the cool grace that comes from goodness.

Phone calls are not the only way to avoid work.

I lean back in my chair to get a better view of the photo.

As I do I find myself thinking of another chair in another office, my father's office, not the little cubicle he rented after the war, with its abbreviated wall partitions, but the office he would retire from, a two-roomed suite on the eighth floor of an established building downtown. I remember it with the precision of a shrine, his desk cornered in an L with his partner's against a wall of venetian-blinded windows (the old wide ivory venetians you could lacerate a hand on), the blond-wood cabinets filled with samples of ladies' wear and swatch-books, the cartoon from *Punch* tacked to the side of one cabinet, showing three emaciated slaves surrounded by maybe half a million Roman legionnaires, with the muscular member of the trio saying, "Come on, friends! They can't stop men who want to be free!"

But most of all I remember the pictures on his desk. There were three of them, black-and-white shots of each of his children dressed in their holiday best. Somehow the department-store photographer managed to get to the truth of those children in spite of himself. My older sister was grave in her picture, my younger on the edge of a helpless laugh. The picture of me showed a dozy six-year-old kid in a white shirt and bow-tie, with a crest of blond hair like an upright waterfall, and his mouth half-open. The photos were the most exciting and disorienting things in the office to me, even more than the telex machine in its clunky wonder, or the wire cups of the ladies' bathing-suit brassieres. In a universe of exotic commerce my sister and I were celebrities but shouldn't have been; we were out of place in all that glamour of work; we were too familiar, where things were meant to be strange.

And we weren't unique. All through history fathers have fled home at daybreak, ostensibly to seek food, or adventure, or war, but in reality looking for *freedom*, trying to touch the people they were before they were domesticated forever. I flee too every day, a much shorter distance than most, just to the basement, but as far as I can get with the home-boy deal I've made. Yet at the same time all of us, from Ulysses to the man in the grey flannel suit to my own father, have carried ritual images with us of the agents of our bondage. We've placed them on our desks, and carried them in our wallets, and tacked them to our walls. And at times inexplicable, we've felt compelled to look up from the Trojan horse or a pile of figures, into the face of our jailers.

Somewhere the father in Raleigh has one, too. Something more permanent than a memory, that is.

A snapshot.

The first family snapshots ever taken were pictures of dead babies.

This is not as surprising or ghoulish as it sounds. Photography's dawn came just before the mid-point of the nineteenth century, a time in history when people lost children regularly, so regularly in fact that the deaths came close to equalling the births. The infant mortality rate in the "civilized" Western World in the mid-nineteenth century was nearly forty percent. Consequently the children who didn't survive were nearly as substantial a part of a family's legacy as the ones who did. The invention of the first permanent photograph, the daguerreotype, by Louis Jacques Mandé Daguerre, in 1839, and of the first reversed negative image, by William

Henry Fox Talbot in the same year, meant that a parent could now preserve the image of that half of his or her genetic material which up to now had been as fleeting as a tear. The opportunity wasn't restricted to parents, but the passion for parents turned out to be addictive. If bereft Victorians became collectors, bereft parents became curators. Photography was *the* parental technology, the trick parents had been waiting for. It let the museum of their memory become concrete.

The result was the post-mortem, or "hieratic" (meaning priestly, or sacerdotal) photograph, suitable for framing and your mantlepiece. Post-mortem photographs were taken of adults as well, but it was the photographs of children, not surprisingly, that turned out to be most poignant and enduring, and not simply because of the predictably sentimental reasons. Infant hieratic photographs were unique precisely because they refused to conform to the aim of the genre: namely, to show people who were definitely deceased. The first hieratic photos I ever saw in my life were in a book of photography I picked up by chance one day in the library. After the initial shock, what struck me was how *un*-hieratic the pictures were. Under the first print in the book, the text-writer had written: ". . . the subject was never to be seen as potentially asleep or in some other attitude that would have disguised the true nature of the situation. It was important — perhaps in some way it was even cathartic — that the deceased look coldly and stiffly departed, the hieratic photograph being all that remained, except memory." To qualify as hieratic, that is, the children had to convince their parents — and us — that they were dead.

But the kids in these photos will not co-operate. To look at them today is to know the limitations of human grimness. A photo of a little boy taken by a Canadian photographer, François Filteau, in 1888 is a perfect example. Lying three quarters on his side on a sheet-draped table, his head resting on a pillow, his arms folded in his lap, the dress's hem covering his feet and its mantilla-like collar curving snugly at his neck, the boy in the picture looks *absolutely* asleep. He looks vaguely ceremonial, true, in an Oriental way, like a little emperor with his head shaved — but still simply *asleep*, and nothing like dead. Similarly, an anonymous post-mortem photo taken around 1850 in Santa Fe, New Mexico, shows a little girl of toddler age in bed, cozily rumpled on her back, the blankets draped informally enough about her that she appears to be hugging them. With the mid-part in her hair she has a Dead End Kid look, maybe, but again, definitely not a dead look. In the end something defeats the hieratic purpose in every post-mortem picture involving a child. It might be the innocence of the photos' subjects, or it might be — and this is harder to think about — the subconscious defiance of the stage managers, the parents themselves, who could not bring themselves to arrange the bodies in positions that might be uncomfortable to a living child. The parents might have been refusing to take "possession" of their children's passing, the same way I hadn't been able to find a way to "own" my daughter Rosie's death, when she was born as still as a statue. Whatever the reason, the invisible fingerprints of parents mark these photos as deeply as the most shameless of modern album snaps. The children in them aren't stopped; they just seem to be pausing on their way to the next day. We look at the photographs and think: *Soon* they will wake up. Soon.

But the post-mortem photos were taken by professionals, not by the parents themselves, and they were a fairly specialized arm of the parental album compulsion. The first true album snapshooter, the father of the family snapshot, was a Frenchman named Jacques Henri Lartigue. Born into a rich, chronically curious, leisure-inventive family with a weakness for hot-air balloons and early go-karts, Lartigue took his first picture, of his mother and father, when he was seven years old. From then on he took thousands, a large number of them of children: first of his brother Zissou and his cousins; and then, after he married in 1919, of his own children. In a dozen studies of Lartigue you can find detailed discussions of the style and spirit of his children's pictures, but nowhere, interestingly, will you find mention of their most obvious singularity to any parent who looks at them: the dramatic difference between Lartigue's pictures of children before he was married, and his pictures of his *own* children afterward. Lartigue's early child-pictures, that is, are almost totally lacking in what you might call the "protective frame." The kids in them are invariably caught in motion, with nothing and particularly no *one* to hem them in, to stop them from ejecting clear out of the picture. Imminent danger is the theme. The most famous of these snaps, "Bichonnade in Flight," shows the young Jacques Henri's favourite cousin, Bichonnade, literally flying down a staircase, tilted at a forty-five-degree angle. To look at this picture is to know that a second later Bichonnade is going to fall flat on her face on the sidewalk.

By contrast Lartigue's pictures of his own children are *all* internal frame. It's almost impossible to find one that doesn't include other people, usually family members, protecting the child from the edges of the photograph and any possibility of external danger. In his celebrated photo of his son Dani's first step, Lartigue draws back to include the woman Dani's toddling from (his mother) and the woman he's toddling to (his aunt). In his most famous photo of all, "My Family," a wide-angle celebration of his extended family in bed, Lartigue has Dani wedged between his grandparents so securely he's almost invisible, and flanked by three more adults on each side for good measure. Looking at this picture, you think: What could possibly happen to this boy? A baby kangaroo would be no safer in its pouch. In his later "adult" pictures, candid snaps of JFK and the Ziegfeld girls, Lartigue remains as playful and dangerous as ever; it's only with his kids that he's not a kid any more. Art takes a back seat to the parental instinct. In "My Family" the *parental* snapshot has truly been born.

Fifty-five years after Jacques Henri took his picture of Dani in bed, I took my first pictures of my daughter in the hospital with my wife. I shot them with a twin-lens reflex box-model Yashica 12, a copy of the old Roleiflex, and developed them in a darkroom at home. Paula hated them. They were too big, she said — like Jacques Henri's — and they were in black and white. True snapshots had to fit into an album, and they had to be colour. Black and white made too much of a comment on reality, when what she wanted was a record of reality. (Twelve years later, when we started to talk about Jennifer's Bat Mitzvah, we had the same argument. "Who cares about

Auntie Selma's soul? I just want to know if she was there, and what she was wearing.")

So we started buying albums. And we started taking pictures. We didn't plan any particular picture, we just took it, Jenny in her high-chair, in the bath-tub, at parties, on the toilet, in a soft leather suitcase, two eyes above the horizontal zipper. By the time Ben was born, when Jennifer was three and a half, we'd filled two albums. Each album contained about forty pages, and each page four snapshots back and front, eight in all. Ultimately we had 640 pictures of our daughter, culled (we only used the good ones) from about 1,200. About, in other words, one a day.

They're there on a shelf in our family room right now, above me while I sit here procrastinating. Up there too are the four other albums we've filled since then, with pictures of the next two kids. Granted, we did experience the usual second- and third-child let-down, which meant we ended up taking fewer shots than we might have. So now all we have are 2,000 photos, carefully selected from 4,000. Of course we'll take more.

We are neither chroniclers of post-mortems nor professional image-creators like Jacques Henri Lartigue. Even by common parental standards we're lazy picture takers. And yet we've recorded the visual lives of our children faithfully enough that you could use the results for time-lapse photography, rippling the snapshots to watch them grow.

Why?

It's not enough to say "to remember." Every parent knows this cliché as profoundly as the latest Kodak slogan. We take pictures, the cliché goes, we record voices, we make videotapes in order to "capture the moment," because children grow so quickly, and before we know it the way they were is not the way they are. A couple goes to Niagara Falls for the weekend, and when they walk back through the door their three-year-old is as tall as a tree and speaking a second language. And a day later — because kids are kids and geniuses at fiddling with time and imposing amnesia — the present *becomes* the past, and the parents can't remember her ever being any other way. "Can you think of a time when she couldn't speak Maltese?" "Not me." What else can a parent do, goes the cliché, than to take the picture that lets him revisit the past his child has stolen?

And of course the cliché is true. In a drawer in our bedroom we have a tape of Jennifer singing — what else? — "Somewhere Over the Rainbow," when she was four. Twice a year my son takes it out and makes us listen to it — he's also on the tape, as a screeching six-month-old in the background. My wife and I always react the same way. We bend our heads to "sink our sight," like Herman Melville's Confidence Man, and we listen to the wispy, tinny voice with complete amazement. Was that her? Did she really sound like that? How could that be her?

The cliché is true, but it doesn't go far enough.

Yichas doesn't either. *Yichas* is a Yiddish word that might be translated as reflected, or at least deflected glory — in plainer terms showing off. *Yichas* is the whisper behind the photo of your child in your wallet, the one that comes out during picture exchanges at the water cooler, always prefaced by, "I just happen to have one in . . ." *Yichas* was also the motivation for an ad that appeared in the mid-eighties in a variety of upscale magazines for Chivas Regal, the vintage Scotch whisky. In the ad, set on the balcony of a Manhattan apartment, one handsome young couple was entertaining another. The caption read: "They don't brag about their children or make you look at slides of their vacation. What are you saving the Chivas for?"

Your better class of people, the ad suggested, refrained from boring you both with slides of their trip and the wonderfulness of their children. In both cases, the message went, you had to "be there" to enjoy the view. As élitist and misguided as the ad was (who did they think they were selling their Scotch to if not boring parents?), it had a point. *Yichas* is based on a unique perceptual set. What's obvious to a parent — that his children are singularly beautiful and brilliant — is not always obvious to the world. That's why we protest too much. *"I know, I know," says every parent at the water cooler, "everyone thinks their kids are brilliant and beautiful, but mine really are. Just look at this face."*

Which brings us to another Yiddish child-directed institution: *nachas*. *Nachas* (pleasure), is the better-known handmaiden of *yichas* (pride). If *yichas* is the bait that draws the little crowd around the water cooler with their wallets out, *nachas* is what keeps one poor jerk there looking down at his wallet long after the others have gone. According to the precepts of *nachas*, we collect images of our children not to show them to other people, but to gaze at them ourselves. The aim isn't ulterior, but idolatrous. The looking is the pleasure. Because in the process we get to exercise a truly unique piece of parental hardware, what you might call the Parental Eye.

The other day Jennifer and Ben were making themselves an after-school snack, when I walked past the kitchen door. Rosie was in the kitchen too, lying on her stomach on the floor crayoning on a piece of paper. The snack was buttered Melba toast, which my younger daughter decided, natch, that she loved too. When Jennifer started walking away with a plate full of toast, Rosie said in a sharp, mature voice, "Jennifer, give me that right now." To a stranger eavesdropping the scene would have sounded typically obnoxious, with Rosie coming across as a purse-lipped Shirley Temple clone. But pausing from my particular vantage point to watch, I could let the scene hit me with its built-in redemption and apologia. I knew Rosie didn't say what she said to be cute, because I knew she was too weird for that; so I knew it had to come from a kind of perverse blitheness, and I could tolerate it. Not simply tolerate it, but get off on it, and laugh at it, with the father's laughter that lives in your jaws and the stretch of your cheeks. Was I demented? Sure, we all are. But I was also seeing with the Parental Eye.

What a parent sees with the Parental Eye is this: the story behind the picture. It's the story that coincidentally could turn the boredom of the people at the water cooler and in the Scotch ad to chauvinism if they knew it. It's the before-and-after story, the unique knowledge of where the face in the picture is coming from, and where it's going to. As a genius, Jacques Henri Lartigue could tell this story with a single photograph; as parents we figure we need to take a couple of dozen to really know it well. Because to know is to understand is to forgive.

Knowledge engenders tolerance; ignorance bias. The Parental Eye doesn't add sentiment, it leaches prejudice.

In the end the explanation could be as simple as this: we are uniquely unprejudiced against our children. In fact our children may be the only people in the world towards whom we harbour no adverse prejudice at all.

So we like to look at pictures of them.

But in the end none of the explanations hold up. Nostalgia breaks down, and pride, and even the Parental Eye. (As uniquely unprejudiced as a parent can be towards a child in the morning, he can be uniquely on his back by the afternoon.) Taken together the stock rationales can account for maybe one album on a living-room shelf, but not half a dozen. They can't begin to explain why we cherish certain photos more than others, or why there are snapshots it is virtually impossible for us to lose, no matter how hard we try. They definitely have trouble accounting for the two most memorable photographs I've ever seen in my life, two pictures separated by forty years of history, but connected forever by their resistance to time.

The first picture was a photo I found in a small tan suitcase that was kept on the top shelf of the hall closet in the house where I grew up. Its location wasn't accidental. Nowadays, when every parental pursuit comes in a package, visual history means albums and videos, and eventually maybe holograms in the living-room. But my parents never kept an official photo album in their lives. For one thing, serious candid photography when we were growing up was still a somewhat specialized leisure activity, and my father (unlike his brother) had never been a hardware aficionado. Maybe more important, the albums themselves were imperfect; snapshots couldn't be peeled and pasted or slipped into convenient plastic windows, they had to be fitted in place using four little black and gold corners that could have doubled as tuxedo accessories. The process was painstaking, and the glue on the corners never held. As a result, instead of an album, what we had as kids was what most of my contemporaries had: a small case — in this instance from an old portable typewriter — crammed full of photographs.

The vast majority of the pictures were black and white; order was non-existent. Pictures of us kids were mixed together with pictures of navy buddies, friends from Labour Zionist summer camps, gag shots, muscle photos of very skinny teenage guys in the late 1930s, smiling goofily into the teeth of World War II. The only chronology the pictures had was the random selection of your hand. Photos could be separated by forty years or five thousand miles of ocean. A favourite pastime of my sisters, in fact, was trying to figure out who the pictures were of, and when they'd been taken. It was a mystery game in which all the faces had a European cast and all the names were for some reason hilarious. "Look, there's Mendel Beck," my father would say, checking in every once in a while. "Look, there's Shaya Gluck!" "Look at that, that's Meema Brunna!" The result was a more realistic echo of a family's history than any annotated set of albums could ever be. It was memory the way memory worked.

After my parents moved from the home we grew up in, the tan suitcase endured a fitful odyssey, moving from sibling apartment to parental house, hall to linen closet. Eventually the case itself was lost; only the photos were left, stuffed into paper bags my sisters divided among themselves.

I ended up keeping only one picture, one of the few colour photographs in the case: a shot of my mother and myself. It was taken at the cottage we rented on a lake north of the city, when I was four or five years old. In the picture my mother is kneeling horsie-style on a fringe of grass in front of the cottage's little beach, with me sitting on her back. The colours are the colours of the old Kodak colour film, saturated and crazily rich; the picture was taken in the daytime, but either the original exposure or the passage of time has deepened the sky to blue-black, so that the impression is of summer in the land of the midnight sun. Against the sky my hair is blond to the point of whiteness — that's as much of me that catches the eye. It is my mother's picture; in the vivid gloom her face glows, and even her tan has a sheen to it. She looks so strong and momentarily beautiful that the picture almost seems illicit. A dazzling young mother looks up into the camera, carrying her son as unselfconsciously on her back as a sister would carry a brother. Whatever nightmares she might have, the world can only guess at.

At the beginning of my second year of university I rented a safety deposit box; I put the photograph in it. I didn't look at it until the week before I got married. Then, for reasons I never completely figured out, I took it out and showed it to my mother.

We were in the kitchen of her new home, a small room with an enormous window enveloped in trees. She looked at the picture long enough that I had the feeling something was wrong. After a little while longer, without looking up, she said, in a quiet voice: "God, you were a beautiful boy."

She wasn't seeing the photograph I was seeing, of

course. She may not have even noticed how eerily powerful, through a fluke of film and light, the picture of the beautiful young woman was; she was just looking at a snapshot of her child. Art didn't matter much compared to the opportunity to gaze at a particular face.

And my mother's look when she gazed was truly directed out of time. It was a hieratic gaze, meant to freeze life in the same way that the original hieratic photos ironically animated it. Her aim was the same as the subversive originals, and Jacques Henri Lartigue's internally framed photos: she wasn't interested in saving the moment; she wanted to save *me*. I was safe in the picture, and the more images she had of me where I was equally safe, the greater the chance that she could keep me that way now, as I headed into marriage and the unknown. The snapshot was a totem; she was a fifty-five-year-old *obeah* woman, practising protective voodoo. It's the same voodoo we all practise when we record the images of our children through processes still magical to most of us, and file them for safekeeping. We aren't trying to preserve their past, but to protect their futures.

As with most voodoo, our success rate varies. On the third Thursday in the month of April 1992, a fifteen-year-old girl named Kristen French set out on the five-minute walk from her high-school to her house in the town of St Catharines, Ontario. She never got there. Two weeks later, police investigators found her body on a country road thirty miles from her home town. She had been raped and strangled, and her hair had been cut.

The day after Kristen was found a photograph appeared on the front page of *The Globe and Mail*. The photo showed three police investigators crouching in a thicket of branches, all looking at something the middle man was holding in his hand. The investigator on the right was young and lean; the man on the left wore glasses and looked finicky. The central man, obviously in charge, was regarding his own left hand with the blocky, solid dignity of Spencer Tracy. The hand was encased in a surgical glove, and in it, gripping it, young and as smooth-knuckled as the glove holding it, was a child's hand.

No other part of her body was visible; it was obscured by the branches the policemen knelt among. Because of the camouflage the photograph was truly hieratic, and touched with grace. As young as the hand was, there was no doubt the hidden body it belonged to was dead. The men gazing at it were undoubtedly looking for clues, but their looks were so reverential, so careful without being maudlin, that the picture transcended itself. By pure chance, it had the biblical aura of Renaissance paintings in which people come upon something limpid and wondrous. It had gone beyond sadness to a kind of devotional peace. Ordinarily pictures like this infuriated me; the photographers, I assumed, were ghouls who deserved solitary confinement on deserted asteroids. But looking at this one I couldn't decide whether it would have been a curse for other parents to see it or, in the most peripheral way, a kind of comfort.

If her entire body had been visible it would have been unbearable, but only her hand was. A hand. A heart. Maybe my sister-in-law was right. Maybe the heart of the Raleigh man's son would have made a terrific souvenir, the ultimate wallet photo to remember him by.

It was just one his father did not choose to carry.

Jacques Henri Lartigue was a man, and with very few exceptions the photographers who took the post-mortem photos were men. Although the trend in professional photography has changed today to a more equitable balance of the sexes, fathers are still the picture-takers in most families. Every time the imbalance starts to shift, a new wave of technology hits the shelves, faster and glitzier than the one before, and men, generally keener on toys than women, exert their numerical dominance again. So fathers have historically been the chief mechanics in recording their families' histories, and by default their main archivists as well.

The greatest father-archivist I've ever known was my father's older brother. A quippy man with a highly developed sense of organization and a Sansabelt wardrobe his daughter razzed him about unmercifully, my Uncle Irv took pictures at every opportunity imaginable, filling carefully annotated trays and lazy susans of slides, everything in those pre-computer days beautifully taxonomized. Slide shows were common, but the picture-taking itself was the main event. At Passover Seders, at Chanuka parties, on vacations and sleepovers, my uncle always had his camera ready. He also had a dry, collegiate wit, and a funny little cackle of a laugh no one could imitate, but the basis for his heft as a family anchor came from his archival mission.

But by far the most famous of all my uncle's records weren't photographs at all, but something called "The Funny Books." Leather-bound volumes which he compiled from weekly notes and transcribed in his office beside the kitchen, "The Funny Books" were simply records of funny things his children — and nieces and nephews — had said or done over the course of their lives. An example?

November 30, 1956:

Mark (six) and Belle (nine) are discussing [my Uncle's] birthday.

Mark: Daddy, are you really forty?

Irv: Yes.

Mark: Jack Benny's forty.

Irv: He's fifty-seven.

Mark: Fifty-seven!! I don't know how Jack Benny could act if he's fifty-seven.

Belle: Jack Benny's fifty-seven? He's *much* older — he's about sixty-nine.

Mark: Hmmm. Something's wrong here — I thought he was forty.

Like any book, the Funny Books revealed as much about their author as they did about their subjects. My cousins emerged from the pages coated lightly in my uncle's veneer: droll and epigrammatic. They emerged in the Parental Voice as much as the Parental Eye. They also emerged with love.

My uncle died suddenly in the fall of 1982, the victim of what one of my cousins, a doctor, called "a galloping hepatoma." He was the first of the older generation in our family to die while we were adults, a step in what we knew would become a progression but still weren't ready to accept as real. At the *shiva* after his funeral my aunt started at the sound of my voice in the kitchen, turned and said, "God, I could have sworn it was Irv." I had never before heard anyone say our voices were similar. To escape I went into the office off the kitchen; my cousins were already there, leafing through the Funny Books as though it was the most natural thing in the world. My father was there as well, reading the last entry. "What we'll do," he said, "is keep the books going for him. We'll pick it up from today."

But no one ever did. The Funny Books still sit in my uncle's office, under his orderly collection of *New Yorker* magazine covers, stopped permanently at October 14, 1982. Or maybe not quite permanently. Some seeds take longer to germinate than others. Five years after my uncle died, I was standing in a crowded room with a glass of champagne and orange juice in my hand, watching a small girl say something droll, when I physically felt a presence behind me. I knew, without turning around, that someone was standing there with a camera.

I could have sworn it was him.

I made my first entry that night.

Jennifer Teitel, aged six, New Year's Day, 1985
(on the trouble with adult parties):

"I hate adult parties. People talk and talk, and recognize each other from twenty years ago. And then you find out the cake has nuts in it."

3

Taking the Baby to the Doctor
Mothers & Daughters, Fathers & Sons

"I don't want to be sexist, but the girls in our school have tribes. It's true. Every tribe has a chief, and the tribes hate each other."

Ben Teitel, 1991

12:30 p.m.

ACT ONE — SCENE 2 — LADY EINSTEIN

INTERIOR, WISE FAMILY LIVING ROOM, DAY
Close shot of JOEY WISE, a small twelve year-old, standing at the living-room picture window looking out.

SEYMOUR WISE
(V.O.)

Joey, are we going to play or not? I've got a purie up for grabs here.

JOEY

I pass, Dad.

SEYMOUR

You can't pass. We're playing Bronx rules. What are you looking at?

JOEY

Nothing.

At the same time, though, the CAMERA cuts to show us what JOEY *is* looking at: CHARLOTTE MILLER, across the road shouting instructions up to the TWO CARPENTERS. She's waving her cigarette with its huge length of ash animatedly.

The CAMERA cuts back to JOEY as SEYMOUR comes into the frame at the window. SEYMOUR is stocky, balding but nice-looking in a chaotic way. He's wearing a STRIPED BATHROBE, and carrying a velvet Seagram's bag filled with MARBLES.

SEYMOUR

It's stuck on. It has to be.

JOEY

I don't think so.

SEYMOUR

Ten to one it's going to fall off in the next thirty

seconds. My immies against your Indian fish-eye.

JOEY
(sticking his hand out without looking)
Done.

SEYMOUR
(as Joey counts)
You're too trusting, Joey. That's your problem. You have too much faith in the people.

"Jay?"

It's Lucy. I almost fall off my chair turning to look at her in the doorway. The baby is standing beside her, holding her hand like an orphan.

"Rosie has an appointment with the doctor, isn't it?"

No. My wife will kill me. "What time do you have, Lucy?"

"Twelve seventeen," She's wearing, I notice, the same watch as Joey Wise. "I got the diaper-bag ready and a bottle, warm warm. You're late, isn't it?"

It is. I thank her, grab the baby and the bag, and, my mind still not perfectly in sync with reality, hustle her outside, throw her in the car-seat, back out of the driveway, drive to the end of the crescent and yank the car into traffic.

To get to the doctor's we have to drive east along a schizophrenic four-lane road that divides the world cleanly into the rural and the suburban: to the left there's farmland, to the right brand-new housing developments. The break is as clear as the Maginot Line. Eventually developers will breach the line and the tailored fields will become lanes and crescents as well, imposing their own arbitrary geometry on a world that's already been geometrized by the farmer's mind. People will import the names of swank downtown streets to the new developments, and other people will decide that certain treeless farmer's fields are more desirable locations than other farmer's fields. What no one will dispute is the time-worn homily that the suburbs are great for kids, when in fact the perks that the suburbs are supposed to provide — fresh air, safe streets, low street-people density — are primarily great for helping parents to relax. The suburbs are for *parents;* there probably isn't a normal child in the world who wouldn't rather wake up on a grimy city street.

"Rosie, look!" I yell suddenly, "The Emerald City!" An architectural prodigy rises in front of us, a huge Eastern Orthodox church, complete with gilded onion domes, stuck in the middle of a cornfield. By the time Rosie looks it's gone; she starts to wail, and I hand her her bottle. She hums around the nipple as we drive fast now, heading along the top of the city into the sun, towards the office of the man who saved her life.

The doctor's office is upstairs in a strip-plaza across from a larger mall, a colonial-trimmed red-brick neighbourhood plaza redeemed by several old cars showing real rust parked in the lot. The waiting-room is packed as usual when we walk through the door. I take Rosie over to a corner so she can play with her favourite toy, a wire roller-coaster with perforated beads you can slide down steep inclines and around loop-the-loops. A little blond boy is already there; she stands and watches him, very still, very interested. Feeling lucky I'm not a little blond boy, I go over to the desk to check in with the nurse, just as the doctor comes out of an examining room, wearing a pair of jeans and a plaid shirt. It's always been strange to see him in his civilian clothes, a bearded, kindly bulk of a young guy, with cornflower blue eyes. His demeanour is invariably modest to the point of apology, as though the power he got to display so dramatically one night was his only arbitrarily, and doesn't rightfully belong to him.

Now he says hi and as usual asks about the baby, noting that she looks fine and that he's convinced we're now "in the clear." Whenever he uses the expression, I see my family moving downfield in a football game, breaking clear of the coverage. Checking Rosie's chart, he adds that she's due to get a shot today, something Paula conveniently forgot to mention. I thank him and go back to Rosie in the corner. She's watching another blond boy now who's joined the first on the floor, the second one the image of the first, both of them beefy in matching striped T-shirts, like sailors on leave in Marseilles. Their mother is sitting on the couch beside them, diapering another kid. She's got henna-coloured hair, and is wearing a man's shirt, jeans, and — maybe because they were handy — rubber boots. There are women all over in the same sort of come-as-you-are apparel. I keep reading that times have changed, but ten years ago I was the only man at Jennifer's Moms 'N Tots Creating Together class, and today, once again, I'm the only man in the waiting room. When I do see men these days, they're almost never the only parent — they're with their wives — or if they are alone they're grandfathers, not fathers. A pediatric waiting-room is still the realm of women.

As such, it's a blessing. Whatever little macho discomfort I've felt at being the only man in "women's" locales — being called "Dad" by nursery-school teachers, as in "Oh, here's Dad now," or "Dad, do you want to take this permission slip with you?" (the teacherly syntax always sounding as dated as it was when Ward Cleaver visited the Beaver's classroom) — all this has been more than made up for in vicarious advantages. If *The Man Who Loved Women* is remade, it should be remade here, in the waiting-room of the Western World. In this place that is ninety-five percent hassle and five percent fear, a man can get to see the opposite sex at its harried best. In the haphazard way the waiting-room mothers wear their jeans, the distracted way they puff their hair out of their eyes while they deposit boots on the bench and haul another little kid onto their laps, in their apparent capacity to make peripheral an army of tasks that should be an all-consuming nightmare, they seem to me like the acme of competent sexiness. It's not that a woman in a tailored suit delivering a closing argument to a jury can't be sexy, it's just that she only has one thing to do. Versatility in women is a powerful aphrodisiac.

What I seem like to *them* — other than a novelty — has always been a mystery.

"Is that your daughter?"

It's the red-headed mother in the rubber boots, smiling at Rosie. She is, I say.

"She's so beautiful. And watchful, too."

"Thank-you." Actually Rosie looks as though she's sizing the two boys up for potential martyrdom. "Your sons are pretty good-looking too."

"Oh, they're not mine; they're my daughter's. I'm just their gran. Their mother hasn't been able to get these two into everyday day-care yet, and there's no junior kindergarten where she is, so I take them three times a week. This little guy's supposed to be in day-care, he's only two months old. But he's the patient today, aren't you, honey?" She squints at the baby on the bench. "It's a long drive for me up from Scarborough, but what are you going to do?" She looks up at me. "What are you here for?"

"A checkup. And a shot." I'm still trying to believe she's a grandmother. She must be in her late forties at most.

"Not that pertussis, I hope."

"No, a booster I think."

"That's good. One of the boys had a bad reaction to that pertussis vaccine."

"My daughter did, too. Not my son, though."

"You have a son, too?"

"Uh-huh. A nine-year-old."

"Uh-huh. Boys are different, aren't they?"

"They certainly are."

There's a lull. Up to this point this has been a classic waiting-room conversation, the kind women have as naturally as breathing, and the kind that is guaranteed to make a man nervous. Rosie has dropped to her knees now between the two boys, and may actually be about to play. "How about yourself?" I ask the red-headed grandmother. "What are you here for?"

"Oh, he has to get his business checked out, you know?" She means the baby. "From his circumcision in the hospital. My daughter thinks he might have an infection. He's got a little cold, too." She fastens a diaper tape, then leans forward a bit. "Tell me something," she says. "You have a son. Do you ever worry about the size of his equipment?"

I'm actually slow enough that for a second I visualize swings and a jungle-jim, playground equipment. She blushes in a workmanlike way. "Do you mind my asking this?" she says.

"This is his genitals we're talking about," I say.

"Actually his penis. Jimmy, *no* —" she reaches out to restrain one of the twins. "I'll tell you what it is. My daughter is really worried about the baby's penis; she thinks it's quite small."

Sometime this afternoon I'm planning to write a scene where a real-estate agent tells a suburban father she's the greatest genius since Einstein. It would help if the father looked pretty much the way I must look now. "It usually is when they're two months old," I say.

"No, I'm talking about really small. Her other two weren't built this way, she's sure of it. Anyway, she told her husband about it, and he got very annoyed. He thinks Louis falls well within the normal range and besides it isn't my daughter's business. This is a man's thing, according to him. He thinks it's perverted for her to be so involved in it." She pulls one of the twins onto her lap, keeping her hand on the maligned baby. "You're a man, what do you think?"

I think about it. "I don't know if it's perverted."

"But it still might be better if she just dropped it, right?"

"I don't know. I just think your daughter may not understand exactly what her husband's thinking. She may not know that what he's thinking about is how his son would feel about it."

"But he's a newborn. And he'll never know, right? She's just worried about him."

"Maybe that's what's bothering him. I mean, how would you feel about a man who told his wife he was worried that his teenage daughter's breasts were too small?"

She shakes her head as though I'm not getting it. "She'd be a teenager, and this one is barely a baby. Also, you can get by being flat-chested." The nurse calls out a name, and she turns. "Oh, that's me. Look, thanks very much for your viewpoint. Maybe I'll ask the doctor."

She pushes the twins ahead of her, carrying the baby with one hand. The door to the office opens as she passes it, like a movie scene dissolve, and a trio of women — two women and one girl — come in. I'm still in a kind of daze, the three of them are hard to ignore.

They're black, West Indian by the accent, and obviously related, from different generations. A grandmother, a mother and a daughter who could be anywhere from thirteen to sixteen; it's hard to tell because of her height. All three are tall and handsome, although the daughter, still gawky, looks as though she one day may be the beauty of the family. From the big boutiquey bags they're carrying they've just been shopping, probably at the mall across the road. The grandmother keeps motioning the granddaughter to take items out of the bag, scarves and sweaters, and hold them up in front of her in an impromptu fashion show. The granddaughter complies with a kind of pop forbearance, obviously embarrassed but not wanting to back down, rocking from side to side with her hands on her hips as she does to show her impatience. Meanwhile her mother and her grandmother deliver a running commentary on the clothes, doing everything but stroking their chins. Because half of what they're saying is in patois, it's hard to follow. But the actual meaning of the words isn't that significant, anyway. What is significant is their *business*: the intimate, cruel, loving, ironic, cozy mix of digs and affection that hold when the principals are female and the ties that bind are blood. Each generation up the ladder is better at it than the next. The grandmother, the maestro, works on the mother, the mother works on the daughter, and the daughter, fighting upwards, doesn't really have anyone to work on, although she doesn't seem to mind; maybe she knows that if she's patient enough her time will come, and in the meantime she can always practise on a man.

I'm still trying to eavesdrop when the nurse calls out Rosie's name. I pick her up from the wire roller-coaster, trying to steal a last glance at the floor-show, and take her into one of the examining cubicles. The nurse comes in, and weighs her and measures her, and then the doctor makes his appearance to palpate her body and answer the list of Paula's questions which I thankfully remembered to stick in my back pocket before I left home:

1. Should she still be drinking 2% milk, or should we be switching to 1%?
2. What are the chances she could still have adverse effects from her birth?

3. What *percentage* of kids have adverse effects from a birth like Rosie's? (this isn't the same as #2)
4. Mention her diet. Is she eating enough?
5. The hunch-back syndrome. Scoliosis runs in my family. Does she have scoliosis?
6. Has he read about the theory that lefties are more likely to die young? That traumatic births can cause left-handedness?

But all the time the doctor is answering Paula's questions, thoroughly and without irony, I'm thinking about another question that isn't on her list. It's been coming into focus ever since I walked into the waiting-room. It's tied to the conversation I had about the relative size of male procreative organs, to the three-woman West Indian tarantella I watched after that. It's tied to the fact that I would never consider writing a list of questions for any doctor, that in spite of my daughter's shaky entry into the world I've always been as convinced of her ultimate good health as her brother's and sister's.

It's still there when the doctor leaves and the nurse comes back in with the needle. She has coffee-coloured skin and a capacious voice.

"Tell me something," I say, as Rosie clenches her biceps on my lap, subconsciously sensing danger. "Who's better in these situations, men or women?"

She looks up at me for a moment, the needle poised.

"Let me think," she says.

But this isn't the question I really wanted to ask. The question I really wanted to ask was: "If the Raleigh father had been a mother, would she have taken the heart?"

The answer is the General Bifurcated-Gender Theory of the Insufficiency of Love.

If you're the parent, try this experiment. Take any normal activity you do with one of your children — going for a bike ride, going shopping for milk, teaching them to tie their shoelaces, asking them to get you a glass of water — and think of how you act during the process. Now imagine your spouse doing exactly the same thing with your child. Now — if you have a son and a daughter — imagine yourself doing the same thing with the child of the opposite sex; imagine your spouse doing likewise. Think about it a bit more. If you've managed not to tie yourself in knots and you're still on your feet, you're construing the General Bifurcated-Gender Theory of the Insufficiency of Love.

I first started thinking about the General Bifurcated-Gender Theory a few months after Ben was born, when it became obvious that the difference between the way my wife and I treated our daughter was child's play compared to the labyrinth of differences when you added a son. Over the next ten years the General theory subdivided itself into three special mini-theories of relativity: the Theory of Relative Worry, the Theory of Relative Torment and the Theory of Relative Salvation. Here the theories are, along with an apology beforehand for any headaches they induce.

I. The Theory of Relative Worry:

Fathers worry about the bodies of their daughters and the spirits of their sons. Mothers worry about the bodies of the daughters, and the bodies *and* spirits of their sons.

In diagrammatic terms:

The Theory of Relative Worry

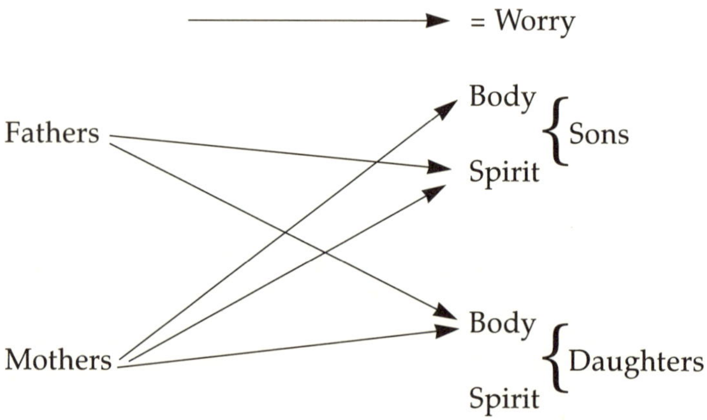

From the diagram, it should be clear — maybe not totally clear — that the spirits of sons and the bodies of daughters are lightning rods of worry, while the bodies of sons are a moderately nagging concern, and the spirits of daughters get no respect at all.

Consider the story of the "Fry Stealer."

About a year ago I got a phone call from the editor of the in-flight magazine for a national airline. The magazine had decided to expand its interest base, the editor said, to include the family traveller as well as the business commuter. She was particularly interested in families travelling to non-traditional destinations (for families). Would I be interested in touring the chateaux of the Loire Valley in France for a week with one of my children? I told her that I couldn't really choose between my two older children — even I wasn't crazy enough to want to take the baby — and my wife would kill me if I went without her. If they'd send the four of us, I'd consider it. I was sure that would be the end of the conversation, but she called back an hour later with a proposal; if I'd pay for my kids' flights, she'd pick up the tab for everything else. A month later Paula and I flew to Paris with Jennifer and Ben in tow, rented a car at the airport, and drove three hours south from the City of Light to the medieval town of Blois.

We got there about lunchtime, parked the car beside the hotel, and went out looking for something to eat. Appropriately, in a town where several famous medieval Frenchmen had been poisoned by Catherine of Medici, we ended up buying hamburgers and fries in the town square at a McDonald's clone called "Pacman." We took our food outside to eat in a cobblestone patio area. A few minutes after we sat down, there was a commotion a few stores away, and a short, swarthy guy, possibly in his mid-twenties, dressed in a tight ratty sweater, shuffled over to our table and stuck a laminated card in my face: the card — as much as I could understand of it — described his plight as a refugee in a foreign land, his destitute family and his need for assistance. In accented French that was probably Algerian he kept saying he was hungry and rubbing his index finger and thumb together manically. All around me French people were shaking their heads *non*, so I said *non*, too. He walked away, jiggled a few times, then came back to the table fast, and stuck his hand into Ben's plate and grabbed half the French fries off it, stuffing them into his mouth immediately.

My reaction amazed me; I don't remember getting up from the table at all, I only remember suddenly having my arm around his neck and shoulders and moving him firmly from the table with a steely kind of discretion, talking to him in English he couldn't understand but that was pure Clint Eastwood to me. "This is no good, my friend," I said to him, or something like it. "You can't do things like that. What you can do is take this money —" I handed him some francs — "and get lost, or I'll call the police. *Gendarme*, you understand?" He took off with the cash, probably laughing all the way to the bank at my bravado, but at least he was gone.

That night in bed at the hotel Paula told me she didn't know what she would have done if I hadn't been there. "I don't think I could have touched him. I would have been afraid of him. Unless he did something to Jennifer, then I could have done something." I knew what she meant. My reaction if it had been my daughter would have been just as quick and probably more violent, but it also would have been more stock. With Jenny I would have gotten up to remove the threat to her skin; her soul would take care of itself.

But when the Fry Stealer's hand rose from his plate clutching half his food, Ben let out a little cry of shock, "Ahhh!" that went directly not to my gut but to my heart. I wasn't worried about his being injured, I was worried about his being haunted. I knew that cry, and I knew that in the nights to come the spectre of the Fry Stealer, and the little piece of the universe he shattered, would be lodged in my son's fervid imagination. I knew because his imagination was mine.

I hadn't known it from the beginning. When Ben was born, the most common comment from well-wishers was that with a son I would "feel differently." More than a few of them, sounding like they were in a thirties drawing-room comedy, actually said that now I would "feel" like a father. Even my wife got into the act indirectly, letting me know it was all right to admit now that I had wanted a son all along.

In fact, if anything, the opposite was true. Before my son was born I was primarily a ladies' man — adult or child. The pluses a son could provide seemed minor and redundant by comparison. As a camp counsellor and later an uncle I'd taught dozens of boys how to throw a baseball and shoot a basketball, and if I wanted to play catch I had plenty of adult friends to call up now. The traditional allure of a male heir, having someone to carry on the family name, seemed as immaterial as fog (I assumed my daughter, like her mother, would keep her last name, anyway). Unlike sons, daughters had skin like flowers and actually seemed miraculous in their creation. Girls were mysterious aliens. Boys were familiar as buddies. I knew exactly what boys were. I was one. Who needed another one?

When my son did arrive there were differences, but not the differences that anyone had predicted. They fell into two unconventional categories: Looks, and Fear.

It's awkward to admit now, but before both my daughters were born I actually spent some real time hoping that I would like their looks. Basically I was rooting for them to be my type. If their mouths were too narrow, I worried, or their fingers were bent too far backwards, I wouldn't be able to love them with a hundred percent of my being. So it was a kind of relief as opposed to delight to discover that both of them had exactly the features, the squished little Betty Boop rosebuds of mouths and the wide dark eyes, that I was a sucker for. What a coincidence!

With my son, though, I expected nothing, and reaped a bonanza. From the moment I first saw him — beat up and slope-headed from his extra time in the birth canal — I thought he was the "handsomest guy I'd ever seen in my life." This became my absolutely deadpan serious appraisal of him, the deadpanness of which was capable of making Paula laugh in a totally baffled way for years afterward. "He's the handsomest guy I've ever seen in my life," I'd say, and she'd look at me as though I was crazy. It was my mantra. I said it like hammer-strokes in case anyone doubted not just his handsomeness but my conviction. There were days, granted, when he looked like the cousin of the toothless idiot savant who played "Duelling Banjos" in the movie *Deliverance*, but they were no large deal to overlook. Even after the blush on the rose had faded, after his breath, in John Irving's phrase, "was no longer as sweet," I could still resurrect my "handsomest guy in the world" faith on demand.

But there was a flip-side: if I had pure faith in my son's physical attractiveness, I had almost none in his psychic strength. From the beginning I was far more afraid for him, far less confident of his ability to ultimately deflect the slings and arrows of the world than I was of my daughters'. Jennifer's six-pound body inside her receiving blankets had an immutable wiriness to it; Ben's nine-pound heft seemed to contain a large measure of bluster.

It was too familiar.

If you examine any of the famous father-son pairings in literature, or look at images of them on film or in still photographs, you will usually detect one common thread: the emotions expressed by the fathers in the books or movies or snapshots are simple. They may be tender or violent, inarticulate or roaring, but they're almost always simple, and simple to read. The simplicity is a function of recognition. Fathers don't need to spend a lot of time figuring out what their sons are feeling, because they already know. They may have trouble dealing with the feelings, or acting on them, or responding appropriately, but they know what the feelings are — because they're boys themselves. They know the limits of their sons' courage; it's their limit, too.

I will never know the parentheses of my daughters' strength, I'll have to guess; but with my son, from the beginning I knew every weak link in his soul — or at least I thought I did — because I knew him. I could get inside the fear in his eyes, and the texture of his goofiness. I knew when he was lying, and when he wanted me to know that he was lying, when he wanted me to pry (practically always) and when he wanted me to "beat him up" (always). His first summer on the planet we had a Jamaican baby-sitter named Val, who would take hourly breaks to smoke Gauloises on the back porch and tell me stories of how many shots were fired at the house parties she went to on the weekend. Val like to sit Ben on her lap like "a big rude boy," even though he was only two months old and he couldn't really hold his big head up properly. While his head lolled back and forth and she tried, like Edgar Bergen with Charlie McCarthy, to get it to stop and stay seated in the saddle of his shoulders with a little bit of dignity, I had the feeling I could predict every sway of his big noggin, and the amplitude of its drop. In the same way that parents feel their mouths moving when their infants eat, I actually felt my head lolling when Ben's did. I knew his troubles even then. What I didn't know was that I was probably afraid of the knowledge, and that it was that fear, and not any bachelor proclivities, that had made me leery from the beginning about the birth of a son. To know a person as thoroughly as a father knows a son is not unlike the pressure of saving another person's life as a Japanese: you become responsible for that person in a way you never will be for anyone else. Any secret deficits you have in your own soul you automatically worry will surface in theirs; if you feel terror in yourself you figure they will probably feel it too. You particularly want to save them because you know how much they need to be saved, but the reason for their need is exactly the reason you're worried the rescue may be so hard to pull off.

This mutual identification society might also be the main reason why sons can drive fathers crazier than anyone else, and why fathers are harder on sons than on anyone else. What's operating here isn't just the Freudian cliché, but the Danny Thomas cliché. Danny Thomas played a harried Lebanese father on the old sitcom "Make Room for Daddy," who was most harried by his red-headed son, Rusty. His daughter on the show was capable of striking him dumb, but Rusty (Russell, Danny called him when he got mad) drove him crazy continually. He did it, Danny said, "with the *little* things."

He was right. It is the little things about sons that drive fathers crazy. Their habits are ours as much as their bodies, so we know what to look for. Ben, an addictive personality to begin with, had a weakness for chants: "I am a garbage truck" was a big one when he was six, along with maddening mis-re-creations of ad jingles: "McDonald's (as opposed to Red Lobster) for the seafood lover in you!" This drove me crazy. He wore his T-shirt hanging out under his sweatshirt like a butcher's apron, and this drove me crazy. He never did his shoelaces up; this drove me crazy. He couldn't play fifteen minutes of catch without digressing; he was hypersensitive to the point of universal paranoia; he worried about offending gas station attendants; he covered his shoes with a washcloth before he went to bed at night, so they wouldn't be cold — and this drove me craziest of all.

The transgressions of sons are small; the anger of fathers is large. One winter night last year after a day of terrible work, when Paula was out with the girls, I had to help my son take a shower. I adjusted the water, fetched him towels, made sure the rubber mat was anchored so he wouldn't break his neck when he climbed into the tub like a wildebeest. I was already in a horrible mood when he called downstairs five minutes later to say he needed help. I went upstairs to find the big bath towel I'd given him lying in the hall, not put away. It was a King Tut towel, a souvenir from the tour of the King Tut artifacts a few years before, that we'd had hanging in our first house as a wall-covering. It was the last straw. I steeled my entire body and brought my leg back to kick it with pure, satisfying rage. As I was on the downstroke, the blanket moved and Ben stuck his big head out, giggling. I went briefly insane — there's no other word for it. "Are you crazy?" I yelled. "What were you thinking? I could have kicked you, I could have really hurt you. You crazy *jerk*. You crazy, crazy *jerk.*" Even as I said it — the novel, terrible combination of words "crazy jerk" — I was already realizing how shocked he was. He went, cowering, into his bedroom, and sat down on the bed, and pulled his blankets over his head. I hoped he was laughing, but I knew he was sobbing. I pulled the blanket back, but he kept hunkering down into it, his breath short, saying "No, no, no." Ninety percent of the time, when his sister Jenny cried, or locked herself in her room — or when she insulted her mother — I had no idea why. But with Ben I always knew; that was the difference. At every step of the crime I had known exactly what he was feeling on the other side of my sadism. Big hero that I was, I had frightened him into speechlessness. All he had wanted to do was to play a joke. He thought I would laugh.

Now, a murderer, I tried to make it up to him. "Shhh, okay. I'm sorry. I was just worried I was going to hurt you. Okay. You're too sensitive, Benny."

"It was a *joke.*"

"I know. Shhh. You're too sensitive, Ben. You're too sensitive."

He was, of course, even though I was saying it to pardon myself. He was a few times too sensitive for his own good — maybe a bit eccentric too. He thought smithereens was a fruit, he loved the sound a librarian made when she closed a book, and he considered travelling "one of his hobbies." He ordered a hamburger with "the fixin's" one day because that's the way it was spelled on the menu. He hated the movie *Lord of the Flies* because the boys killed Piggy. He danced like Henry the Eighth. He had a gleam in his eye like a pirate.

He drove me crazy.

> Raleigh, N.C., AP — "Grieving Mom's Heart-Tugger." A woman waiting for a heart transplant agreed to take the heart of her daughter, killed yesterday in an accident. "It was the only heart that could have saved me," said Edwina Reid, 45, "and I know Linda Sue would have wanted me to have it . . ."

II. The Theory of Relative Torment:

Sons torment fathers and mothers. Daughters torment mothers. Mothers torment sons and daughters, and fathers scare sons. Fathers wouldn't mind being able to scare daughters too, but even if they did, chances are they'd never know about it.

Again, representationally:

The Theory of Relative Torment

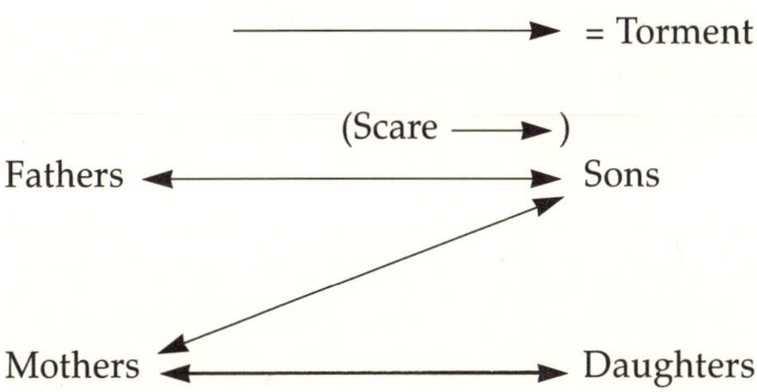

Once again the diagram complicates what most families already know: fathers and daughters get off lightest in the mutual torment department, mothers and sons the worst.

In fact, this "torment differential" is probably the most visible part of the difference between the way mothers and fathers react to their children, particularly their sons. My son drives me crazy, and I respond by scaring the daylights out of him. My son drives my wife crazy, and she reacts by driving him even crazier in return. She does this with a simple tactic the average father couldn't duplicate even if he wanted to: being personal. The words "You're not treating me very nicely" or "*You're* not fair" out of my wife's mouth are enough to do it. They have an even longer-lasting effect than the "You crazy jerk" from me. Where fathers lose their minds, mothers get personal. Where fathers grow distant, mothers get under your skin. Where fathers yell *at* you, mothers talk *to* you.

Mothers and sons, that is, have a complex relationship. When it comes to mothers and daughters the complexity moves off the chart.

In one of the great moments in the movie *Moonstruck*, Olympia Dukakis, playing an Italian mother, pinches Cher, playing her daughter, on the fleshy part of the arm as she walks out of a room. At this point in the movie the room also contains Nicholas Cage, the man who wants to marry Cher, whom she also wants to marry, but whom her mother *does not* want her to marry. The pinch, a hard one, is so authentic it's hard to believe it was in the script — it has the feel of tactile reality. It's a complex pinch, pregnant with a complex message: "What are you doing? This guy's a baker. Forget about whatever's bothering you. What is bothering you anyway? Love? Forget about Love. The brother is reliable, for God's sakes. You know what I mean. He's a man, but at least he's reliable. *Capisce*?"

And that would only be a précis. By contrast at another point in the movie Danny Aiello shoves his brother with two hands in the middle of the chest. This time the double message is fairly simple. "I love you, asshole," is close. What is certain is that no father ever gave any son a pinch as telegraphically prolix as the one Olympia gave to Cher on the movie screen.

To me at least, the relationship between my wife and my daughter is the mysterious centrepiece of our household. From the time Jennifer was old enough to speak, her communication with her mother has been a matter of speculation. It's characterized by energies of love that seem incredibly powerful half the time, and terrifically entertaining—but inaccessible—the next. And it grazes on the apparent the way well-fed cows graze on clover. Nothing is ever as it seems, precisely because so often it *is* what it seems. Like the pinch in *Moonstruck,* like the comment that created the crisis of the day this morning, the message is always simultaneously more obvious and less obvious than the words obviously imply.

It's *personal.* The word is impossible not to come back to. "I'm getting tired of doing things for people who hurt my feelings," Paula will tell me. The statement mystifies me as much as her habit of asking our children periodically if they "love her." (This is an impulse that apparently starts early: a woman I know pinned a set of photos of her four-month-old son up on her bulletin board after she went back to work, all of them including the penned-in caption, "Mommy, I love you.") "Do you love me?" and "You hurt my feelings" are two messages which are not in the native fatherly vocabulary. Your children can be didactic, a father will acknowledge, and reveal things to you about yourself, maybe give you pause with the truth, they can tell you you swear in the car too much, or that you sound like an idiot when you lose your temper, or even cause you to lose your temper and act like an idiot — but hurt you with rudeness or insults? With fathers it doesn't happen. Whatever else their failings are, most fathers know that a parent needs a glassy conceit to survive. You can't take things personally, because half the time children, especially older ones, aren't even aware you're there. The critical thing to remember is the source of the censure. Children are idiots in their own right.

The difference is in the valence of intimacy. It makes sense to talk of bonding between fathers and sons, but mothers and daughters are already bound. The knowledge I share with my son is knowledge of ourselves, setting out together naked from the starting blocks of life, a couple of yokels aiming to move forward to try to figure out how the world works. The knowledge my wife shares with my daughter already has the feel of how the world works; they're starting halfway down the track, with so much more already understood that they might have been running for days. They're like an old married couple, a pair of crony partners from the garment industry. You could measure their relationship in dog-years — every minute they spend together is like seven. Is it any wonder they sometimes get on each other's nerves?

The difference is knowledge, who has it and who wants it. I know Ben, and because of that knowledge half the time I want to kill him. I want to kill him because I'd rather not know him so well, but he wants me to know him even better, a combination that can drive you crazy quicker than anything. Ben is always hugging everyone, going on love rampages. "Dad, I love you," he'll say spontaneously, like a refugee from an EST experience. "Mom, I love you." On the other hand my wife would love to get to know my daughter even better than she already does, but Jenny doesn't want to be known. Jenny's response is silence, the cruellest move on the block. "She's so beautiful, but she's so cruel," Paula says, her version of "He's the handsomest guy I've ever seen in my life." My love is over-requited. My wife's is under-requited. (In the end we may have to turn to each other.)

The difference is dialogue. The conversations I have with my son are fledgling versions of the conversations men have in locker rooms, less boring but almost as dumb in their obliqueness: no matter what we say to each other we're only saying one of two things — I love you, or I'm going to kill you. The conversations my wife and my daughter have are denser versions of the conversations women have in restaurants or medical waiting-rooms — fascinating, on-point, and always about people and feelings. For me to listen to my wife and daughter talk is like listening to boustrophedon, the ancient Greek language that was written on city porticos in a zig-zag, "as the ox ploughs": first left to right, then with reversed letters right to left. Just when you think you know what's being discussed, the conversation heads in another direction, with words no longer meaning what they meant a second ago and nuances capsized to their flip-side. In the layered haze you realize that you have to listen to the silences as acutely as to the words now, and even then you will probably never catch the drift completely. And that, too, is no doubt just as well.

But all the difference between the sexes — mother-daughter/father-son differences, differences in dialogue, differences in confidence, differences in relative torment — take a back seat to the third special theory of relativity: The Theory of Relative Salvation.

In a gem of a short story called "The Mission," the American poet Reginald Gibbons describes coming home one day to find his five-year-old daughter crying, apparently over a minor crisis that occurred with a friend at school. She keeps crying, longer than the problem merits, and then suddenly blurts out what's really bothering her: "You and Mommy left without even saying good-bye to me!" Gibbons is dumbfounded. "When?" he says. "The first day of kindergarten," says his daughter. "But you wanted us to leave!" Gibbons says. "You were lined up with the other kids to go into class behind the teacher, I thought you were happy to go in!" "But the other parents were still there!" his daughter wails, "And you left without even saying good-bye!" And as his daughter begins to cry in earnest, standing on the porch step above him, Gibbons realizes he has just been given an on-the-spot lesson on the limitless scope of his love for her, and the very real limits of his capacity to save her. "I understand again what I must do as long as she and I live," he writes, "and how much I want to do this, to love her, and need to, and how too it is not enough. It is in the way of things, and no blame on anyone for it, that it is not enough."

It's a nice sentiment, and a nicer story, but somehow you can't help hearing his wife telling her daughter through the screen door behind her: "Okay, enough, sweetheart. We're sorry we left you, but we're here, and there's nothing we can do about it now. So if you want to watch 'Star Trek' before supper you better dry your eyes, and have a glass of juice and get moving."

The Theory of Relative Salvation

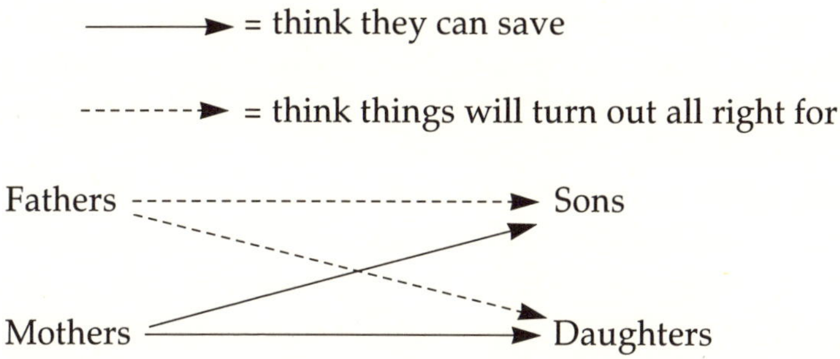

It's fathers, Reginald Gibbons included, who feel they will ultimately be unable to save their children. We feel it from the moment we have children, and we're doomed to feel it at regular intervals after that. We know our kids will ultimately be thrown onto their own devices, but deep down we don't think they'll be able to handle it (we don't think *anyone* can handle it), and even worse we don't think we'll be able to do anything about it. This doesn't stop us from trying to save them globally, with grand gestures like bringing them into the business or sitting on the porch steps holding their hands and writing stories about it afterward. We do this because at heart, paradoxically, we're diehard optimists; we're sure everything will work out in the end.

Mothers for their part *do* believe they're powerful enough to save their children; it's just the interfering world that won't let them. Being practical, though, they continue to do the small things that can be done to help protect their children. At the same time they're the incurable fatalists on the parental see-saw. Mothers are the vocal worriers. But where mothers can become hyperactive in their pessimism, fathers can be immobilized in their optimism. Fathers can be paralyzed by love.

Up until two years ago I played basketball every Sunday afternoon in a pick-up game in the basement gym of a downtown hospital that was trying to supplement funds by renting its facilities to outside groups. The game attracted a mixed bag of players in ability and age; half of us were friends of the person who had done the renting, the other half were on staff at the hospital. One of the best hospital players was an older man, a burly Australian-born orthopedist, a good six-five in height and more than sixty years old, who was a relentless rebounder and on-court competitor. Off the court, though, he was from another generation, with lovely old-world manners and a total lack of hubris no matter what the subject of conversation was. Most of the conversation we had took place at an oyster bar across the road from the hospital, where half a dozen of us went for beer after the game. The majority of us talked the classic male hierarchy of talk, sports, business, cars, breasts, and only ultimately, because we were "liberated," families. The orthopedist tended to start at the other end. After a few months he knew something about all our home lives, and we had a clear, if reserved picture of the members of his family: his wife, who was a semi-retired actress, a daughter in medical school, and a younger son who was starting up his own software business.

At the last game before the Christmas holiday the turnout was small, and the two of us ended up drinking alone at the bar. He was in the middle of talking about his son's latest advertising brainstorm — he was going to direct-mail software disks — when he stopped himself and said: "Here's an interesting thing. Brian got a call from his brother yesterday." I thought I'd misheard. I thought he only had one son, I said. "No," he said. "We have an older boy, too. Our first. He's in Miami now; I'm not sure exactly what he's doing. We had some problems with him a while back, and he doesn't speak to us any more. Not directly, anyhow. We'll get a cryptic message through his brother every once in a while. But he hasn't spoken directly to us in, what, it must be seven years."

And that was essentially the story. Without being asked he filled in what else there was of it. When his family had moved from Australia to Canada his son, high-school age at the time, had been "angry about the move" and had fallen in with a "rough crowd." No rougher than in Australia, he said, but he'd never been "that kind of boy." And things had deteriorated from there. He'd gotten angrier, and his father had gotten angrier. And one day, just before his son's high-school graduation, the orthopedist had come home with his wife from the cottage and he was gone. They hadn't seen him or heard his voice since.

"He was married for a while to some infant of a girl who was still in high-school. I think that's over now, thank God. No children, fortunately. This is not a person you'd want raising a brood right now." He shifted in his seat and took a sip of beer, looking up at the TV set over the bar tuned to a late NFL game, a huge man in a crew-neck sweater and a greying, boyish haircut. There was no indication of how he was feeling, other than the fact that he didn't seem to be able to get comfortable in his chair. "My wife is just broken up by it, of course. You can't even talk to her about it. She's still trying to make contact, through his brother. She doesn't sleep nights worrying about it, and then when there's some hope she doesn't sleep nights hoping. I've given up. He's too angry. He's just totally unreasonable. My son." He looked up at the football game again, and then he looked back at me. His gaze was without defence. "I have no idea what happened," he said.

Who could say he was being dishonest? Not me. Not then, and not now. That night, lying in bed, the odds were good his wife would say her wish out loud twelve different ways because she was afraid it would never come true, while he would refuse to mention it, like the name of God, because he thought there was a chance it might. A mother, she would lie awake afterwards, her mind racing; a father, he would fall asleep. But her waking dream would be the same as his sleeping one: that three thousand miles away a grown young man would have mercy on two people dying for love in the dark; that somehow on the other side of the million light years of interstellar space he had erected between them, their child would pause on his way to the bathroom or the front door, pick up the receiver, and phone home.

4

A Father's Phone Call

"When I was eighteen years old I thought my father was the dullest man on the planet. By the time I turned twenty I was amazed to see what he had learned in two years."

(attributed to) Mark Twain

1:50 p.m.

According to legend, William Faulkner wrote *As I Lay Dying* in forty-seven nights, while he was on his down-time from shovelling coal in a powerhouse. It's an intriguing statistic. The Library of America edition of *As I Lay Dying* contains 178 pages. Figuring 400 words to the page, Faulkner would have to have written six pages or 1,500 words a night to finish the book in a month. Fifteen hundred words is approximately the length of an article in *Sports Illustrated* or a J.D. Salinger short story. Later in his life, after Faulkner secured a family of his own, and became an alcoholic, his output dwindled. People blamed the alcohol; I was never convinced. What I wanted to know was this: in those dark, blazingly creative hours at the steel foundry, while the sparks were flying from the furnace floor and Bill's mind both, did he have a phone in the room? Was there someone depending on him to pick up supper? Was there a black-eyed little girl in the back seat recovering from a booster shot and singing a song like a cross between Frances the Badger and Alice Cooper: "I like to swing with a monster's head in a big basket, not a bad monster, a witch, a wicked witch called Missus Skultch, with *green* skin in the sky..."?

On the way back from the doctor's I make two scheduled stops, one to get gas and money from a bank machine — eighty dollars as opposed to a hundred to fool myself into thinking my account isn't plummeting as fast as it is — the second to shop for supper: chicken, green beans, cucumbers and bread. There's a Bi-Way in the same plaza as the grocery store, so I also drop in to buy Ben a couple of pairs of sweatpants, which Paula mentioned he needed last night, because he was starting to look "mouldy" again. By now I'm used to buying my son's clothes by myself; I can eyeball his size at a glance. He keeps threatening that he's going to come with me one of these days, but he always finds something to do at the last minute. The only exception was one Saturday last summer, when I took him to buy a suit for his aunt's wedding. We went to a store that specialized in fancy dress for boys, the kind of mini-gentlemen's shop that was common when I was his age, but that nowadays is as rare as jade. He loved it; the racks of suits and sports jackets, in particular, all his size, all the same but for colour and fabric. He even loved the hunkering old salesman, who slipped the jackets on his shoulders, tweaking out the pads and smoothing down the back vents, laying on the "perfects" as thick as sour cream, doing everything but asking us if we wanted an extra set of pants. This was a "real" store, my son informed me, taking a tweed double-breasted number off the hanger and closing the lapels tight in front of him as though he had a bad chest cold. "This is the way they do it, Dad. James Bond." The light of passage was in his eyes; he would remember this day for a long time; suits would always be magical.

For me it was underwear. When I was eight my father took me to Spadina Avenue to buy clothes, a wide, raunchy, "textile" street downtown that could have come out of New York's Lower East Side, jammed with street-cars and diagonal parking. Specifically to a long, dark bowling-alley of a shop owned by Frank Shore, a Slavic jobber who had huge gaps between his teeth and couldn't say "V." Never without a cigar, Frank would welcome my father, a supplier of his, with a big, beaming "Abie! What do you want? Some boxes underwear? T-shirts? Wee-necks?" At Frank's the box was the basic mathematical unit; buying less than a box was unthinkable. You bought two boxes, four, maybe half a box if you were a particular *schnorrer*, everything in the boxes white and a bit too big — Stanfield briefs, sweatsocks, snowy white T-shirts with "wee-necks." For me, going to Frank's was like going to visit a Ukrainian oracle in his cave; he was always asking me short, fecund riddles I couldn't answer. "So, *boychick*, what's the plan? Any funny business below the belt?" For my father, Frank had the advantage of not only being cheap, but also being far enough from our house that we could keep the details of how much we were spending hidden from my mother, who worried about such things.

Times have changed.

My only unplanned stop is at the neighbourhood library, to pick up a book on marble-playing they're holding for me: *The Great American Marble Book* by "noted" marble aficionado Fred Ferretti. "Everything you forgot about immies, mibs, purees, pee-wee's, etc., and how to play Last Clams!" boasts the front cover. I check it out, along with a book for Rosie which she won't let go of: Robert Munsch's *Love You Forever*. We have *Love You Forever* at home already, but the redundancy doesn't bother her. She's adamant: "This is a *different* book," she says.

I'm looking forward to heading downstairs as soon as we get home to challenge Faulkner's record, but there's someone on the porch when we pull in the driveway. A missionary group, a family I see when I come up the stairs with Rosie and the parcels: Jehovah's Witnesses if the magazines in their hands are an indication. On the verge of ringing the doorbell, now they step aside apologetically to let me through to hand Rosie to Lucy for lunch and her nap. There's a thin freckled man in a black suit, a more ample woman wearing blue, and, surprisingly — this is a school day — a blond boy in a blazer who looks as though he could be about my son's age. Because of the boy I find myself not being able to be as curt as I want to — which may be the idea. I mention that I'm busy, but it seems to have no effect.

"We'd just like to have a little chat with you about God's place in your life. And possibly leave you some of our literature."

"Actually," I point to the *mezuzah* on the door jamb, "we're Jewish, as you can see." This is meant to make them feel guilty, but also to give the boy a kind of out, a reason for rejection other than simple irritation. He's standing very stiffly, like an automaton, looking down at the pamphlet in his hand.

"Why don't you just take these? There's no charge of course. You can look at them at your leisure."

"I really don't think so," I want to close the door, I have work to do, but the boy is stopping me. His head is still stoically down, just a faint rim of red tingeing the downy tops of his earlobes.

"Could you hang on for one second?" I say. I let the screen close, and, not quite believing what I'm doing, I go into the living-room, to the shelf where we keep our High Holiday prayerbooks, our "religious" section, my son calls it. Rummaging, I find what I'm looking for, a hardcover book called *A Treasury of Jewish Thought*.

I walk back to the front door with the book in my hand.

"I'll make you a deal," I say to the father. "You take this and read it, and I'll take your material and read it. Does that sound fair to you?"

The boy looks up, involuntarily, and glances from the book to his father, his face flushed. The older man looks only at the book, not flustered but intent, calculating something at adding-machine speed, more like an accountant than an arm of God. "I don't think we can do that; that's an expensive book."

"It's all right, yours is expensive as well."

Time stretches a little more. The father calculates; his son watches him, either because he can't believe what's happening or to see what his father's going to do — I can't tell which.

"Fine," the mother says suddenly, a message for her husband in its peevishness. There are souls to be saved. "That's fine. Thank-you." She takes the *Treasury of Jewish Thought* and puts it in her valise. "Eric, give the gentleman our material." The boy hands it to me, avoiding my gaze.

"Would your son like a glass of juice, or pop? He looks thirsty."

"No, he's fine. Thank-you for your interest. God bless you."

They leave, a bit anti-climatically, going down the steps and onto the sunny street. I wait to see if the father will ask the mother to see *The Treasury of Jewish Thought*, or if the son will suddenly clamour to get a look at it, in a delayed reaction to the little incident on the porch. None of it happens; it's as though people offer them barter all the time; they continue on beside the curb with the dignity of people inappropriately dressed for the suburbs, the son's bowed head and gangly energy once again yoked to the common cause.

I'm going to have to explain to Paula what happened to her *Treasury of Jewish Thought*, which I think we got for our wedding. And I forgot to ask them — the perfect survey group — about the Raleigh man.

JOEY and SEYMOUR are still at the window.

SEYMOUR

All right, so I owe you every immie I have. Let's play some Last Clams.

The doorbell rings

JOEY

Jehovah's Witnesses again. Five to one. I'll get it.

JOEY half-runs to the FRONT DOOR, and opens it. CHARLOTTE MILLER is standing on the porch. JOEY is too excited for a moment to open the SCREEN.

CHARLOTTE

Hi, hon, is your Dad home?

SEYMOUR

Right here.

CHARLOTTE

Could I have a word with you, Seymour?

SEYMOUR

Sure. (He steps outside)
What can I do for you, Charlotte?

CHARLOTTE

Seymour, I want you to just listen to me for a moment, and accept what I'm about to say to you with an open mind. I want you to banish doubt from your heart, Seymour. Can you do that, Seymour?

SEYMOUR

As long as there's no real-estate involved.

CHARLOTTE
Seymour, I want you to accept that I'm a greater genius than Albert Einstein.

I stop. Not because I've heard anything but because I sense something behind me: I turn and see Rosie standing alone in the doorway this time. The playroom lights are dark behind her and she has the look of a waif who's been fending for herself for the past six months on the surface of Venus. She's holding her book in both her hands like a wedding-ring cushion.

"Dad, read me it," she says.

"Rosie, I don't want to read you it. I'm busy. Where's Lucy?"

"It's a *different* book, Dad."

"It's the book you got at the library, Rosie. It's the same book as one we have here."

"Dad, do you have hazel eyes?"

I call upstairs, but there is no answer. Lucy must be doing laundry.

"Rosie, if I read you the book, you leave me alone, all right? Come here."

I pull her onto my lap, and open her book on the keyboard, thinking that it's unusual of her to like it so much — a book, *Love You Forever*, my kids can usually take or leave. The reason its author, Robert Munsch, has sold so many copies of it — over five million world-wide to date — isn't kids, but parents. *Love You Forever* has a fairly stock story-line — about a little boy whose mother rocks him every night as he grows up and tells him she'll love him forever — and one of the eeriest illustrations in any children's book I've ever seen. I flip to it now, over

Rosie's objections. It's a picture, by Sheila McGraw drawn from above in that dated Golden Book Middle-American Gothic style, of a car driving through the night with a ladder roped on top. Meanwhile the story is telling us that the boy has grown into young manhood, gotten a place of his own on the other side of town — but that sometimes in the middle of the night, his mother gets into her car...

I turn the page, to the next picture, of, of course, the mother sitting on a bed now, holding her big strapping sleeping son in her arms, the ladder propped on the open window behind her. This picture isn't as successful — somehow the mother has mutated into a white-haired granny with wire-rims and a bun. But together with the illustration of the ladder on the car, it forms a whole idea that's both insane and perfectly logical. To a parent, that is. Most non-parents I've shown the book to either think it's insane or pathological. Who would use a ladder? My Aunt Barbara, I tell them, who liked to cruise past the poolhall in her curlers and housecoat every night to check on my nineteen-year-old cousin. It's a thing mothers do.

"Read me it," Rosie says.

"No." I dump her off my lap hard. "That's it. Go to Lucy. Get out of here."

A beat. Then she turns, her face breaking up, and heads out the door, with that stiff stumble that comes before the collapse. As if in retribution the telephone rings.

I figure it's going to be my wife, psychic avenger, but it's my father, calling from Florida. Checking in, in his phrase. The least nosy of parents, my father still manages to call twice a week from their winter address to see how things are with me and my work ("So when are we going to see something in print?") and to wonder if Rosie's awake. This is his standard Florida agenda, although he probably reverses his real priorities out of politeness — what am I now after all but a machine that produces grandchildren? With the gentlest pressure imaginable he prods me, my old man, to give him something to be proud about. A little something, anything, so he can call my mother: "Shosh, come here, listen to this!"

Today is no exception. He asks me about the "movie business," and a fairly well known character actress who called him a couple of months ago by mistake, looking for me. I tell him that I've found out the actress calls everybody, so he shouldn't get too excited. We laugh about that, but he's still waiting. I can't resist it.

"We sold the game in France last week, Dad, did you know that?"

"You did? You didn't say a word. Shosh, come listen to this! Your son's got something to tell you!"

My mother gets on the extension. I tell both of them about our latest coup in the toy-business world (besides the writing "business," I've been inventing board-games with a partner for the past few years). At the same time, before they can ask about Rosie, I take the opportunity to tell them the story of the Raleigh man.

With my parents, too, there's a pause when I'm finished. Then my father says: "Fortunately, with the heart I've got now I don't have to worry about that problem."

He's talking about his recent bypass surgery, but my mother isn't impressed. "How can you say that? Is there any question? How could anyone do a thing like that to their child?"

"So you wouldn't take the heart, Mom?"

"Definitely not."

"Dad?"

"I don't know. I'm not a theologian. I'm not any kind of logian."

My mother actually laughs. "Is Rosie up?" she asks.

I put my daughter on the phone, watching her breathe with noisy graveness into the receiver, listening as intensely as one huge ear, naturally refusing, after a morning of garrulousness, to say a word. While I do I think about my father's joke. "I'm not a theologian; I'm not any kind of logian." As corny as it is, there's no arguing with it — it is a father's joke. Lately I've found myself becoming more and more prone to the cheesiest puns imaginable, actually enjoying it when I can make my kids groan instead of laugh. A biological imperative is invading my sense of humour. Until she was seven or eight, my younger sister actually believed that all people who passed the age of sixty lost the facility to speak English, and gained a sudden fluency in Yiddish — it made sense; she didn't know any older people who were native North Americans. Similarly I don't know a single father (now grandfather) of my father's generation who doesn't share his sense of humour. A lot of them are quippy, lively guys, canny and innocent at once. The difference (between them and me) is that when they tell their groaners, or speak Yiddish, or do accents, they manage it with a solid legitimacy that no contemporary of mine could duplicate. How to be unshamedly corny is just one more thing our fathers know that we do not.

What did my father and his cronies always know that my peers and I don't? Stylistically, how to *be* fathers.

Illusion or not, they had the routine down pat. They wore houndstooth slacks instead of jeans (at least until they became grandfathers), their sneakers were strictly for handball at the Y, and they rarely missed work. They believed in the triumph of good and in people with Dr in front of their names. They never complained. They didn't indulge in the public acknowledgement of fear. They always managed to pick up the check first.

And most critically, they gave us our "moments." If every father has one instant in his life when he realizes what his relationship to his child will always be, every child has a whole repertoire of moments when he realizes what his relationship to his father can never be again.

In my ham-handed way this may have been what I was trying to give the Jehovah's Witness boy: a better moment with his father than the one he was having.

The most revealing "son-father" moment ever recorded for posterity probably occurred on the afternoon of July 31st, 1970, in the thirty-third year of the writer Geoffrey Wolff's life. That afternoon, Wolff was sitting in a wicker armchair drinking black rum and tonic, along with his wife's brother-in-law, on the terrace of the home of a friend in the village of Narragansett, Rhode Island. One of his young sons, Nicholas, had just left for a car-ride with his grandmother in her old black Ford sedan; the other, Justin, was with Wolff's wife at the beach. At one point the phone rang, and his wife's brother-in-law, whose name was John, was called to the phone. When he came back out a moment later he stood thirty feet away on the lawn, shifting from one foot to the other, obviously extremely nervous. Wolff rose to meet him, feeling a terrible premonition.

"Your father's dead," John said to him.

And Wolff said: "Thank God."

It was an astonishing reaction. In the book in which he eventually described the incident, *The Duke of Deception*, Wolff gave two reasons for it, one direct, one indirect. First, when he saw his wife's brother-in-law standing on the terrace, he'd been sure that it was with bad news about his sons; he walked toward him, in fact, to "learn which of [his] boys was dead"; any other kind of news would have constituted a reprieve. And secondly, even if he hadn't been concerned about his son, chances are he would have felt undeniable relief hearing about his father's death. Wolff's father, Arthur, *was* the Duke of Deception himself, a Great Imposter with a family, a brilliant sociopath who had spent his life pretending to credentials he never had, ultimately reaching positions of great responsibility in his "chosen" field, aeronautics engineering. He was a man continually on the make, even with his loved ones; he never acknowledged the fixing hand of reality, he refused to be pinned down. Death was the only thing he ultimately couldn't finesse or deny. After reading *The Duke of Deception* it's easy to see how Geoffrey Wolff's "Thank God" might have been not simply an expression of relief that his son was all right, but a prayer of gratitude that something had finally caught his father in the x-ray of truth, and forced — or helped — him to stop lying.

As unique as Geoffrey Wolff's experience was, it happened to contain in it the kernel of most major "son-father" moments, that split-second when a father, by intention or accident, is revealed in a way he would rather not be. Not all fathers are geniuses of deception in the class of Arthur Wolff, but virtually all fathers practise a subterfuge that's as native to them as after-shave. What makes the whole transaction typically paternal is the fact that the fathers involved are usually totally oblivious to their own involuntary con; they think they're just being themselves.

Listen to Professor Marvel's monumental line of palaver in *The Wizard of Oz;* then watch the little man working feverishly over the levers when Toto pulls the curtain back. They are one guy and the same — the universal Old Man. Remember the famous plea for clemency?

"No, no, my dear. I'm a very good man. I'm just a very bad wizard."

It doesn't have to be scandalous or vast. The first "moment" I can remember having with my father happened when I was five. It was his birthday, and my sister had walked me down our street and out to the main drag where the neighbourhood Woolworths was located to buy him a gift. I remember the walk we took being hilly, a series of giant dips and rises; I remember also that the mission wasn't undertaken in ease, but with a tension that wasn't totally unpleasurable. Part of the reason might have been that my father had given me the money for the present, a quarter (I'm sure I didn't invent this detail) that morning before he left for work. For some reason the circularity of the deal injected an edgy thrilling anxiety into the trip. At the store I agonized for a while, then finally settled on what I could afford: a package of Gillette Super Blue Blades, five blades separately wrapped in tissue, stacked in a tiny rectangular cardboard box, navy blue, with a bearded man and the same Gillette symbol they showed on the Friday night fights on TV. I took the box home over the same mountain range, and waited for my father to get back from work. He finally came in the door, as youthful and gangly as a young Dick Van Dyke. I couldn't wait to show him my present; I'd been too anxious to wrap it. He took it in his hand, looked at it, and looked back up at me with a bemused expression. "Thank-you," he said. "But I use an electric razor."

He could have said, simply, "Thank-you." Or he could have said, "You know, it's amazing, but just the other night I was telling your mother how my electric razor was really irritating my skin and that I wanted to go back to using my trusty old safety razor, but what I really needed were some good blades. And now look what you get me. You must be psychic!" But he didn't. He stood there squinting down at me, his hairline scooped out clean and young on both sides of his dark, curly widow's peak, maybe beginning to regret what he'd said, but either not being able to cancel out the words or not knowing enough to try. Either way, I only remember what I felt. I was obliterated, wiped off the surface of the earth. In future years if I wanted to feel a dying swoon all I had to do was remember this moment. By then, though, the little vacuum in the pit of my stomach would have been replaced by an important new piece of information: this was someone who could do me harm.

And what, really, had he done? In the rush of the moment, a young dad coming through the door, his son running to meet him with the disguised universe in the palm of his hand, my father had been caught out on a technicality. Logic had been neglected, and it just seemed natural to point it out. He *did* use an electric razor, after all. What was he going to do with blades? And so he said what he said, maybe because the apparent smallness of the scene reduced the visible stakes. Or maybe because looking down at my avid gaze he found himself kicked into that paternal fugue state where suddenly below you is not the product of your loins but a little person holding up a little box: father-amnesia. A friend of mine once walked six blocks to buy a pack of cigarettes before he realized that he had a baby daughter sleeping in a crib alone at home.

But children don't care about fugue states. Children aren't just tyrants of the present, they're tyrants of the conservation of style. Even more than mothers (who at least get to change their fashions) fathers are expected to be constant, as constant as a suit. Lapses are always penalized. The younger the child, the worse the penalty, because the penalty is memory, and the sentence the length of time it lingers. And if annihilation lingers longest in the childish memory, a close second is mortification of the soul.

Maybe fittingly, the second "moment" I clearly remember having with my father came under the guise of revenge, when I was twelve years old, in the car on the way back from a Passover Seder. It was the second night of the holiday, and instead of going to my uncle's house, on my father's side, we'd accepted an invitation to celebrate with my mother's brother and his family. This side of the family struck me as noticeably rich, and half the crowd, relatives of my aunt's, were virtual strangers to me. Most different of all were the tunes sung at my aunt's Seder, which harked from a Polish *shtetl* instead of a Russian one, so that they sounded more like actual melodies and less like Cossack drinking waltzes. The tunes concerned me, not because I didn't like them, but because I was worried that my father, who loved to sing and was known in family circles to have a fine voice, wouldn't be able to restrain himself and would interrupt at one point to suggest a "good Russian song." Worse, I was afraid that he'd end up singing a solo in his attempt to lead the crowd, complete with his classic, looping Myron Cohen finger points. (I actually *liked* the finger points when he sang Seder songs at my uncle's house, the same way I liked his annual Passover joke, including the one about the parrot who was training to be a cantor. But my uncle's was my second home. Like certain wines, there were items in my father's repertoire I was convinced would not travel well.)

And of course, what I feared most happened. On the second to last song, "Who Knows One?," the Passover equivalent to "A Partridge in a Pear Tree," my father held up both palms and said, "Excuse me everyone, may I suggest a different tune, just for a little cross-cultural seasoning?" and launched into "our" version of the song, a droning lament that sounded a bit like a European ambulance. When he was finished everyone was so charmed (stunned, I thought) that he led the table in his version of "One Kid That Father Bought for Two Zuzim." It took a long time to be over.

Seven years later Philip Roth would write *the* definitive magnum opus of a child's mortification by a parent, *Portnoy's Complaint*. I would read it, along with most of the male Jewish teenage population of North America, half of whom would claim that Roth had stolen their lives. They would be thinking of the similarities between Mrs Portnoy and their own mothers; what haunted me most in the book was Alex's father, Mr Portnoy, who was stricken with terminally chronic constipation. As far as I knew my own father was as regular as a clock; but I still resonated with Alex's dilemma. I knew exactly how he must have vacillated between sympathy for his father and fear that one of his friends would come into the apartment while his old man was on the can, and overhear the groans and wails of his all too human condition. Alex's mother was actively horrible; his father would mortify him without even trying, with the exercise of his natural bodily functions. He would embarrass his son by being himself.

In fact the singing at the Seder probably had been pretty awful, and my father did have a beautiful voice. And chances were also, it would occur to me later, that my mother had put my father up to it and that my father would not have imposed if he hadn't felt welcome. All I knew that night, though, was that I was cringing in a way so unbearable it was almost delicious. In the car on the way home the air was funky and close with the lingering smells of matzoh and stuffing, and I managed to restrain myself only until we got onto our street. Then I said something censorious, something about how my father really shouldn't impose himself on other people, it wasn't polite, and it was embarrassing. I remember starting off with the phrase, "You know, Dad, you shouldn't . . ."

And I remember his reaction being astonishing — not because it was so immediate or explosive, but because it was so *personal*. He said it was none of my business where he sang and when he should be embarrassed, and he wasn't going to let some twelve-year-old jerk tell him so. I should just close my mouth and think a bit. He said I should close my mouth more than once, enough that my mother said his name. It was totally uncharacteristic of him; this was a gentle man. In the back seat, wedged between my sisters, I didn't feel fear, though; I felt suspicious. I suspected that he suspected he had been embarrassing too. I thought he was protesting too much.

What I was sure of was revolutionary: this was a person *I* could harm.

In the late 1970s the makers of Chivas Regal ran another famous "parental" ad that appeared regularly on the back covers of a number of American magazines. The ad consisted of an entire page strewn with cheques, the way a desktop might be, written over a twenty-five-year period by a Mr John R. Spencer; the payees, in various amounts, included the C&M diaper services, Phil's Toyland, Camp Wakananga, Marvin Honig MD and State University. To look at the cheques in 1978 was to read a life — a strictly middle-class life granted, but a life so real in its implied affection it was irresistible. The copy at the bottom read: "You'll never repay him. But at least you can give him Chivas."

Looking at the same ad today is like looking at a dinosaur. The chances that a father will write the totality of cheques for a given child in the future is skimpy; if Chivas Regal ever wants to update the ad today the page will have to include cheques signed not just by John R. Spencer, but by Paula Spencer, or more likely Paula *Osborne*, another last name added to complicate the pitch and obscure the joke. And while equality will be served in the revision, something else will be lost: the poignant if perverse fascination of watching a man in a full suit of armour trying to convey love. In being so apparently all-sufficient, in having the steadiest signature alive, John R. Spencer and his generation of fathers weren't just showing us that they had the scratch; they were revealing how trapped their souls were. If they had the power to write the cheques, it was virtually the only power they had when it came to finding avenues for their regard; the rigid role-demarcation lines of the times made sure of that. This isn't to suggest that there weren't fathers who didn't embrace the cheque-writing option of fatherhood as a cop-out to avoid getting involved in more active parenting; they were probably legion. But invoking the "limitless" power of men to explain all our choices is always too easy, no matter how politically correct, to be close to the whole truth.

When I was in my last year of high-school the mother of one of my best friends died of breast cancer. I went to the funeral and to the *shiva* at his house afterwards, I remember, feeling uncomfortable and scared; I sat on a couch in the corner so that I wouldn't have to say anything, particularly the wrong thing, to any of the mourners. A minute or so after I sat down, though, my friend's father came out of the kitchen with another man, and stopped in front of me. Both of them had drinks in their hands. My friend's father, who was in his socks according to custom, looked drunk, which was extremely unusual for any *shiva*, and especially for my friend's father. The two men held their glasses up to each other, both bleary eyed, and my friend's father said, by way of a toast: "She was a hell of a gal."

Even at eighteen I was aware of how inadequate the statement was. "She was a hell of a gal" seemed more like something you would say in a public farewell to Sophie Tucker or Mae West than about your wife. It was awash in not just sentimentality, but generality. At the same time I had the feeling that my friend's father would have liked to say a lot more about his wife, but the linguistic template he had to speak through, father-talk, would only let it emerge in one particular stilted way. In that sense it was like the verbal equivalent of the desktop of cheques John R. Spencer wrote. Both of them were a kind of interrupted discourse. If there were fathers who groused, "I'm the breadwinner in this family," and "Who pays for the goddamn groceries around here anyway?", there were also fathers who said, "What do you think I am, a money tree?" holding out as they did in their outstretched hand a bill or the car-keys. For them a signed cheque was the dual symbol of limitation and love.

My father was not a typical postwar paterfamilias — he wrote his cheques with discretion, for one thing, and he was lavish with his affection. Still, the "paternal" moments I enjoyed with him as I grew through adolescence were as neatly tailored as the shortsleeved Egyptian broadcloth dress shirts he bought from

Stollery's on Yonge Street in boxes of only two (Frank Shore would have been shocked). I remember him visiting me in the hospital after I severed two tendons in my wrist by accidentally putting my hand through our glass storm-door on the way to the bookmobile (and then having my distracted mother roll her Vauxhall into the ditch on the way to the doctor's). "You can have anything you want," he said simply. "Anything." I asked for a pastrami sandwich instead of a Cadillac. I remember driving with him down a curving, ritzy city street one Saturday, on the way to help him pack samples at his office, talking to him about erections. "Do you want to know about erections?" he asked. "No," I said. "Are you sure?" he said. "Yes," I said. I remember standing at the foot of his bed at two-thirty in the morning while my mother was asleep, telling him about a girl I'd just taken out, who I could have done more with than I had. "Sometimes the more manly thing is to restrain yourself," he said, squinting into the darkness, maybe forgetting it was the same line he'd used when I chickened out of fighting a bully named Mark Champagne in the fifth grade. I remember the glasses he sent me when I was working at summer camp and broke a pair, perfectly packaged in a perfectly sized tough cardboard box meant for a Dymo-tape machine, along with three chocolate bars and a twenty-dollar bill. I remember the letters he sent me that summer, all of them written on his salesman's letterhead, with the "T" in his name shaped like a hanger.

I remember him trying to find a psychiatrist for me at the end of another summer, the summer I turned eighteen and suddenly started worrying about losing my hair. In fact I was losing my hair — my only craziness was in the timing of the panic — and the shrink he found, young and highly recommended, was bald as a billiard ball. The comparison must have been salutary. After a few sessions my father told me he was so grateful for my improvement he was considering sending a donation to the American Psychiatric Association. Fortunately he held off. By Christmas I was back driving my mother's car around the block at fifty miles an hour and washing my hair five times a day. One night during Christmas exams, when I was too anxious to study, he took me out to a movie for distraction — the movie: *2001: A Space Odyssey*. In our seats near the back I sat slack, utterly wiped out, too tired to cry. "I can't stop thinking about it, Dad," I said. "I just can't." He put his hand on my shoulder, the base of my neck actually, and gripped it. "All I can tell you is what my brother used to tell me when I was getting started in business, and things were tough: 'God grant us the strength to change the things we can, the courage to accept the things we can't, and the wisdom to know the difference between the two.' " Up on the screen HAL the computer was malfunctioning, singing a drawling version of "A Bicycle Built for Two," and in the audience my father was squeezing my neck and mouthing platitudes. Perfect platitudes, guided missiles of maxims. He had shown me how to countersink a screw and hang a ceiling fixture, but now I had another piece of evidence to back up the surprising possibility:

This was a man who could *teach* me something.

The calendar pages flip now past graduations and trips to Europe, past weddings and births, to a fall afternoon in the late 1980s. I'm meeting my father for lunch downtown at a cafeteria a few blocks from his office. In fourteen days he'll be retired for good; this is the last downtown work-lunch he will buy me; no longer will his place of business be a way-station for me to drop in on in the course of city errands.

A few years ago he was diagnosed with angina. He reacted typically, with pep and resolution, getting himself admitted to a recuperative exercise program previously restricted to recovering heart-attack victims, walking two and then three miles a day, modifying his diet, and generally getting into the best shape of his life. (He'd started to remind me of pictures I'd seen of him in high-school when his nickname was Bunty, a small, quick guy, skittish on the base-paths.) Lately, though, the pain has returned — he can only play doubles on the tennis court, not singles. A recent stress test indicated increasing artery blockage; an angiogram he took a week later confirmed it. His doctor has recommended a bypass, he tells me as we sit looking at the menu, and he's decided to go ahead with it as soon as a bed's available. According to the experts he's in excellent shape, and this type of procedure has become as routine as gall bladder surgery.

"So if it's so routine, why not have two?" I say. "Are you getting a second opinion, at least?"

"I will if I think it's necessary," he says, in his careful way. "We live in a technologically marvellous age. I'd be a fool not to give myself every chance it can give me. My father couldn't do anything about his heart condition. I can. I don't want to wake up in five years and say, schmuck, look what you could have done for yourself."

"Because then you wouldn't be waking up."

"That's right," he smiles, refusing to take offence. "Then I wouldn't be waking up."

A woman sits down beside us, a blonde in her mid-forties, attractive in a brassy way. The tables are very close, and she asks if she can put her coat and sample case on a chair at ours. Partly because I'm irritated with my father, for his stoicism, for his reverence for authority, for reasons I can't figure out, I strike up a conversation with her. She sells housing brick on the road; she's got her samples with her, and with a little prodding she lays them out on the table in front of her: slices of clay brick and some calcite (although she tries not to push it, "inferior durability") in various colours, like enlarged tempera squares in a child's paint-by-numbers tin. She's got an appointment in an hour, she says, for two guys building a "theme" gas station. What do I think she should recommend? I can see that she's flirting, not just with me but with my father too, liking the idea of monopolizing two men in this small space. When she gets up to leave a few minutes later she says she hopes her clients will be as good-looking as the two of us. My father and I both watch her leave from behind.

When she's out of earshot my father says: "You know I don't know if I could have done that. Talk to her like that. I have to tell you that. I really admire you for it."

It is a statement delivered with candid surprise. He isn't acknowledging brilliance in an area where he lacks training or talent; he's delivering praise for someone's success in a field to which he is privy. He's facing eternity, and all he can think to do is to compliment his son on being good with women.

But he's telling me more than that; he's telling me I have something to teach *him*.

He had his bypass that May. The morning of the operation I drove downtown to the hospital to sit with my mother and my sisters while the "procedure" was done. The waiting-room was cavernous and filled with light, like a library or a set from a movie located in Limbo. Spaced sparsely through it were little clusters of people waiting for the same operation to be performed on the fathers and husbands in their lives. Every thirty minutes or so a masked doctor would come out and approach a group soundlessly on the thick carpet; they would rise to meet him, the women reaching for their purses and lagging behind on the uptake in that way women have, the men — sons mostly — on their feet immediately. The conference would be low and discreet to the point of inaudibility; when it was over the family would either sit back down nodding, or follow the doctor like chastened monks through the door that led to the ICU.

My father's doctor had said he'd be through at about eleven. At eleven-thirty he still hadn't appeared. My mother put her hands in her lap and sat up a little straighter. Finally, just before noon, he came through the door, pulling off his mask as he did. The second artery had been kinked as well, he said, so while they were at it they'd decided to do a quadruple bypass instead of a triple, to really up the blood supply. Farming for the fourth vein from my father's thigh had taken the extra time. The machine would be breathing for him for another twenty-four hours, but if we wanted to see him now — two at a time — we could.

I went in with my mother. The unit was brighter and busier than I'd expected; friendly vigilance was in the air. My father lay on his back, shirtless, an enormous tube down his throat, another draining the chest cavity, his entire torso rising and falling with a rush like a mechanical waterfall to the clacking sound of the respirator. What struck me most was how large and vigorous his features looked. There was a glow about them that my mother must have noticed as well. She reached out and touched his forehead with the backs of her fingers. "He's always had such young skin," she said.

According to Freud, the most powerful moment in any man's life is the death of his father. Looking down at my father, I figured my most powerful moment would have to wait. The respirator's rhythmic clicking didn't echo the precarious dependency of his body on a man-made artifact, so much as the pulse of his own determination, his dapper ingenuity and his plan to live. Without ever approaching extremis, he'd invited a stranger to open his chest and stop his heart. And the beneficiary of his gamble wasn't just him, but me, too. I had a vested interest in every breath the pleated accordion took: the longer he lived, the sunnier my family medical history would be, and the greater the odds I would live longer, too.

But it was his bravery in the protection of his own life that I coveted at that moment. "What are you doing in Montreal?" he would ask me the next day, when he swam into consciousness. "Trying to pick up a few pointers," I said. He nodded blearily, not really getting it, but hanging tough anyway, the last blocker between his children and the infinite.

And that, I assumed, was that. Outside of the ultimate moment he had dodged and I preferred not to think about, I figured I had been through all the moments with my father: mutual destruction and instruction, humiliation and admiration, belated hero-worship. All I had to do now was go to the synagogue with him on Yom Kippur, call him up once or twice a week, and learn how to tell corny jokes in dialect.

A week after my father was released from the hospital, and was at home recuperating, I rented a video for my family to watch. The movie was rated PG, but through some brilliant piece of PR one of the trailers was for the remake of the horror film *Return of the Living Dead*. Ben, who was watching, caught about thirty seconds of it before we realized what it was and fast-forwarded. He swore he loved it, but that night he came into our bedroom, racked with nightmares that wouldn't let him sleep. I fed him hot chocolate and let him watch TV. I offered to sleep on the floor in his room with him. Nothing worked. Finally, exhausted, I tried one last, desperate resort: I told him a story about myself as a kid, being as scared as he was. I told him specifically about the night I'd slept over at my friend Ryan Ginsberg's duplex apartment when I was seven years old, and watched an episode of *The Twilight Zone* called "The Eye of the Beholder."

The episode was a classic; telling it to my son, I saw it clearly again myself. The show opened with a close-up camera shot of a woman who had just undergone surgery, to repair what was apparently a horrible facial deformity. Sitting on the floor in front of the TV, Ryan and I saw the woman's face swaddled in bandages and heard the doctors discussing their past failures with her. This would be her last chance, they made clear — failure again would mean her banishment to an island colony of similar grotesques, a kind of St Elba's for losers. As an adult I might, *might* have noticed that at no time during the half hour that followed did the camera actually clearly show anyone's face, that the whole show was shot either in shadows or from the rear. As a seven-year-old in the Ginsberg living-room I didn't have a chance. The bandages came off, scissors were thrown in disgust on the floor, a doctor hissed, "Failed again," and the camera swung to the face of the horrified woman, who of course was beautiful. Then it careered to the faces of the doctors and nurses, who looked like pigs with hangovers — snout noses pushed halfway across their faces, twisted mouths, dewlapped cheeks, beady eyes. Rod's little homily when it was over was no comfort at all. An hour later, with the apartment pitch black and filled with sleeping Ginsbergs, I slipped out of bed and went into the kitchen and phoned my father to come and get me. I wouldn't even wait inside for him. I stood on the duplex balcony in the dark in my pyjamas, and willed his headlights to appear.

Back in our own dim kitchen the story had obviously hooked Ben, the details on the balcony in particular. How high was it? he kept asking me. Could I have jumped? Where were my shoes? Were my pyjamas short-sleeved? Looking down at his squint I had the same uncomfortable feeling I'd had before with him, that he'd gotten tired of messing up my present, and now he was invading my past. It was more than his usual voyeuristic pleasure. I kept getting the feeling that he was actually there waiting with me, on the balcony.

And then I realized that of course he was there that night: I just had the roles confused. My son was *me*, looking down Wilmington Avenue for a pair of headlights. And I was my father, driving to rescue him. In all the times I'd told the story of that night, I'd never seen it from my father's point of view. But now it was effortless to imagine how he must have felt: irritated at being pulled away from the eleven o'clock news, swearing at the chilliness of the car, and then turning the corner and seeing the little boy standing on the second-storey balcony in the dark. For a moment of anarchy the apartment stairs might have seemed as irrelevant as reason. There might have been a flash, however brief, of the ladder at the back of the garage. Hurry, hurry. You can race home to get it. You can put it on the car.

5

Driving Carpool
Other People's Children

"... and you see other people and you think, 'Gosh, they have kids, too.' It's kind of like when you get a certain make of car, and you drive down the street and see all the other cars like it and think, 'I didn't realize there are so many of these around.'"

Annie Lennox, lead singer of the Eurythmics,
after giving birth to a baby, July 20, 1992

3:46 p.m.

In 1967 the British writer and parapsychological aficionado Colin Wilson published a science fiction novel called *The Mind Parasites,* which within the space of a few years became an underground classic. Purportedly the journal of Gilbert Austin, a professor of archaeology at Oxford University, the book chronicled the discovery — by Austin and some scholarly cronies

— of a communal race of invisible virus-like alien beings who for the past two hundred years had invaded the minds of human beings and sapped the very "life force of mankind." One of the more annoying by-products of these "mind parasites" was the common writer's, or thinking, block. The aliens were determined not to let any human being ponder too long or clearly on any particular event, just in case someone rooting around in his own mind happened to stumble on them and sound the alarm. The pain of thinking, the torture of getting an idea to sit still, this was just the mind parasites scraping their fingernails on the blackboards of our consciousness. It was a fantastic leap of imagination; anyone who'd ever stared at a blank page could recognize the logic of it instantly — better, he didn't have to blame himself any more for being a lazy moron.

To call children mind parasites is too easy. Children and carpool *combined* are something else. I'm on the verge of finishing the scene on the porch between Seymour and Charlotte, and more important, figuring out what's still bothering me about it, when I look down at my watch, and the day swims back into view. It's 3:30, and it's Thursday. I'm driving carpool. Only science fiction can get me to the school on time.

I make it by 3:45. The parking lot is already half-empty, but there are enough jeeps and mini-vans left sitting in the sun that it looks like an RV convention. Carpool, like the doctor's waiting-room, is still largely a woman's world; the difference is in hairstyle and slickness of make-up. By the afternoon, women who were chaotic in the morning have managed to find the time to put their sartorial houses in a little bit of order, and to get discreet.

There are a lot of trim pony-tails and sunglasses threading their way through the parking lot at this time of the day, which is fine with me, too.

Inside the school I head directly to Paula's office, navigating the remnants of the kid-river to do it. Nothing can jolt you out of the solitariness of a sedentary job like a school corridor at dismissal. Ben and our two carpool regulars, Annie and Miles B_____, are waiting outside the office already, in a welter of jackets and packs, but Jennifer's nowhere to be seen.

My wife is on her feet taking a phone call when I lean into her office, writing something on a pad on her desk and simultaneously motioning to some eleven-year-old boys in the playground outside her window to do something, probably to get their palms out of their armpits and stop making farting noises at each other. When I knock on the open door she shakes her head. No time.

"Where's Jenny?"

She motions out the hall.

"Am I taking her to skating or what?"

She covers the mouthpiece and looks at me with friendly encouragement, albeit a bit impatient at my obtuseness. "You're driving, you decide. I trust you."

I walk out of the office, a bit confused — I thought we had a crisis here — and I'm almost run over by my eldest daughter, who's hustling down the terrazzo at a fast dancer's walk.

"Dad, I have to ask you something," she says urgently. "Can I go to Mia's after skating? She asked me to dinner, and they're going to the Promenade after. Her mother said she'd pick me up from the rink and bring me home. I know you hate to drive."

I look down at her. She's flushed, but not from embarrassment as far as I can tell. There's something irresistible about her spiel. I'd be willing to bet there's nothing calculated in it. For some reason I remember her admitting to me, about a month ago, that up to the day before she'd thought "prima donna" was spelled "pre-Madonna."

"Aren't you forgetting something?"

"What?"

"This morning. Something happened, remember?"

She looks about two inches to the side of my gaze, and starts tapping her sneakered foot, her heel, on the tile floor. "All right, I apologize. Can I go to Mia's?"

I think about it. I could say yes and solve everything. She's right — I do hate to drive. But something, not exemplary parenthood, stops me. More the chance to waylay well-laid plans. She has this all worked out so well.

"I don't think so," I say. "Mia's is a privilege, especially on a week night. I don't think it's really coming to you."

"Then I don't want to go skating either. I wouldn't mind quitting."

Now we're all doomed. "Ah, Jenny, Jenny," I say. "Now you have to go skating, Sandra will be waiting for you. It's — " I look for the word, " — a *commitment*."

I round up Ben and the B______s and herd them through the gym and out to the car, Jennifer lagging behind. It isn't until the other kids are buckled in and I gun the engine and roll forward a foot or two that she deigns to get in the front, sitting down heavily.

"I won't go in. I'll just sit outside. Or I'll take the *bus* to Mia's."

"Fine," I say.

"Dad, *no*," this is from Ben behind me, "She can't take the bus, it's *dangerous*. You can't, Jennifer."

"Oh, Ben, leave me alone."

"Be quiet, Ben."

"*No*. I can express myself; I'm just worried about you, Jennifer."

"Yippya-dee doo da."

"Dad, I can't believe how mean she's being."

"Be quiet, *everyone*." I say.

We get to the rink in five silent minutes. Jennifer gets out as soon as the car stops moving, slams the door, and then walks over to the steel-rail fence in front of the rink entrance and sits down on it, staring into space and swinging her legs. If I were my wife, I realize, she'd be staring at me; there are always things to be thankful for. I look at her, trying to figure out the proper, dignified, satisfying thing to do. Finally I put the car in gear and drive away.

"Dad," says Ben, "I can't believe you did that. Go back!"

"Be quiet, Ben," I say. "Your sister will be fine. She'll go inside as soon as we're gone."

I turn on a tape deck and put in a James Taylor tape. I hate arguing with my kids, I realize. It's like arguing with their mother; the air becomes unquiet. When we reach Finch I make a right instead of a left, apologizing to Annie and Miles in back, and drive back past the rink. The railing is deserted.

We drive on. The little knot in my stomach doesn't dissipate appreciably, despite James's pure tones, rising now to crest a series of terraces of sweet pain. In the back seat my son is tormenting his buddy Miles with his

Gushti-Gushti voice, a private dialect consisting of over-enunciated consonants and dramatic long vowels. "*Mi*-les," he says, pounding on the "l," "I feel it's time to demonstrate your wonderful talent for gassy explosions at this time." For some reason the accent improves his grammar. "Ben, stop," says Miles mildly. "I mean it." "But *Mi*-les," Ben says, "Those explosions are intense. Thy fans await thee." "Ben, I mean it, I'll do something." "*Mi*-les, this is carpool. You can't *do* something here." There's a thud — Miles has done something. My son makes a crepitating noise with his mouth and starts cackling hysterically. "*Mi*-iles, what a blow. It sounded like a gassy explosion to me." "Ben, I'll smash you again."

I stop the car by the curb, put it in park, and get up on my knees on the driver's seat in one motion, twisting around to look back at him. "Stop It" I say, the two words coming out equally weighted. I'm an inch away from grabbing him. "Someone asked you to stop it, so you stop it. Are you hard of hearing? *Stop It*."

I sit back down and pull the car away from the curb. If we were alone Ben would be a lot more upset by my outburst; now pride won't let him be. The three of them wait a respectable length of time — to accommodate the idiot in the front seat — then slowly they start whispering again, this time about a playground game called "Red Ass," the boys sounding equally idiotic, Annie, two years younger, trying to inject some reason.

Now that I've exploded I can listen again. The world they're talking about, I'm aware, is one in which I have less and less of a function lately. It's peopled by friends of my son's, the majority of whom I don't know well; the circle of his life is moving farther away from the circle of mine, the area of intersection shrinking. His is a universe populated by other people's children.

Two of those children are in the car, the B_____s themselves. I've always gotten a kick out of both of them: Miles, a year older than my son, has the sobriety and work ethic of an old-time ballplayer named Preacher. Absolutes are his bailiwick: "We *never* have dessert at our house," he's told me more than once. Also: "We *never* go out to eat." To hear Miles tell it his family-life is only one degree less austere than Fagin's house.

His sister Annie, on the other hand, a sloe-eyed first grader, is one of the sweetest oddballs imaginable; she speaks in a steady monotone about issues of great and minor import alike, like Howard Cosell or one of the Monty Python laundromat ladies; I can see her crossing the English Channel on a raft to go see Jean-Paul Sartre and ask him what he meant when he said life was meaningless.

And interestingly, the farther Ben draws off into the sunset, the less contact I seem to have with his private life, the more relaxed and entertaining my relationship with the B______s — ironic camp-counsellor kind of relationship — seems to become. And the harder I've gotten on my son.

It's more than just proximity. Lately, I have to admit, whenever my son's with a group of other kids, I've become a perpetual critic. Driving carpool, going into the change-room at his judo school, I find myself monitoring him one degree tougher than I might if he was alone with just me or the family. I'm more aware of his faults, his brashness, his loudness, his failure to stop and consider the alternatives. What's with him? I ask myself, thinking at the same time that Miles and Annie seem like paragons of rectitude. In the process I end up cutting Ben's friends slack that I would never give to him. It isn't that the weight of my attention has shifted, just the direction of my generosity. Whether it's because I know my son too well, or it's supposed to be good breeding to give the guest the benefit of the doubt, my good will has a habit lately of attaching itself to other people's children.

Which may not be such a bad thing. Because ultimately it's the kid in the golf-cart, and not the kid in the back seat, who can bring out the best in us. It's other people's children — and not our own — who might be the key to the salvation of the planet.

Consider this:

On a sunny October day in 1987, an eighteen-month-old girl named Jessica McClure was playing in the backyard of her aunt's Midland, Texas, home with two older friends, when one or both of the friends moved a rock in the yard, uncovering an abandoned oil-well shaft, eight inches in diameter. Jessica's seventeen-year-old mother, Reba, unaware of the danger, went inside to answer a phone call. When she came back, Jessica had apparently vanished. In fact her daughter had somehow managed to fall into the narrow shaft, coming to rest on a pile of debris twenty-two feet down. For the next fifty-eight and a half hours, during which Jessica sang nursery rhymes to herself, slept, and cried, one of the largest rescue operations in the history of the state of Texas was set into motion in an attempt to save her.

I was in New York City when the accident occurred, meeting with a toy manufacturer. I saw the first report on the TV in my hotel room, and followed the Texas drama for the next two days, turning on the set whenever I had the chance and trying to catch glimpses on TV screens in the appliance stores I passed on Sixth Avenue; when a TV wasn't handy, I found myself asking cabbies and librarians and bellboys if they had heard any more "Jessica" news. And I wasn't alone. In coffee shops, on the streets of America's busiest city, the fate of the little girl down the well in Texas was paramount. Interest crossed borders as well. Back in Toronto the news from Midland was just as relentless.

Nothing I could remember — certainly no single incident involving a non-celebrity — had captured the world's attention as effortlessly as Jessica McClure had by falling down the well; and nothing would come close to it in the future until, ironically, a pair of bow whales became trapped in pack ice off the Bering Sea. But the bow whales were another species, and the reaction to their plight wasn't just sentimental but anthropomorphic. Jessica was a child, not a bow whale, which meant that her case ended up being not just *intra*-species, but intra-*parental.*

In fact on the surface nothing seemed more obvious than the identification of other parents with Reba McClure and her husband, Chip, a house-painter. Watching the dark young teenage mother hug herself in the flat Texas backyard, we (parents) figured we had an unbreachable connection with her, because momentarily we knew, we thought, exactly how she felt. In our minds and hearts we were plugged into a homogeneous parental network of concern, where all the compassionate givens were the same. But in reality we were missing one critical ingredient from Reba and Chip McClure's world-view, an ingredient that, as Jessica's immediate parents, only they were privy to. It was the ingredient whose absence paradoxically let us react to the unfolding story with pure good will. Call it the flip side of the Parental Eye: the *Jaundiced* Eye, or maybe the Will To Rage.

Consider this: On a sunny October morning in the town of Midland, Texas, a seventeen-year-old mother named Reba McClure is trying to help her sister run a mini-day-care centre in her backyard, wash the dishes, and answer the phone, all at the same time. Her daughter Jessica — "Juicy" by nickname — isn't helping any; she keeps taking off with two other kids Reba has to take care of, to parts of the yard she's not supposed to play in. Plus, she keeps humming the same song over and over again, so that Reba finds herself gritting her teeth and thinking, "Can't she give it a rest?" Now the kids are playing with the wash-stand pole behind a big rock at the end of the yard, where it's practically impossible to see them. The phone rings — perfect, Reba thinks, and runs inside to get it. It's a pre-recorded voice selling time-share units in Galveston; she waits too long to hang up, though, and then has to wait another minute or so, checking the line to make sure it's clear, in case one of the day-care parents calls with an emergency. Finally the dial-tone resumes, and she goes back out into the yard, seething. *Now* where is she? Jesus Christ. It never fails. Jessica. Goddamit, Jessica . . . !

Only saints are immune to the Will To Rage, and saints as a rule don't have children. How many times has the average parent said, "I don't know how, but he/she knows exactly what to do to drive me *crazy* . . ."? And how many times have all of us suspected that the talent wasn't unilateral, that it didn't lie in the driver alone, that fifty percent of it might be our unique readiness to pick exclusively at the flaws of our unique children. Abusive parents know this better than other parents, because they carry the impulse to a pathological conclusion, but the *excuse* for the conclusion, the tiny, supreme irritation, is there in all of us. As uniquely talented as our own children are at eliciting our love, they are expert at getting under our skin. Because of course, they *are* under our skin. We know them too well. The same familiarity that washes out our ordinary prejudice injects a specialized bias back into us. The result is an *un*peaceful co-existence that these days is liable to be labelled "dysfunction" or family "toxicity," but which may simply be a natural law. Parents need to make the same deal with civilization everyone does. The Will To Rage may be the price we pay for love.

As disinterested parents watching Jessica's ordeal, though, we lacked the Jaundiced Eye *and* the Will To Rage, because she wasn't our specific child. We had the "grandparent" advantage — we got to see her best side, and then to go home at night. Distance took care of anything perverse; what we lost in intensity we made up for in tolerance. Becoming a parent lets you into a new room with two new views, not one. The first, the view of your own child, actually diminishes your moral horizons while it sensitizes you; you become a powerful special-interest lobbyist with a constituency of one. But the other new window opens on other people's children, and that view is all-expansive; it diverges to include the world.

The universal view takes the ambivalent game of parenthood, light and dark, and increases the margin for error for the light, like widening the "out" lines on a tennis court. In cases like Jessica McClure's, it can create a potential force for communal good, close to the compassion the Greeks called *agape*, that may be unparalleled in history.

Why then aren't we living in Camelot? If as parents we're such a force for good, why is the world, particularly the world of children, such a disappointing and deadly place? Why, to put it in sci-fi terms, haven't parents ever managed to get organized?

I can think of two possibilities: Sentiment and Sheepishness.

The fact is that for better or worse the world, and parents themselves, have never really been comfortable with their own sentiment — which may in fact be the greatest weapon they have in effecting any kind of historical change. The sentiment of parents has always been regarded as simplistic in the "real" world — as opposed to just simple — and weirdly infantile somehow, as though, because parents spend half their time preoccupied with immature life-forms, they must be immature, too. (Either immature or irrelevant, which accounts for the historical fate of women and teachers.) For any parent, especially a man, to try to insert a parental perspective into a discussion of *realpolitik* — the Gulf War, say — is a conflicted proposition. Just after that hallucinatory night when smart bombs started falling on Baghdad I wrote an opinion column for the newspaper about my own ambivalence towards the fighting, which contained this sentence: "When it comes to war, though, which ultimately involves killing babies even if we're not aiming at them — simply being right isn't enough. War has to be the *only* thing that will work." I was planning to make the killing of babies a lot bigger issue, but even in its stripped-down version it gave me pause. Was I being soft? Was I being naïve? Was I being "womanly"? Similarly, there isn't much that's soft about an IRA bullet or a ICBM silo, but when Catholic and Protestant mothers get together in Northern Ireland to march for peace, or English mothers rally to block the road to a nuclear installation, the report usually ends up in the inside, softer "women's" sections of the newspaper. When some people voiced concerns about child fatalities during the Israeli invasion of Lebanon in 1981, one celebrated American journalist used his column to upbraid them for their bleeding-heart myopia — then went home to minister, tenderly from all reports, to his handicapped son. Like the columnist, most fathers are only comfortable emoting about children in private; in public they stick to baseball. Lately, women have started showing their own squeamishness about exploiting the "sentimental" side of the parental psyche. And any general will tell you it's hard for an army to mobilize when half of the troops are too embarrassed to come out of the closet.

But there's a second, more important reason for the global ineffectiveness of the parental instinct that crosses gender lines: the tendency of all of us to turn our pluses into deficits. As "universal" parents we may not suffer from too little empathy, it turns out, but too much.

The night of the day Jessica fell into the well in Texas, another "children" story appeared on television, not on an official news program but in a public-service infomercial. The story was the continuing "saga" of the famine in Ethiopia. As of October of 1987 the famine, brought on by a combination of a quarter-century of Sahara drought and the kind of African civil war that seemed as mindless and murky as any Balkan bloodbath, was in its fourteenth month and showed no signs of waning. Every day thousands of children were dying of malnutrition or from drinking contaminated water. Fourteen months for news is an epoch. The crisis was such an old item now that it no longer appeared on a daily basis in broadcasts or on front pages, despite the fact that on an objective level an ordinary day in Ethiopia was far bigger news than practically anything else on the planet. What the famine had become was late-night programming, the feature event on a number of donation-solicitation shows, run by World Vision and similar organizations, most of them religiously affiliated, all of them asking for money. As a rule the shows were hosted either by "niche"-celebrities — game-show hosts like Alex Trebeck — or ex TV stars like Sally Struthers. One of the most persistent hosts was an astonishingly lovely All-American beauty of an actress, who looked like a gaunt Phyllis George. Night after night you could see her on the screen opposite David Letterman, her big ravishing face growing more immaculate as the scene behind her grew more abysmal. Her "co-star" was a skeletal little boy lying draped across his mother's lap, with the obligatory flies buzzing around his huge-eyed face. This was a boy, the actress would tell us in a later voice-over, who had died the next day. It was too late for him, but not for the others. The point was clear: it was a children's famine she was showcasing. The stars of the show were kids.

Yet despite the terrible recurring reminder of the boy's death, despite the thousands of other kids dying every day, despite the hostess's sexiness and all the Band-Aid concerts, nothing in the famine in Ethiopia ever riveted the attention of the adult world, the parental world, the way the drama to save Jessica McClure did those four days in October.

The stock culprit is indifference. Human compassion is limited, goes the argument, and to stay sexy in the public mind an event has to be both specific and graspable. Ethiopia was ultimately faceless, while the Texas drama was as specific as you could get. "Don't tell me about the death of millions," the poet wrote; "Tell me about the oak that will no longer bloom outside my door." The religious charity organizations had obviously bought the argument; they were trying as hard as they could to put a face on the tragedy. They thought their problem was numbers.

They were only half-right. The famine hadn't simply committed the crime of being too large, it was guilty of being about children and being without hope. For parents this wasn't an aesthetic mistake, but a gut issue. The famine didn't have too little impact, it had too much. It had targeted its audience, parents, perfectly, but it had hit us so hard in the universal instinct it had us diving for cover.

In the parameters of parental pain, Jessica McClure was manageable. She was one child, on identifiable terrain. She was still alive while we watched her, and it was more than possible to imagine a happy outcome. She came from a comfortable, relatively affluent life, and if she was rescued she'd be comfortable again, other than having to endure the sure-fire TV mini-series chronicling her close call. Her dilemma was a blip on an acceptable sea. She was a safe thing to worry about.

The children in the famine, by contrast, were part of a skein of tragedy without any end in sight. There had been droughts *forever*, it seemed to any news watcher, going on in Africa, and children had been dying forever. If they were fed today, chances were they would starve tomorrow. When the famine did become specific, in the person of a fly-tormented boy who died in his mother's arms, the specificity was so utterly sad it was impossible to watch. At our house, in fact, a routine developed over the course of the famine. I would walk into the family room to find one of the kids, Jennifer or Ben but even sometimes Rosie, watching World Vision, staring at the screen transfixed — I would end up being the one to change the channel. My reasons sounded logical even to me — we should send money or turn it off, I told them, it wasn't entertainment, and to think so was to insult and exploit people who were suffering. In fact, I just couldn't watch the shows. If, as T.S. Eliot said, "Human-kind cannot bear very much reality," parent-kind can bear even less. The irony of ironies is that when it comes to the suffering of other people's children parents may end up being *less* responsive than non-parents, because we're so much more sensitive to start with.

The implications come on little cat feet, like the fog. Nazi Germany is the acid test. In six years one million children died in its concentration camps, while millions of German parents sat idly by and did nothing. Or maybe they didn't sit so *idly* by. This is not to excuse the impulse or the indifference for a moment, only to suggest an awful possibility. Maybe those German parents were sabotaged by a mechanism other than apathy, one that clicked on the moment they suspected the unspeakable truth. Maybe they were ambushed by their parenthood. What was monstrous was how far they retreated to avoid the pain. On the continuum of responsibility and guilt we sit at the low end of the crescent watching the gaunt woman on TV, while they stand at the pinnacle, listening to whispers in the candy-store. But their reasons for inaction might have been the same as ours: They may have turned inhuman because they were all too human to start with.

My wife's late grandmother had a habit of scanning newspaper reports of disasters for Jewish names. The message seemed to be: "No Jews; all right, it's bad, but not *so* bad." As parents we do the same with the names of other people's children. If a disaster, a plane crash or an earthquake occurs and no children are involved it is horrible but bearable (the next names we look for are those of people who *had* children). This is why the American air-raid on Mohammar Kadhaffi's palace turned poisonous when it was revealed that the dictator's adopted infant daughter had been killed in the attack; why it's so hard to swallow the word "freedom" when Palestinian "freedom-fighters" blow up a busload of children; why, after you read a magazine story about Jay Leno's rise to the "Tonight Show" throne, the first thing you tell your wife about it is that his manager had a three-month-old baby who died of AIDS (until you mention this, it's as though you haven't told the story).

This is also why, when a story you hear has a happy ending, God — to paraphrase Sir Lancelot — in his mercy lends you grace.

Four and a half years after Jessica McClure slipped down her version of the rabbit hole, a three-year-old girl named Amanda Ashley went missing from a family picnic at a tourist farm just north of Toronto. As the family was getting ready for a hayride, her mother turned around momentarily, and when she turned back Amanda was gone. All night, in a heavy downpour police and family searched for her, with her mother sure that she'd been kidnapped. Then just before nine the next morning the weather cleared, and a police helicopter spotted something lying on top of a hay bale about a mile from the farm. It was Amanda. She was fast asleep, perfectly safe except for puffy eyes from crying, and a few mosquito bites. "Mommy, I went for a walk," was all she would say to anyone afterward.

Reading the newspaper story, though, a parent is transfixed by a detail that isn't there. A police officer climbs out of the helicopter and approaches the sleeping child. The air smells of humid hay and sun. She looks, as the policeman will later say, "protected by angels." But the question is: Does he wake her right away? Or does he let her sleep? If so, how long does he let her sleep? Does he watch her? Does he reach out to touch her cheek?

Until the moment he does she is his child, and more; she's a child abandoned. She is everyone's child.

Do you wake her?

Do you take the heart?

This isn't to deny impersonal evil. This isn't to pretend

that the Pol Pots and the Saddam Husseins don't exist, that generations of African children weren't stolen like chattel. This is only to say that for most of us, the parental instinct is the best instinct we will ever have — and that the parental instinct customized a bit, stripped of its dysfunctional possibilities and the Jaundiced Eye, can become something even better.

For parents, the "other" when it comes to children has always flown in the face of what the "other" has always meant in history. Children won't go into that mould. In 1970, Mark Harris, the author of a famous fifties trilogy of baseball novels about a pitcher named Henry Wiggen (*The Southpaw, Bang the Drum Slowly* and *A Ticket for a Seamstitch*), wrote a clinically cool novel called *The Goy*. The title was ironic in more than one way. Historically the Hebrew word *goy* has mutated from its straightforward Biblical definition of "other nation" to the epitome of otherness itself — a *goy* in modern vernacular is an outsider, outside the fold, and outside the secrets of grace and touch. In Harris's novel the *goy* of the title is the hero, a Gentile professor of history named Westrum who's married to a Jewish woman, and who has three sons "Jewish by half." In the seminal incident of the story, one that actually takes place before the book begins, Westrum in a moment of frustration (literally over a broken dish) strikes his youngest son Terrence so violently that he breaks his spine. What the protagonist wonders afterward, what he's never sure of — even as Terrence recovers — is whether or not he said what he thinks he might have as he struck his son: the words "Jew" or "little Jew," or "you little Jew." He wonders, in other words, whether his anger was sufficient to let him turn his own son into a true "other," to see him as something less than a human being.

It's a moot point. In doing what he does, out of rage, Westrum makes his son his own more irrevocably than he could with any embrace. Fury is an intimate emotion when it comes to children — this is something every parent knows within a month of becoming a parent. It's the guilty secret we all hope is shared. Sadism has its allures, too pure to be total nurture and no nature: there are moments when only the tiniest slice of patience separates the harried single mother who hits her kids and the harried "liberated" father who just turns around in a car and yells at his. What binds the two, again, is the fact that they're dealing with their own children. And what's interesting is how on a certain level we can sympathize with, or at least understand, that inner-family crankiness unto rage, while the crimes of strangers are harder to absorb.

In November of 1970 a little girl, who would become known to the world simply as "Genie," walked — or hobbled — with her mother into a social services office in Temple City, California. A biological thirteen at the time, she looked like an autistic, although strangely lovely, six- or seven-year-old. She spat indiscriminately, had two full sets of teeth, and a hard ring of callous around her buttocks — this last because she had spent virtually her entire life, since she learned to walk, tied to a potty seat by her father (with her mother's acquiescence) in one room. The circumstances of Genie's ordeal were enough to make headlines anyway, but what made her a sensation in the academic world was the fact that she was language-immaculate; Genie was virtually speechless.

As a result, she was the most perfect subject for tests designed to prove or disprove prevailing theories of language acquisition since "Victor," the famous French "Wild Child" of the nineteenth century. (In this sense, Genie was also a scientific ancestor of the psychological subjects of King Frederick the Second of Germany, who in the thirteenth century had a group of orphaned babies raised in total silence to see which language they would end up speaking: German, Latin, Greek or Hebrew. The babies died.)

Genie's life before the fact of her discovery would have been heart-breaking enough. What happened to her afterward was like a low moan after the shouting was over. Despite promises made by the linguists involved with her to conduct only "ethical testing," and to place Genie's interests before those of science, ultimately she ended up a pawn in the world of publish or perish. The only person who might have been able to "save" her, a woman named Jean Butler who was her teacher at the rehabilitation centre at the Children's Hospital of Los Angeles, was disqualified as a potential adoptive parent on the grounds that she was "bad for the research."

But that was Genie's life. One of the most fascinating things about Genie's story is how quickly people who hear it mentally file away the authors of the truly horrible abuse she suffered — her father and by association her mother (incredibly enough, she was eventually returned to her mother in the end) — and redirect their anger at the scientists, the strangers who exploited her in an infinitely milder way. We do this because we believe reflexively that her natural parents were obviously insane, while the scientists should have known better. Genie's parents had distorted access to the Will To Rage; the scientists had neither access nor a right to it. Reading about Genie, we don't excuse her parents because of any privilege to go crazy — they were self-created monsters — but we recognize where they started down the road to damnation. The callousness of other children's parents, who had a chance to try to repair what had been done to her, strikes us as almost as unforgivable as the intimate monstrosity.

Before my in-laws moved closer uptown to us, they lived in a large older house on a tree-lined street farther south in the city. The house was old and large enough that it had a secret basement vault / wine-cellar accessible only by a staircase that was itself hidden behind a carved wooden panel in the den. To open the panel you had to press a discreet little black button in the small built-in bar adjacent to the den. This was the button the original occupants had pressed when they wanted to slip downstairs to throw back a contraband gin and tonic or two during Prohibition days.

One Friday night we were over at the house for dinner, and halfway through the soup course someone realized that Ben was missing. I went to look for him, getting more irritated with every empty room, sure that he'd taken off somewhere to watch TV or play with his He Man figures. Walking past the den at one point I heard a faint, birdlike cry. It came again. I pressed the button in the bar, and the panel swung open. Ben was standing at the top of the stairs, so frightened he couldn't cry, only gasp. It took a long time to calm him down; even when he did, the wide-eyed, startled, blank look stayed on his face.

It was only later I realized where I had seen the look before: on Jessica McClure's face, when she was carried up out of the well after fifty-eight and a half hours of solitude. A plan to have a man who could dislocate his shoulders squirm through and rescue her had been passed over in favour of a new high-power water drill. With the white bandage wrapped around her head like a dressing from the Paris barricades, her look was white, too, in the floodlights as they hustled her, too ordinary to be true, into a waiting ambulance. A tremendous lassitude of joy settled over the crowd around the site in Texas, the same release of joy that I (and probably millions of other parents) felt watching it. At the same time, the little girl's face was locked in a disorientation too acute to ignore; it was blank, like my son's. But he was mine, and she was everyone's. So where with him I felt guilt that wouldn't fade and a helplessness that would, anger at myself and worry about how he would remember this night, towards her I felt the peace of angels.

"Dad, what are you doing, slow down! Slow *down*!"

It's my son again, doing a little more back-seat driving. I resist the impulse to kill him, and hit the brake-pedal instead, the tires squealing. Red brake lights are going on all around us, traffic slowing from fifty miles an hour to a halt in the space of a hundred yards.

"Dad, what is it? An accident?"

"I don't know."

But it isn't an accident, I see now. Five or six cars ahead of us a school bus has stopped, its hexagonal stop sign flipped up on the driver's side. Although the road, more countryish than suburban, has been widened here to an ample four lanes, true highway width, traffic has come to a halt going both ways, stretching ahead of us at least a hundred yards. As we wait, the school bus door opens and a little boy, five or maybe six, gets off. He's wearing a pack and carrying a Star Wars lunch-box — a hand-me-down? On his head is a yellow visor-style cap, with no top, just a brim, so his hair shows through like a golfer's. He makes his way now slowly across the shoulder of the road to a wire gate, which he opens, awkwardly because he has to reach over with the lunch-box hand to get at the latch. The house in front of him, the last remnant of a farm, looks like a small whitewashed cottage. It's a scant twenty feet from the busy road; there isn't another house within half a mile of it.

Behind the screen door of the house the main door opens now; through it I can make out an adult's shape, but the screen obscures the face and the sex, like layers of pentimento in a painting. The little boy walks slowly, up the walk. Slow but steady. He is small, and the world is large. A kind of suspense grows. In the line of waiting cars angry hearts slow in expectation. Everyone is in a hurry, but now we will wait. We have no time, but we will give him all the time he needs. Will he make it?

He reaches the door. It opens. A figure stoops briefly to usher him inside, a woman; the door closes; he's safe.

"Hey, let's go!"

"Yeah, Dad, I got things to do!"

6

Figure Skating
The Little League Father

"Mirror, mirror, on the wall, who's the fairest of the mall?"
Rosie Teitel, 1991

"Winning isn't everything; it's the only thing."
Vince Lombardi, 1962

4:30 p.m.

In my second year of university I volunteered at a youth drop-in centre in the inner-city of Toronto called St Christopher's House. At St Chris's I ended up working with half a dozen ten-year-old boys, a racially mixed group, all the members hailing from a housing project five minutes from the centre. Of the four boys whose adult fates I kept track of, one became a policeman, one a pimp and another the head cook at a large downtown hospital. The fourth was a beefy mulatto kid with reddish hair and freckles, whose nickname was

"The Foodman." The Foodman had acquired his nickname not because he liked to eat — despite his bulk he was actually a picky kind of nosher — but because he could tell you the price of virtually any supermarket comestible you could name, at any *supermarket* you could name, off the top of his head. The Foodman — I'll call him Jerry — was a grocery genius; towards the end of our time together he was even branching out into heating-oil prices. He also had one of the truly original vocabularies I'd ever encountered: if something was a gyp or cheaply made it was "chinchilla"; elderly ladies he didn't like he called "bingle-bats."

The Foodman was single-minded enough to have made a great broker on Wall Street, but he never got the chance. Three years after I stopped working at the centre, I got a call from a friend of mine who was working for legal aid, letting me know that the Foodman had just been arrested for making one of the most offensive series of obscene phone calls the local precinct had ever investigated. A little while later I heard that he'd been caught doing it again. Over the next couple of years it became his *modus operandi*. What made it even sadder and less explicable was the fact that of the group the Foodman had been the most laconic conversationalist. He used to sit for an hour like the Buddha in the back of my old Volkswagen 1500, and then suddenly ask: "What potatoes, Duane?" — usually a good twenty minutes after Duane had mentioned potatoes. "What muffler, Kenny?" the Foodman would ask. "What eggplant, Doug?" "What red light, Jay?"

In the car now, six-year-old Annie says something that makes me think suddenly of Jerry the Foodman, at the same time as it jolts me out of my current daydream. What Annie says is: "What party, Ben?"

"Donny Morrison's," Ben says. "It's at Skyscrapers."

"Cool," says Kevin.

"What's this about a party?" I say, coming all the way back to reality.

"I've got one. Donny Morrison's birthday party."

"What do you mean, you have a party tonight? It's a school night."

"Not tonight, today, now. It's an after-school party. Dad, don't tell me you didn't get a present. You can't tell me that."

"I don't know anything about Donny Morrison's party, Ben. Who has a party on a school day? Are these people unbalanced?"

"Dad, I told Mummy about it, it's on the bulletin board. We have to have a present."

"Mummy didn't tell me anything about it, Ben. How can I get you to this party? I've got to pick up Jennifer. This is insane. The gift is the least of it."

By this time we're at the carpool's house. Annie, having done her damage, gets out along with her brother with a smile, taking an incredibly long time to close the door, it seems to me. "If you'd like to see our new computer, Jay, you could come in now," she says. "I think it would be okay with my dad." I thank her, ask for a rain check, and back out of the driveway, taking the corner a block away with a squeal, feeling real satisfaction when Ben has to grab the door-handle for balance, and say "Dad."

"Don't Dad me, Ben."

"Dad, calm down. You asked me to tell you the next time you got like this."

"I can't tell you how pissed off I am about this, Ben. This is the last straw."

It's true. For some reason the birthday party, as innocuous as it is on its own, is the trip-wire for the afternoon's frustration. It's not just losing the hour and a half of work I'd counted on between dropping off the carpool and picking up Jennifer. It's not even the general chaos the day has disintegrated into, the defeat of the plan. What's really bothering me, I realize, yanking the wheel around and heading for Skyscrapers, is the feeling of privilege surrounding my family's preoccupations for the day, which are diametrically opposed to the values I always thought were mine. Figure-skating, a "theme" birthday party on a school night, even carpool, are not things that I would have ever considered "me." My kids have turned me bourgeois in a way I don't remember being, either at twenty years old — when I worked with the Foodman — or at ten — when I walked home from school every day. Granted, my father drove me to hockey practice in those days, and baseball after that, but I had to beg him to do it, and eventually I took the bus. Parties were at the kids' houses in the neighbourhood, and we walked home from those too. The world was half as diffuse, and a quarter as packaged. In *my* day, I want to tell Ben . . .

I don't get a chance to do it; we're at Skyscrapers. Through the windows of the commercial plaza unit we pull up to I can see children in sweatpants and T-shirts going up and down from an unseen source, as though they're sealed in a little plastic snow scene filled with water. Skyscrapers is a trampoline club. This is a trampoline party. Bowling parties and miniature-golf parties have given way to something more exotic in this, the waning decade of the North American twentieth century. More exotic anyway than Steven Kwinter's recreation room with the marimba players on the walls. But where do you play "Seven Minutes in Heaven"? The world has become both slicker and less mature for an eight-year-old. And I have become a cabbie.

"Thanks for driving me, Dad," Ben says, leaning over and kissing me on the cheek goodbye, and then getting out of the car fast. "He likes G.I. Joes. Vehicles, not figures."

I watch him go through the door of the club, ahead of a woman in flowered leggings. He kissed me goodbye, it occurs to me — he does it without thinking. Through the waiting-room window I see him throw an arm around one of his friends shoulders from behind, turning him around so they can laugh with each other like a couple of dwarfs at a bar.

I take Leslie Street south for a mile, deke into a Toys "R" Us to pick up a G.I. Joe Rescue Wagon ($11.95 plus tax), a gift bag as opposed to wrapping paper (save the planet), and a funny card (he should have made his own), and get to the skating rink on Yonge Street in thirteen minutes flat.

At the rink there's warm autumn sun outside and the incongruous mound of snow where the Zamboni piles it up in the parking lot. Inside the air has the dank, slightly fusty smell of rinks everywhere — at least everywhere in Canada. Once on Long Island I watched the New York Islanders practise in an arena that smelled like an amusement park.

To say the figure-skating scene is different from the carpool scene is to play with understatement. At the rink pony-tails are at a minimum, and adult egos, at least the female ones, are either on hold or on loan. The mothers, dominating once again, sit at scattered levels in the stands, reading their books and doing their knitting and drinking their coffee with the kind of weary forbearance that men always have trouble figuring out. There are fathers here, too, mind you, a handful of regulars, one of whom, with his moustache and balding, fine brow, overcoat and exquisite briefcase, looks like a South American diplomat. He's in the glassed-in viewing area when I come in today, sitting on the middle step with a portable computer in his lap. His daughter, dark like a young duenna, is changing into her skates on the bench below him. I see the diplomat every week — in fact I've seen him at other lesson sessions, dance, swimming — but we've never spoken, just exchanged polite shrugs that acknowledge our secondary status. We are no longer the centres of the universe, our shrugs say, we just drive the centre of the universe from place to place. We are the moveable audience.

Today when I see him, though, I realize that I wouldn't mind talking to him; I'd like to ask him about the Raleigh father. I have the feeling he'd have exactly the right answer, delivered with Latin sadness — like a *fado* singer — and maybe the exchange of business cards.

Instead I get a cup of chicken soup from the coffee-dispensing machine, and walk through the glass door to the non-climate-controlled perimeter of the rink itself. From the boards I look out on the face of beauty.

For different people true beauty, the meshing of grace

with goodness, comes in different forms. For me, it happens to be figure-skating. It's not simply that skating is a spectator sport made in heaven for fathers: sensual but chaste, provocative but inviolate; it's the oblivious purity in the air all over the ice. "My skates were *white,*" remembers Cleo Birdwell, the fictional author of *Amazons,* and the first woman to play hockey in the National Hockey League. Every skater in front of me is coated with the same brand of wistful, transient innocence without being aware of it at all; it's a kind of radiant stunned-ness that goes perfectly with the miasmic nature of a figure-skating practice itself. Who can figure this crowd-scene out? The last thing figure-skating practice is is practice as men know it, regimented and geared towards camaraderie and games. After fifteen-minute lessons with the group and similarly short private lessons, everyone becomes a solo act, practising at will. Because jumps are the riskiest and spins the loveliest, spins are what get done most, that slow arm-extended windup for the tight inexplicable spiral being the favourite. The girls skate a bit and talk a bit, and everything else is done, of course, backwards.

Some of the girls are dedicated, but just as many spend their time looking over at their parents in the glassed-in stands, to see when they can get away with loafing. I watch one of the dedicated ones now, a blonde-haired girl in a black turtleneck and tights practising jumps at the far end of the rink. I watch for a few moments more. Then I realize it's my daughter.

She catches sight of me just as I reach the opening in the boards, and skates over fast, her cheeks flushed with the cold and the sport. Amnesia has blessed her again.

Her little performance on the fence railing outside has been consigned to history along with her morning imitation of Linda Blair.

"Hi, Dad! Did you see that last one?"

"Uh-uh." I'm trying hard not to be too nice. "Go ahead. I'll watch."

"Okay, and thanks so much for the soup, Dad! Watch, okay? I'm pretty sure I didn't two-foot the last one!"

She skates out to try her axel. Named for the Scandinavian who invented it, I know, Axel Tuborg or Sunderstrom or maybe Bergman, it's the hardest of the single jumps, a one and a half rotational manoeuvre that represents the shift from the level she's at, doing single jumps, to the next, doubles. Like all esoteric sports lingos, the language of figure-skating is dopey, but she gets — *I think* — a kick out of the fact that I pretend to share it. She backs up into the jump and does it, then looks over hopefully.

"I don't know." I couldn't have told her if she landed on three feet. "It looked great to me."

"It wasn't. I did a great one before." I always miss her great ones, it's a given. "So what should I do?"

The invitation on her beaming, panting face is obvious. She wants me to coach her. Mind you, she also dreams of my wife sitting in the stands with a skein of wool.

"You have to set the edge more," I say. Isn't this skiing talk? "Which foot do you take off on again? Okay, sink down twice as far as usual and do not raise your left leg at all till you jump, okay? Keep it straight."

"Okay," she looks a bit confused, but eager. "Do a couple."

She moves out to the centre of the rink, skates backwards, and co-operatively does two more jumps, landing one shakily and falling down on the next one. I'm trying to pick out what she's doing wrong, but the moves happen so fast they're impenetrable. I also find myself being distracted by a voice beside me, a man's voice. The voice has a pedantic, pleasant quality, almost a singsong. It's repeating one word over and over again. "Coward. Coward. Coward." I look to my left and see a compact, handsome man leaning over and speaking to a dark-haired girl in a purple and black skating suit. The girl is the man's daughter; he is methodically berating her.

I've seen both of them before, but never from so close. The daughter has a slim, pale face — like the face of one of the Irish girl singers in the movie *The Commitments* — and a quick, sudden way of getting up on one hand when she falls, so it's always seemed to my untutored eye like part of her routine. Her father looks Milanese; he's wearing a fashionably baggy leather jacket and expensive loafers. There's something very professional about him, professional too about the space between his frowning face as he leans over with both hands gripping the sides of the open gate and his daughter's downturned one. Pedagogy and seduction are on the same tonal continuum. He could be her coach or her lover.

"If you're not going to do the double, you might as well give up. Your competition's in a week. You want to be a suck, be a suck. Cowards pull out like that." He's making no effort to either lower or raise his face. "You want to be a coward, or you want to have a chance?" She says something low and shrugs her shoulders, something with "can't do it" in it. He squints at her. "So give up. I don't mind living with a coward so much if you don't. Or maybe you want to try again?" She shrugs again. "Go on, get out there," he says. "And *stick* it this time."

She glides out with her head still low, coincidentally choosing the same corner of the rink as Jennifer. They jump at about the same time, and both stay on their feet. The dark-haired girl pulls out of her landing, though, with a quick, forlorn spin and heads back, on one foot, to the boards. Her father hits the open door hard with his fist when she gets there. His voice is too low now for me to hear.

"Did you see that, Dad?" Jennifer is back, panting. "Did you see that one?"

"I saw it. It was great."

"No you didn't." She follows my gaze. "Who are you looking at? Oh, Jessica."

We both look at Jessica. She's looking down at the toe of her skate. It wouldn't surprise me to see tears on her cheeks, but all that's there is dark surliness.

"What's he so upset about?" I say. "It looked perfect to me."

"Her double sal's too spinny," Jennifer says. "She's afraid of jumping high enough to extend it."

"A spinny double sal?"

"Double salchow. The judges look for that." I feel her hand on my elbow. "My jumps don't look like that, do they, Dad?"

A spinny double salchow. I watch Jessica's father lean in a little closer and talk mean and low to his daughter because her double salchow is too spinny. Don't worry about her spinny double salchow, I want to tell him, you've got something a lot worse to worry about. Your antsiness about your daughter's double salchow may come from somewhere natural, but it's gone somewhere poisonous. We know all about this transformation, we fathers in the stands. We know the little rush you get when people come up to you at the local pond, and ask where your daughter learned to skate so well, or when they tell you at judo how strong your son is, or at school how sensitive he is. It's so *seductive*, the ease with which your kids' accomplishments can attach themselves to you. But the next step, to actually try to make their limelight yours, isn't just illogical, it's doomed. Forget about the fact that the way you're butting into Jessica's life is grossly unfair, I want to tell the natty man beside me, it's tactically disastrous. You're thinking you'll get something back for it, when, as the Jewish mother says, you will get nothing but heartache. And in the process you'll probably begin to disappear yourself. A good rule of thumb for fathers is this: any time you find yourself abnegating your ego to try to control a pint-sized vessel of your own genetic material, it's probably an acknowledgement of failure.

I want to tell him all of this — at the same time I'd like to go over and kick his Giorgio Armani ass halfway across the rink. But before I can do either I happen to glance over at my own daughter. Her hand still perched on my forearm with *noblesse oblige*, she's watching the little drama unfold in front of her with extreme attention, and curiosity, and something else: something undeniably like envy.

Scratch a parent *or* a child deep enough, and eventually you get to the thing with feathers.

In the spring of 1987, a nine-year-old boy from New York City named Joshua Waitzkin competed and won in his division of the National Elementary Scholastic Chess Championship of the United States, held in Charlotte, North Carolina (a short two-hour drive from Raleigh). He won the championship with a stirring come-from-behind tie in his last match against an eight-year-old named Jeff Sarwer, who shaved his head and was known for chanting "Kill, kill, kill" while he launched his attacks. In attendance with Joshua at the championships were his coach, Bruce Pandolfini, his mother, Bonnie, and his father, Fred. Pandolfini and Bonnie Waitzkin were obviously nervous for Joshua, but it was Fred Waitzkin, his father, who was the most nervous. When it appeared early in the match that Joshua stood a good chance of losing, Fred Waitzkin realized that this was the single moment he had been "dreading for a year." This game between two children was more than a game, he would realize later, it was a "leap into chaos," a struggle about "life choices, happiness and failure." When the game was over and Joshua had won, and also distinguished himself by comforting a friend who hadn't, his father started wondering what he would do eventually with his Saturday afternoons, when his son grew up. He wondered so much that he decided to write a book about the question, and about the "chess life" he had "shared" with Joshua since his son was six years old.

The book, called *Searching for Bobby Fischer,* was published in 1988 by Random House. I first became aware of it when I read an excerpt in *Sports Illustrated,* entitled "My Son, My Master." It was a fascinating article, partly because it was such a perfect microcosm of the times

— the latter 1980s. But it was most fascinating because of what it was in itself, not an article about a shared life at all but a monumental apologia for the progenitor of the most silent, "respectable" form of child abuse: the Little League Father.

It's hard to think of a single self-contained piece of writing that could function adequately as a manual on how to be a parent — but "My Son, My Master" was probably the perfect anti-manual on how not to be one. It was amazing. Not only were almost all of Waitzkin's parental "instincts" terrible, but every time he thought he was being contrite, turning an x-ray on his flaws, he ended up betraying how clueless and dishonest he was. Either he had no idea how much inappropriate pressure he was putting on his son, or he did know and he didn't think it was so bad. Or he knew it was terrible, but he thought that by somehow confessing it he could get some sort of dispensation. The fact that he was obviously intelligent, even thoughtful, made the whole story seem that much more cracked.

You didn't have to go much beyond the first page to witness the carnage. After describing how he played his son's first chess games with him at the age of six across the coffee table in their apartment, Waitzkin wrote: "Before long, Josh had a professional instructor. His teacher, Bruce Pandolfini, would arrive at our apartment at 6:30 in the morning, and Josh would stumble out of bed in pj's, wearing the same dreamy face as his infant sister. But within a few seconds he would assume the position — two hands under chin, staring bullets at the chess-board. My little Karpov. Watching him sit at the board concentrating like a miniature master had become more exciting to me than watching Michael Jordan whirl 360 degrees and jam." What Josh's father neglected to mention was exactly how Josh had come to just "have" a professional instructor at the age of six — the implication was that he'd either looked one up in the Yellow Pages himself, or a teacher had appeared organically, like pubic hair. At the tournament itself, when Joshua confessed he was "afraid" of playing Jeff Sarwer, his Atilla-esque opponent, in the final, Waitzkin (who'd been noting with a certain satisfaction that other kids had often gotten "sick to their stomachs at the prospect of having to play Joshua") told him that Bobby Fischer was "never afraid of anyone" — then, to show his "better" instincts, he "immediately regretted it because Josh was only being honest." This was a man who would eventually berate his son's coach for having the *chutzpah* to wonder whether plotting the downfall of another nine-year-old boy was right, and who was totally unable to comprehend the equanimity of another father at the tournament, whose son Joshua beat. When Joshua had started displaying truly alarming symptoms in the weeks leading up to the tournament — telling his father he was feeling the walls closing in on him while he played chess in the park, pulling out the hair at the front of his head enough to create a bald spot — Waitzkin actually had to ask a psychologist friend to figure out why; the psychologist told him that unlike adults, children usually hadn't developed methods to handle pressure situations. Admitting he didn't "feel good" about the reply, Waitzkin responded by going full steam ahead with plans to take Josh to Charlotte, and once they got there, by making sure Josh didn't play ball (something he loved to do) with the other kids between rounds. ". . . it's my job to say, 'No, Josh, you don't want to knock yourself out. Why not go over your openings?' " (What other job could a father have?) Meanwhile, back at home Waitzkin's own mother, Josh's grandmother, was screaming regularly at Fred that he was "a terrible parent for allowing [his] son to go through such torture."

It wasn't that Waitzkin wasn't being honest; he was being brutally honest, but only up to a point. You could stop at a secondary level of honesty, he seemed to be saying, and so excuse your larger lie. The whole exercise seemed rotten with baby-boom autism, an adolescent self-indulgence only a terrible parent of my generation could get away with.

The day I read Waitzkin's article, I sat down and wrote two letters to the editor of *Sports Illustrated*, the first a paragraph long and meant for the magazine, the second running five pages and intended for Fred Waitzkin. Not surprisingly, the magazine didn't publish either. The next few issues carried only a couple of reader comments on the article, all either laudible or about chess. I wondered briefly why no one else felt the way I did, then I put both letters and the article in a manilla envelope and stuck them into a filing cabinet.

It didn't occur to me that there were two critical things in the manilla envelope I had overlooked, a pair of items that Fred Waitzkin, a master of ellipses, had also managed to leave out. The first was his son. Fred Waitzkin was a terrible father — I would never think otherwise — he was self-deceptive, weak, and probably a coward. But what did Josh think about him?

The second thing Waitzkin failed to mention was that

to a greater or lesser degree he might have been writing about all fathers. He might have been writing about me.

I would never have believed it myself. From the day my first child was born, the whole idea of the Little League Father hadn't just repelled me, but had seemed irrelevant. The supposed upside, the fantasies and dreams, left me cold. As prone to most parental clichés as I was, I thought I'd finally found one I was immune to. When my first daughter was born I didn't once imagine her receiving her Best Actress Oscar, and when my son was born I didn't dream of him hitting the World Series winning home-run or finding the cure for cancer (I didn't dream about the non-sexist reverse either). Fred Waitzkin had described a moment in his book, after his son had just won a tournament, when he made a "gaudy high five across the room. My son was a little embarrassed, but it was impossible for me to be casual. At such a moment, a parent is truly the child, giddy and dancing like a fool with fantasies of glory and immortality that he will carry to his grave." As of 1988 I was convinced I hadn't had a moment like that, and I didn't plan to start. I thought my children were beautiful and smart, granted, but my fantasies for them had nothing to do with the future at all. My wife used to ask me: "Don't you wonder what they'll be, aren't you intrigued with what they'll be like when they're older?" Half the time she was wondering which one would grow up and buy her a retirement condominium in Florida, but I didn't even have that daydream. Thinking about my kids older meant thinking about myself ancient. Thinking about them glorious meant thinking about me less so.

I also felt no huge compulsion to teach my kids any of the athletic or creative things I knew. This was probably more surprising, because I'd always loved to teach children things; in my pre-fatherhood days I'd spent hours helping my brother-in-law play running bases with my nephews. But alone with my own kids coaching was more complex and less compulsive. It was fun to show Jennifer chord progression on the piano, fun to teach Ben to throw a baseball — even if I did have to wait for a state of the union address before I got the ball back — but it was usually something I had to remind myself to do.

It's possible that my reflex reaction to anything that smacked of Little League parenthood was atavistic. As a kid myself, I'd grown to dread the idea of my parents coming to watch me do anything; they just made me more nervous than I already was. It got to the point where I actually asked them to stay away from my ball games, and by and large they were pretty good about it. It was only when I was an adult that my father admitted to me that he'd spied on my games intermittently as I was growing up, catching an inning or two from the car or the sidewalk across the road from the park. The last time he did it was when I was in university, and playing quarterback for my college in an intramural football league on the back-campus at the University of Toronto. The field was bordered on the north by a main street, and my father got out of the car and watched over the snowfence, long enough to see me throw a screenpass for a touchdown and then get creamed by a two hundred and fifty pound defensive end. By the time he told me this story I had brains enough to be touched by it, and to realize it might have been better if he'd felt free to put in a public appearance. But later, when I had children of my own, I listened to my ten-year-old counsel. Children needed to know their parents were willing to be there — maybe even *wanted* to be there — but their actual presence was something else. The absent-minded father, I thought, was preferable to the rabid Little Leaguer every time.

This isn't to say I didn't like to show my kids off; I just had my own style. Essentially, I took them everywhere I went. When Jennifer was a baby I lugged her from magazine editorial offices to libraries to sports arenas, toting her close to the vest in her Snuggly, or tucked into her car-seat, affecting a casualness that I figured would be irresistible to the world because it was irresistible to me. I wasn't invading her life, I was just using her as costume jewellery for mine. She made my star shine brighter, and besides, she smelled good. I took her to meetings and squash games, propping her up in her car-seat at the latter outside the big glass wall so she could, at the age of eight months, absorb the finer points of the game. After she learned to walk I liked to amble down the street into an ice-cream shop with her and ask her what she wanted as though she was twelve, and not two. I figured I was being subtle. When she got old enough to get her hair cut I took her to the fancy salon my wife recommended, and got mine cut at the same time. Even then she had a lot more to cut then I did, golden Shirley Temple ringlets to go with her big cheeks. I on the other hand had larger muscles. Sitting side by side in our swivel chairs with our plastic smocks on, her perched on a stack of towels, me the comfy lummox, I had the feeling I was a member of a perfectly balanced vaudeville team. I felt shot with smug sun. A bad collaborator from way back, I had never been more content in my life to have a partner.

She was with me, as it happened, when we got our hair cut one day just after she turned four, as part of an extended birthday treat that was going to include a movie afterward. The main room at the salon was being used for a fashion shoot, and we ended up in a little sunroom, where the proprietor, a quizzical zeppelin of a man with every node of colour bleached out of him, was doing hair for two of the models and a third older woman, a TV producer who was organizing the shoot. In the show-biz ambience Jennifer quickly took on the mantle of mascot. The TV producer, who had hair like Lucy Ricardo, turned out to also have a daughter about Jennifer's age who was crazy about *The Wizard of Oz,* so they had a lot to talk about. At any rate, my daughter somehow ended up standing up in front of her chair with her hands at her sides and belting out her version of "Over the Rainbow" for the assembled crowd. She was a big hit — the proprietor called her "unique." When everyone finished clapping, while she was flushed brightly enough to heat the room, the TV producer asked if I'd consider having her come to a casting call for a commercial that was being filmed in a month. I thanked her but said no thanks, ignoring my daughter's look, adding that our "theatrical" policy for our kids was that they could go to auditions when they were old enough to get to them themselves. Then I collected Jennifer, said goodbye, and walked out past the merely beautiful people, happy with the duo we were, the little golden girl and the father who would not be pushed into being pushy.

In the litany of damning exhibits provided by a parent's revisionist memory, the evidence starts small and gets bigger. The first piece would be the level of satisfaction I remember feeling as we left the salon, the proud warmth of the "we." What credit could I take for the curl in her hair, the quaver in her voice? The second would be the behaviour of my lips as I sat listening to my daughter sing, with the hairdresser's scissors poised motionless above my head: they mouthed every lyric of Harold Arlen's classic along with the little girl, willing them to emerge perfect. But the most damning would be my own little ellipsis: ". . . she somehow ended up singing 'Over the Rainbow.'" This is what I just wrote, and in fact my memory remembers it that way, too. But of course Jennifer didn't just end up singing "Over the Rainbow" at age four in the cutting room of a ritzy hairdressing joint. Someone who knew she could pull it off suggested it. Fred Waitzkin had no monopoly on the strategic omission. Listening to myself now on tape-recordings coaxing my kids to sing or recite for posterity I can hear that "casual" suggestive quality in my too-arch voice, subtle as iron, enough to make anyone cringe. But I resisted the evidence of my crime then, the same way I would have resisted the suggestion that I had a four-year-old accomplice all along.

I still thought children were innocent victims in the Little League syndrome, that is, and I still thought I was closer in parenting style to Marie Orser or Jim Redmond than to Fred Waitzkin. Marie Orser was (and is) the mother of the Canadian World Champion and Olympic silver medallist figure skater Brian Orser, who during his performances was famous for being so worried about her son making a mistake and being disappointed in himself that she couldn't bear to watch, and so paced the hallways of a hundred arenas trying to link crowd noise to the course of her boy's performance. Jim Redmond was the father of Derek Redmond, a British 400-metre runner who had a celebrated fall after tearing a hamstring in the backstretch of a semi-final race at the Barcelona Olympics in the summer of 1992. Seeing his son struggle to his feet and start hopping down the track in a crazed attempt to at least finish this race he had been dreaming of for four years, Jim Redmond, a large man, charged down the stadium steps, threw a Spanish security man out of the way like so much cotton batten and ran to his son. "You don't have to do this," he told his son while he hugged him. "Yes, I do," Derek said. "Well, then, we'll finish this together," said Jim Redmond. Which is what they did, fighting off officials in the process, the son's head buried in his father's burly shoulder. By the summer of 1992, when I read about Jim Redmond, I'd gotten enough humility not to try compare myself with him. By the summer of 1989, though, when my kids were just starting to "come out" on the stage of life, I would have wanted him and Marie Orser for prototypes.

It was that summer that Ben turned old enough to play real house-league baseball, five-pitch as opposed to T-ball, and I volunteered to coach his team. It seemed logical — I was going to have to stay with him at the games anyway, and this way I could minimize my driving. It also figured to be different than coaching Jennifer. Jennifer and I were cut from similar sporting cloth; coaching her was like coaching a smarter version of myself. Coaching Ben was an exercise in bewilderment. He had good size, plenty of athletic ability, but elusive passion. He didn't, for example, care to dwell on the event of sport at all; the event took too long. After ten catches or so of a game of catch he'd want to try hitting, and after a few hits he thought maybe we should toss the football around. "You know I really love to fish," he actually said to me one day in the middle of a curve-ball. Up to this point he'd been fishing exactly one day in his life.

And he never stopped talking — not while he was catching or throwing. This amazed me the most. Sports for me had always been a serious delight, with the accompanying conversation usually superfluous or even a little shy. As an adult I'd watched the rite of silence become even more inviolate; talking about the sport you were playing seemed childish; talking about anything else seemed jaded. The solution was off-track sports talk — if you were playing baseball you talked about basketball, if you were playing basketball you talked hockey. With Ben the talk ran the gamut of topics, on and off track; almost always, though, his observations — usually coming at the moment he was going to release the ball — were about feelings. Happy feelings, sad feelings, weird feelings, outraged feelings, sexy feelings. The result was an unevenness of performance that made me gnash my teeth. One day he would hit the ball a ton, with a whiplash swing; the next he couldn't hit a balloon. But it was nothing that an ice-cream bar or a board-game or a discussion of Chuang Tse's butterfly dream couldn't cure. What took me a long time to realize was the simplest thing: my son wouldn't have minded being a sports superstar, but he was too interested in the human comedy to spend time practising. He was more human than fanatic. A stubborn maniac at times, at heart he was more mature than I was. He just didn't care — I thought — about sports as much as I did.

So it was gratifying when he turned out to be into five-pitch — he liked our team's caps for one thing. It was also gratifying to find out that I could maintain my objectivity with him, at least relatively. When he came up to hit I took a few extra seconds to admire how much he looked like a ballplayer, with his million-dollar squint, and his hat bent into a lunatic roof-peak which the kids swore was the major-league fashion. But my partiality was for the team, not him. With Ben my obsessions were mild: I wanted him to avoid the embarrassment of striking out, and I wanted him to make at least one field play per game so that he could keep his baseball self-image intact.

Unfortunately our team, sabotaged by the luck of the house-league lottery, had one of the weaker line-ups in the league, and by the next-to-last Wednesday night we hadn't won a game. It bothered Ben as far as I could tell, when he thought about it, but I was pretty sure it bothered me more. It was the second last week in August, a muggy night with a high sky, and half the players on both teams were away at the cottage or on vacation. We managed to field nine a side, but there were no parents who felt willing or qualified to umpire, so the coaches drew straws, and I ended up the short man out. It seemed like a safe predicament. The other team was the second worst team in the league, with one win to their credit, and their coaches were laid-back and nicely endomorphic in their jeans and team shirts. And because it was five-pitch, I didn't have to call balls or strikes. Things went well at the beginning, too. Our team scored the maximum six runs in each of the first two innings and actually held the other team to only three in one of them, so all we had to do was "hold serve" for the remainder of the game to win. Ben got a couple of hits early and was a pure sportsman when I had to call him out at the plate on a stylish one-foot stab in the third inning. "Sorry, buddy, you're gone," I said jerking my thumb up, and he kind of humphed and went back to the bench like a big-leaguer, getting into it.

But then in the open fourth inning we hit three line-drives to their best player, scoring only two runs before we were retired. With the few parents on the bench getting raucous, the opposing team came up trailing by only five, an insecure margin in five-pitch at the best of times. Amazingly we got two quick outs, and I was praying I would not have to make a critical call. One win was not a lot to ask, I thought. It was at this point that our defence fell apart; the other team scored four runs on a variety of errors, and had runners on second and third. Ben, playing first base, was yacking even more than usual, going crazy exhorting his team-mates one second and lecturing them the next. A little blond kid who had struck out four times already came up; he missed three times, then with his chubby coach excited enough to come out and help him, he dribbled a grounder to our pitcher, who fumbled the ball, then threw it to first, where Ben made a dramatic stab and held onto the ball. To a person who hadn't watched much baseball it might have seemed like a close play, but to anyone who knew the game it was an open and shut case. I called the runner safe. While our players were caught in the chaos of protesting, the second opposition runner scored and the other team won the game.

I felt terrible, but noble, and my son's behaviour seemed to bear me out. He quickly recovered as far as I could see, lining up to jeer congratulations to the other team and then clamouring for post-game Eskimo Pie. The only thing I noticed at all unusual as I walked him to the car was that he seemed a bit quiet — at least for Ben.

And then we reached the first corner past the park, and checking traffic to turn I looked to my right and saw that he was sobbing in his seat, behind his seat-belt. The sound of his distress was pure and intense; there was a wail in it of anguish, devoid of sentiment, enough to tear your heart out.

"Ben, what's wrong?" I said.

"You didn't have to call him safe," he said. "He was out."

"No, Ben," I said, "he was safe. I saw he was safe. I couldn't lie."

"Just *one* game," he sobbed. "I just wanted us to win one game. We were so *close* to winning."

"But I had to be honest, right? What did you want me to do?"

"He could have been out. You could have said he was out. The other coaches do it all the time."

"No they don't," I said.

"They do. Why did you have to umpire? Why did you do that? He would have been out if you weren't the umpire."

"Ah, Ben, don't."

But he was inconsolable. All the way home he sobbed, with as much of his soul as I had ever seen him show before. It was a good hour and a half before I got him to come around, and then it was only by promising to take him to the Dairy Queen to buy whatever he wanted. "Did you have to call him safe?" my wife said in our bedroom, deserting me too while Ben waited in the car. "Come on," I said. "He *was* safe. You're a vice-principal. What was I supposed to do?"

She had no answer. In the car on the way to the ice-cream shop I kept my hand on his leg, feeling the occasional lingering tremor of a sob run through him, while he told me it was all right, and got in a few shots of his own. He'd eaten the Eskimo Pie because he didn't want people to know he was upset, he said. And he walked behind me on the way to the car because he didn't want anyone to know I was his father. (Ah, Ben, I was their coach all year, who else did they think I was?)

But it wasn't all right. *He could have been out. Why did you have to umpire*? He wouldn't be a big-leaguer, my son, but I had still failed him. I'd failed him by refusing to fail myself. I had done the right thing — I would do it again now — but in some corners of blood-relations morality is not a welcome guest. I had failed to enter into the conspiracy of loyalty at all costs between parent and child, an unholy conspiracy maybe, but real nonetheless. So that when our team ironically put it all together a week later and won its last game of the season by ten runs, and Ben forgot the hurt, I wasn't so sure. I had refused his unspoken invitation. But at least I was starting to know its name.

Two months or so later Jennifer took her first skating test, the preliminary figure. Perched on one foot like a blonde flamingo, she traced her careful, slightly absurd backwards eight on the ice, while a dumpy lady in a wool coat made notations on a clip-board. Watching through the glass I was sure she was outside the line; I just hoped she wouldn't take failure too hard. When her coach came in with the news that she'd passed with honours I was honestly amazed. "It was a nice change watching someone who was obviously thinking about what they were doing," the judge had written in her evaluation. Looking up at me when I congratulated her, her face showed a mixture of delight and impatience. "Come on," she might have been saying. "I can do this stuff. Get *with* it."

Over the next few years I had more than a few close encounters, professionally and privately, with the Little League "conspiracy" and its fallout. One winter I researched an article about minor league hockey, watching a half-dozen games in a suburban arena where one entire half of the stands, the half behind the team benches, had been roped off, a no-man's land, because of abuse and interference from the parents of ten-year-olds. A year later I wrote a review of the "autobiography" of Elizabeth Manley, the Canadian skater who had won a silver medal at the Calgary Olympics, overcoming her own history of nervousness, bouts of stress-related disease, and the challenge of a subtle stage mother and an absent father. (The book in a way was a less polished reverse Fred Waitzkin tome; every time she thought she was complimenting one of her parents, Manley was zinging them backhandedly, paying them back for wounds the depth of which only she knew about.) A while after that I watched my son fight his first public exhibition match in judo class, tripping his opponent a dozen times, but losing the match because of an arcane scoring system that seemed as arbitrary to me as the weather. In the car afterward he explained it calmly (one *waza-ari* beat ten *kokas*) like a mature expert, while I ranted at the injustice of it. A few nights later Paula and I went to the movies and saw *Dead Poets Society*, in which a boy fired a revolver into his temple to avoid becoming the doctor his father wanted him to be. A while after that I played the piano for the Grade Five production of *Les Misérables* at my kids' school, holding my breath while my daughter — the star-crossed Eponine — stretched out on a piece of plywood that read "Liberty or Death!" to sing "On My Own," then watching my son — the waif Gavroche — falter at the beginning of his song, before he looked up, caught the eye of his grandmother, and got "a boost," enough to let him carry on and bring down the house.

Adults don't codify what they learn as quickly as children; things take a while for us to sort out. If I had been able to itemize what I was slowly finding out about the Little League "conspiracy," the list might have gone like this:

First — the urge to invade the next generation is universal enough to be a biological law. Almost all parents are guilty of living through their children at some point or other in their lives. We're all capable of shucking off our identities as shamelessly as a stripper sheds her clothes, slipping in behind our kids' eyes, their mouths, their limbs, with alien deftness. We do it for a number of reasons, almost none of them healthy: to make up for lost opportunity, to distract ourselves from unliveable lives, to control at least something in a runaway world, to steal back fresh time from someone we feel stole it from us in the first place. But almost always under the bad reasons lies one that is not so easy to condemn: the forestalling of doom. Scratch any stage parent and you will find not an optimist, but a fatalist. This may be why Little League parents have such an abiding faith in perfection. Tackling the dark forces takes powerful medicine; perfection is other-wordly magic, and our children need help from whatever world they can find to survive life in this one.

The second thing about the Conspiracy was this: it *is* a conspiracy. There are undoubtedly cases of pure abuse, of blanket pressure being exerted on a totally resistant child, but those cases are relatively rare. At least as often, the invading parent is welcomed in some way by the invaded child. For all the terrible things Fred Waitzkin did, by commission or omission, to his son, the truth was that his son also did damage to himself. It was Joshua Waitzkin who had nightmares about chess first; it was Joshua who played speed chess with kids when tournaments were over, just to have fun; it was Joshua who, when his father worried aloud about the bald spot he was making by pulling the hair out at the front of his head, got angry and accused Fred Waitzkin of interfering with his concentration. Kids are as jealous of their neuroses as anyone, and just as talented in hanging on to them.

The third thing was this: in spite of the invitation to come through the door, it's always a mistake to do it. It's a mistake because to live in the house of a child's soul a parent has to lower his level of maturity to fit. It's a mistake because neuroses are a child's prerogative, but not ours; a parent's job isn't to encourage his child's obsessions, but to try to rescue him from them. Joshua

Waitzkin couldn't help himself; Fred Waitzkin could. That was the difference. It's a mistake because unless our timing is impeccable, we'll invariably end up losing ourselves as well as our children, at exactly the moment of triumph we think we're working towards. And the timing of parents is never impeccable. Parents don't understand time.

Six months ago my daughter started studying for her Bat Mitzvah. The first evening I sat beside her at the piano, giving her the starting note on the keyboard, I realized she was remarkably quick at picking up the note structure of the chanted Bible portion, the *trop* it was called; her voice, sweet and unaffected, made the rote chant sound beautiful. The more I listened to her practise, the more convinced I was that we were in for something special. She obviously suspected something similar; her questions had a professional pragmatism: should she sing high or low? Should she use her "head voice," or not?

At the Bat Mitzvah rehearsal the night before the big event, she was halfway through her portion when the *shammas*, the synagogue attendant who was helping out at the pulpit, stopped her to ask her something — later she told me he'd asked her, jokingly, if she wanted a job. When she said it my chest actually grew tight enough that I had trouble breathing. The next day in the synagogue the lump was still there when she mounted the stairs for the real thing. She was wearing a white straw hat with a black ribbon attached, and every time she looked up at the congregation she grabbed it while she sang so it wouldn't fall off.

I can't say that I exactly invaded her body at that

moment, but I certainly moved out of mine. I ended up hovering somewhere between the pulpit and my seat, bodiless and willing her to perfection. It was suddenly very important — it had always been very important, I realized — that she be flawless. When she finished the last blessing with its theatrical *Amen*, my hand punched the air in front of me of its own volition and I whispered "All right, not a mistake!" My wife elbowed me hard and looked at me as though I were vaguely crazy. And I was. For a moment I was truly "the child, giddy and dancing like a fool with fantasies of glory and immortality that [I would] carry to [my] grave." I was Fred Waitzkin. I was a fool.

My only redemption was that the beautiful young girl beaming out at the congregation didn't care what I was. She didn't know I existed.

And rightly so.

"Okay, Dad, I'm going do them till I get it right," Jennifer says now. "*Watch.*"

She pushes herself away from the boards, coasting backwards to the centre of the ice where the rink is clear. I notice, though, that her glance keeps straying to the spot where her friend Jessica is talking to her father.

"Okay!" I call. And dutifully I watch while she goes into her backwards windup, head craned around to help her pick a launching spot. But as clearly as I see the jumps she starts to do now, in the chill yeasty-smelling air of the rink, I'm remembering something else I saw a long time ago.

It was my last year of high-school. I was playing for

the senior basketball team, and we were in the middle of a playoff game against a traditional rival, a school from a swankier suburb east of the city. The game was close. We were being kept in it mainly by our two stars, one a guard, one a forward. The forward — I'll call him Mark Miller —was the only black player on our team, and one of the best natural athletes I've ever seen, then or since. Despite his skin-colour, he bore an eerie resemblance to a young Gordie Howe; he had the same sloping shoulders, and the same economical efficiency on the court.

The game was in the third quarter, with the score tied or close to it, so there wasn't even the excuse of time-significance for what happened when it did. We'd missed a shot at the other team's end of the floor — it may have been me who missed — and their centre had taken the rebound and thrown a long outlet pass to a team-mate who'd been cheating downcourt, and who now appeared to have a clear lane to the basket. Just as he was extending for his lay-up though, an arm came out of nowhere, Mark's, perfectly timed with the guard's jump, knocking the ball away cleanly. The referee didn't think it was quite so clean; he blew his whistle and signalled Mark for the foul. There was a little hiatus while all the action slumped to a stop on the court. Then before anyone knew what was happening, Mark's father, who'd been watching in the stands, ran out onto the court in his jacket and tie and grabbed the referee from behind, holding him like a baulky child or a calf in a rodeo. "You can't do that to my son!" he shouted. "You can't call a foul like that! That's a clean play, you can't call that foul on my son!"

The memory turns as surreal now as the moment. Most of us knew Mark's father vaguely; he came to about half of our games, a trim man, much smaller than his son, who spoke with a West Indian accent and had a business that had something to do with truck parts. But nothing like this had ever happened before. The players on both teams were frozen. Only Mark and our coach, Mr Purcell, seemed able to move. Mark walked over to his father and put both hands on his chest. By this time he was crying, and his movements seemed uncharacteristically wasteful. "Dad, please leave," he was begging his father. "Please get off the court, Dad." In the end it took Mr Purcell and the opposing coach to get him to leave completely.

We lost the game. My memory isn't clear on whether Mark returned to play or not — things only become vivid again in the locker room afterward. We stood huddled together in the centre of the room, still in our uniforms, only dimly aware of the score. The larger world had intruded on the game, but we didn't want to admit its presence. In the nervous laughter that prevailed someone blurted out that it was a race thing, a black-white thing; someone else said they'd die if their old man ever did something like that; a chorus agreed, and suddenly there was a cacophony, a spooked jamboree, with fingers windmilled at temples, with Mark as the mark and Mr Miller as the loon. We were thinking we were warding off a curse with chaos, the ju-ju medicine perfected by adolescents.

But what we were trying to hide, I know now, was the other thing buried in Mr Miller's momentary craziness, the deep thing, distorted but brilliant. It was the same thing my daughter would feel a quarter of a century later, gazing across an ice-rink at a dark-haired friend. For a moment in the gym, our friend's father had ceased to exist for himself; there was only his son and the world that was doing his son wrong. If someone had come up to him and told him his child had just been killed in a golf cart crash but his heart beat on, he would have looked for an angel to assault. In that instant we knew that whatever other reasons Mark's father had for running down on the court that afternoon — old grievances, newcomer's wounds — he was there to save his boy.

7

The Birthday Party
The Death of the Weekend

"When you were a little kid, and you went to school and you drank from the water fountain, did all the other little kids used to make fun of your moustache?"

Dick Cavett to critic
John Simon

5:30 p.m.

The term "synaesthesia" technically refers to the mixing of sensory applications — i.e. describing something you see with a touch word (a "velvety glance") or a food with a sight word (a "gleaming taste") — but in psychological circles these days it more commonly designates the syndrome of applying colour descriptions to stimuli which ordinarily have no colour. People who are synaesthetic see hue in everything. September might be red, the number five blue, and your next-door neighbour pale amber. One woman who was the subject of a landmark synaesthetic study in Britain described her waking hours as a "walking rainbow," and herself as an artist-in-reverse, someone who instead of creating colours in unexpected contexts, absorbed colours no one else had seen. She also thought her "malady" was just the opposite, a terrific advantage. Life was a lot more technicolour in her mind than ours; as far as she was concerned, we were stuck in the silent-movie black-and-white era. She regarded the non-synaesthetic world with more than a little pity.

As it happens, her pity was probably misplaced. We're all synaesthetics, it occurs to me as I pull up to the front door of Skyscrapers, with Jennifer in the car beside me. At the moment my daughter probably sees me in basic black, maybe with some surgical green or blood red thrown in. I'm seeing her in terms of brown. Primary brown, if that's possible; a colour devoid of humour and light. It was probably inevitable. As soon as she got back in the car, in the balmy late afternoon air, she asked me whether she could go to Mia's for supper after all. I thought: What is it about kids, that their powers of denial are so strong? Where does this blind optimism come from, that everything is reversible? How did religion ever flourish on the earth when people are so ready to question the immutability of divine powers?

Instead of saying it out loud, I asked her about this morning again. "There was a *reason* for that," she said. "So tell me," I said. She made a self-deprecating little noise. "You don't want to hear it, I know it." "I do, I do." "You'll just agree with Mummy's side," she said. "Probably," I said. "But tell me anyway. Set a trend." I gave her a little noogie on the shoulder as I said it.

"Don't," she said. "Set a *trend*," I said, a bit crazily, noogying her on the word. "Set a *trend*, set a *trend*!" I thought I saw her lip curl at one corner on the last "trend," but she just said "Don't" again, forcefully, and moved her shoulder away. Before, even this morning, I had always been able to get her to laugh. Now some adolescent immunity was setting in, an antidote to humour. Things were changing.

Things *are* changing. In the sharp clear light coming through the window, my daughter's face is stubborn but somber; her chin is resting on her hand. It's a pose that already seems different from her gaze out her bedroom window this morning; it's less theatrical and less defiant at the same time. More may be there, but less is identifiable.

About a month and a half ago, seized with one of her sudden private missions, she'd decided she wanted to learn to play the guitar. Paula had an old instrument someone had given her when she was teaching kindergarten, but that she'd never been able to get interested in; Jennifer took it into her room and stayed there every spare moment for a week, figuring out the fingering for the chords she already knew on the piano, preferring to reinvent the instrument as opposed to buying an instructional tape or doing anything official. One night at the end of the week she came into the baby's room when I was putting her to bed to show me what she'd figured out. She was in her best of moods, open and self-ironic; I couldn't decide if what she'd done was really as amazing as I thought it was. When she was finished showing me her stuff, flushed with success, she handed me the guitar and asked me to play something. For Rosie, she made a point of saying.

"A *scary* song," Rosie put in, par for the course.

"Puff the Magic Dragon" wasn't scary enough, it turned out, so I ended up playing "The Klan." "The Klan" was a song I'd learned when I was twelve years old from my eighteen-year-old cousin Ricky, a lanky banjo player who in my opinion at the time was the coolest man alive. (In fact, for a long time Ricky had me convinced he had written "The Klan," "If I Had a Hammer" and "There Is a Ship.") The song was a melodramatic exercise in fast-strumming from the Civil Rights era — "The countryside was cold and still, there was a cross upon the hill" — that had a chorus meant to be the words of the young man who was the victim of the Ku Klux Klan on the night the song took place. Rosie loved it — her eyes stayed huge throughout. But Jennifer wasn't as sure.

"Does it mean he dies?" she said when I was finished.

"Well, I don't know for sure," I said, "But 'blood flows down like the summer rain' seems to point that way."

"But does he *die*?"

"Either that or he's got a bad bruise," I said.

"Don't," she got up, half-laughing at herself, and walked fast down the hall to her room. "Don't play it, please, Dad."

Who can tell you why you tease your daughter? The rest of the night I made sure to let her know I had a lot of even sadder folk-songs, whaling ballads and Civil War tunes to sing to her if she really wanted to break down. But when I was watching the late sports and she came downstairs in her pyjamas and sat on the couch beside me, weeping softly while the Blue Jays loafed through a spring-training split-squad game, I finally had the sense not to say anything. And in the morning when I went down to my office, the guitar, the culprit, was there, back in its stand, a reminder to me to flagellate myself occasionally over the course of the day, for being a fool.

Inside Skyscrapers there's a post-party melee that's more intimate than the carpool chaos and more irritable than the skating rink. At least half the parents doing pickup are now men; the day's finally caught up with them. Their suits and shiny loafers are somehow out of keeping with their restlessness — they seem like a bunch of high-school guys forced to dress up like their fathers. Their five o'clock shadows seem unearned, like Hallowe'en make-up. That I probably look the same to them is as impossible to believe as ever.

Ben is laughing his head off with some friends next to the birthday boy's mother, who's talking to a grizzle-haired guy wearing an open white shirt and a Star of David, and a hefty blonde woman. Synaesthetically the blonde woman strikes a chord more caramel-coloured than golden; the frizzy-haired man she's with looks naggingly familiar. When my son sees me he runs up and plants his big palm directly in my solar plexus.

"Dad, I've got a great joke to tell you, do you want to hear it? Actually Iggy told it to me." Beside him Iggy, who has a blond white-man's fade, is going wild with anticipation. "This is it. Okay." He takes a breath. "Okay."

"Okay."

"Okay. Here it is. There are three sons, and their father has the Holy Grail. And he says to his sons — "

"He's a king," says Iggy.

"Oh, right. He's a king — "

"A *mean* king—"

"Right, a mean king. Iggy, don't budd, I can tell it myself. So there's this mean king, and he says to his sons, 'You can each have a drink out of the Holy Grail if you do three terrible things.' That's three things each, not one thing each. Nine altogether. So the first son comes back and says 'I killed two people, I robbed three banks, and I stole a Lamborghini.' So the king says good, take a drink out of the Holy Grail. And the second son comes back and he says 'I killed thirty people, I robbed forty banks, and I stole a jumbo jet.' So the king says that's even better, take a drink out of the Holy Grail. And the *third* son comes," his eyes are maniacal, "and he says, 'I only did one thing, but it was even worse,' and the king says what, and the son says — "

" 'I peed in the Holy Grail,' " I say.

"How did you *know*?" he says. Iggy is holding his hand over his mouth beside him. "I can't believe he *knew*," Ben says. "He knew the joke."

"Ben, did you get your loot bag?" asks the birthday mother. I take it for him and give her her son's present. "Your son is so enthusiastic," she says. "Is he always like this?"

"Only when we forget to feed him."

"Oh, he ate all right here."

"I'm sure he did." Beside the hostess the familiar-looking man is kneeling to tie her son's shoelaces. Before I can figure out who he is the door to the "office" opens and the "trampoline-master," who looks like a swarthy compacted version of Arnold Schwarzenegger in a red track suit, comes out with his palms up.

"Attention, parents," he says with a heavy Israeli

accent. "We have a special invitation to offer you, for being our guests at Skyscrapers. We have five minutes before the next class starts, so any parents who would like to try out the trampolines are invited to go ahead. Parents only, please. No shoes allowed. If you have some problems with your spine or discs it's advised you should watch instead. Also if you're pregnant. Parents, let's go!"

It is not ordinarily something I'd do. Ordinarily I'd stand at the window watching the parents brave enough to try with a mixture of superiority and envy. But today there are inducements: One, the gym windows are visible from the parking lot, and if I jump high enough I can embarrass my daughter. Two, it strikes me as the kind of thing Seymour Wise would do to impress his son Joey, and I wouldn't mind seeing what it feels like.

I end up on a trampoline in the centre of the room, between a youngish guy on my left who looks like he's done this before, and, coincidentally, the familiar-looking grizzled-haired man on my right. The mats are set right into floor level, with bounce space beneath, so there's nothing to fall off, only onto. The familiar man is taking extremely modest, deadpan hops.

"I hate this," he says.

"Trampolining?"

"No, five o'clock. Five-thirty, whatever it is. I hate the end of the day. I still think it should be free time, you know. Time to go have a milkshake or watch TV. But it's worse than the rest of the day. My clock's still on high-school time."

High-school. Clocks. "The orchestra," I give up the pretence of bouncing, too. "You played those percussion instruments, the triangle, that big kettle drum."

"The timpani," he corrects me. I recognize his name the instant he tells me. "I recognized you right away, too," he says. "You look the same, except for your head. You still writing?"

People are always asking this, as though my profession is a kind of passing seizure. I say I am. "Whatever happened to that girl you went out with, she sold sweatshirts under the stairs?"

"I married her." He inclines his head at the viewing room. The abundant blonde woman is standing on the other side of the glass beside the boy whose shoelaces the man was tying. I would never have recognized her. Beside them Ben and Iggy are pointing at me, motioning at me wildly to jump. "We're not married any more, but we're civil. Tonight we got our chauffeuring schedule mixed up. That's my son, the chauffee. I spend my life driving him places."

"I know what you mean."

"Uh-huh." He takes a little test hop. "I hate the end of the weekdays, but I hate the summer even more. The summer's really bad. I can't get it out of my mind that the year doesn't just stop for July and August. I begrudge every business deal I have to do."

"Summer is bad."

"But weekends are worse," he says. "Weekends are the ass end of expectations. Who can look forward to the weekend any more? You know what I look forward to now? Monday morning." He does what looks like a deep kneebend. "This is my weekend now. I've got a million things planned, and I do maybe two of them. Or I say I'm going to relax, but I don't. You can't relax, because you're spending all your time driving. I end up on Sunday night with nothing done, and feeling like a train wreck."

"You didn't happen to read the front page of the *Star* this morning, did you?"

"I don't read any more, I forget how." He does another kneebend. "You know what ragtime music is? You played in the orchestra, you should know. Ragged time. One rhythm that sort of lags behind another. That's what having a kid is." He glances around the gym. "Look at us."

I look. There are four of five trampolines occupied, a couple of youngish matrons in leggings and three old-young men with our fathers' hairlines and enough *chutzpah* to do something ridiculous — and I'm only here for ulterior motives. He's right, of course. We are jumping, some low, some higher, but no matter how lofty our jumps become they will never launch us into the stratosphere of freedom we once knew; we jump tethered by a cable woven from ragged time, obligations and the pattern of another life indelibly imprinted on our own.

Synaesthetically, I still see the days of the week as five little black notches marked vertically along a horizontal plane. For some reason the days run right to left, with a slight upward slant into the future off the left side of the "screen." From wherever I happen to be situated in time, Tuesday, Wednesday, etc., I can usually see ahead a week and back half a week or so, which on a piano keyboard is the equivalent of about an octave and a half. The weekends are like the binary black keys on the keyboard, the E-flat and D-flat, a double set of thicker, longer demarcation lines every five days. Since I was in Grade Three

I've visualized the weekend like this, fixed as an internal constellation; I expect to see it this way till the day I die.

The Week

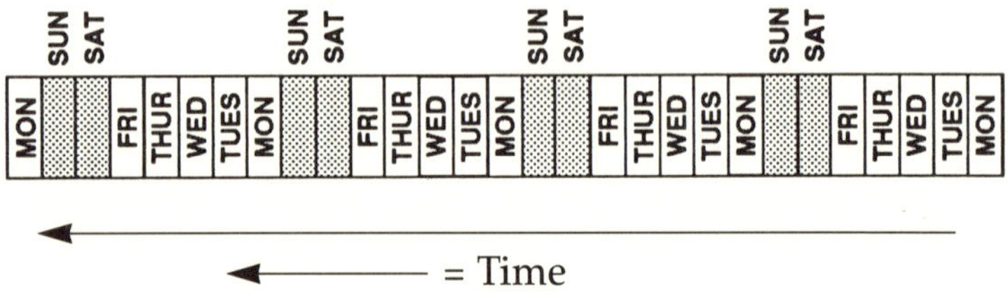

Actually the darker weekend shading bleeds into the upper half of Friday, because that was when school ended and the weekend officially started. Three-thirty on Friday was the crest of a downhill run; the world wound down; in class we couldn't wait for the second hand to hit the six, but paradoxically we didn't want it to. (An irony of the weekly school rhythm — which holds in some offices today — was the fact that I remember being in the least hurry to leave on Friday afternoon and the most on Monday.) Ultimately, though, we made our way home, inflated with a forty-eight-hour future. I usually went over to my friend Larry Ginsler's house to play on his driveway before supper: ball-hockey if it was winter and ball-hockey or basketball if it was summertime. At 5:30 or so I headed back home to wash and get ready for Friday-night dinner, complete with the obligatory chicken soup and candle-lighting. (Ours wasn't a traditional Jewish home so much as a Danish-modern Jewish home, but until the time I was thirteen we had Friday-night dinner every week.) After dinner we all went into the living-room and listened to folk-music albums on a boxy teak RCA hi-fi: Harry Belafonte, Oscar Brand,

Odetta and of course Peter, Paul and Mary — in particular the debut album with P.P. & M. standing in front of a brick wall and Mary holding flowers in her lap. The back liner of the album commanded "No dancing, please," but my sisters and I did dance, executing the odd gymnastic routine as well, using the wedge-shaped back cushions from a pair of uncomfortable nubby horsehair-filled sofas as mats. In temperament our Friday nights were Chassidic with civil-rights overtones; they were suburban bacchanals; we weren't sure what we were worshipping, but we knew it was progressive. My father I remember watching us from his spare two-piece Scandinavian easy chair with roguish encouragement, a cute, middle-aged shit disturber. (After dancing we watched the Gillette Friday Night fights from Madison Square Garden and the Jack Paar Show — Oscar Levant and the scarred bandleader, Bill Cosby and his Noah routine — and went to bed late, for Friday night's sleep, the sweetest of the week.)

Saturday mornings meant one of two things: reading or watching television. Reading we did in bed, until ten or eleven or even noon, consuming the hardcovers we'd taken out at the bookmobile — Chip Hiltons for me giving way to Black Stallions giving way to everything — sliding the ones I'd finished under the bed, where eventually they shared space with dustballs and *Playboys.* If we watched TV instead, we watched it *entirely*; Saturday morning orthodoxy decreed that you could not mix reading and the tube. The shows lined up inexorably, half-hours short on cartoons and heavy on mammals: "Mighty Mouse" (mice singing opera), "My Friend Flicka" (horses), "Circus Boy" (Mickey Dolenz, who would later be a Monkee), "Sky King" (airplanes and horses), "Fury" (horses), and "Lassie" (dogs). If TV-watching bled into the afternoon, it did it with "Shock Theatre" (mummies and zombies), and wrestling, then at its fabulous, tacky apex, a fringe sport for the lunatic fringe, fat ladies with goitres and pre-pubic boys, coming to you live from War Memorial Stadium in Buffalo. Saturday afternoon was for sports, at the park or on Larry Ginsler's driveway again. Saturday night was pizza and the hockey game. After the game we groaned through "Juliette," Canada's songstress, and went to bed late again (Saturday night's sleep, the penultimate sweetness, rimmed with silver).

Sunday morning was darker, more compulsive, with time running out, which may have been why we usually ended up in my parents' bed. It was in my parents' bed, in their downstairs rec-room of a bedroom that my younger sister, four years old, sat on my chest one day, so that for a moment I couldn't breathe. "I can't breathe," I said. "Try," she said, a line that worked its way into my uncle's Funny Books. Breakfast, after we got up, was usually bagels and rye buns and blueberry buns, a homage to wheat. Sunday afternoon was miasmic pre-doom, hypnotized hours of TV (church shows and Tiny Talent Time, Andy Hardy movies and Cleveland Browns games from gloomy Municipal Stadium on Lake Erie) alternating with fitful car rides, to the country or my cousin's house, and the foreplay of homework. Sunday dinner, the last supper, was pizza if we hadn't had it Saturday and delicatessen if we had. In the dying hours of freedom, humour itself fossilized: one night my father stuck my sister's bare foot in a hot-dog bun and covered it with mustard —this made it into the Funny Books too. After supper came homework, followed by "Ed Sullivan." Ed himself, sepulchral and enigmatic, was the perfect bus-driver to get us from the Elysium of the weekend to the week's underworld. The show's mix of zany miracles — balancing a hundred plates on five poles — wasn't bad either; it had a Brueghel-esque foreboding to it. After Ed we went to bed, at an hour that always seemed too early and too black to sleep.

The weekend was over.

And this was the party, the temporal map, my children crashed when they were born.

But what were they really intruding on? As Witold Rybczynski points out in his book *Waiting for the Weekend*, the week, and the weekend, actually measure nothing at all, at least nothing "visible" or "natural." In fact the week and its pre-packaged conclusion are completely human constructs. The year on the other hand bears a relation to the sun (as the month originally did to the moon) and a lifetime of years, at least as far as we've come along the life-line, is attached to our own mortality. Synaesthetically, this is the sort of mental map — a whole *life*-line — that you'd figure children would leave a much heftier footprint on, in a parent's psychic road atlas.

And for most of us they do. Researchers studying cognitive maps have discovered that most people "see" their personal life-lines as a version of the week-line with a forty-five-degree rotation. Instead of being horizontal, life-lines tend to run vertically, from bottom to top, calibrated like a thermometer by decades. The only place the

The Personal Life-Line

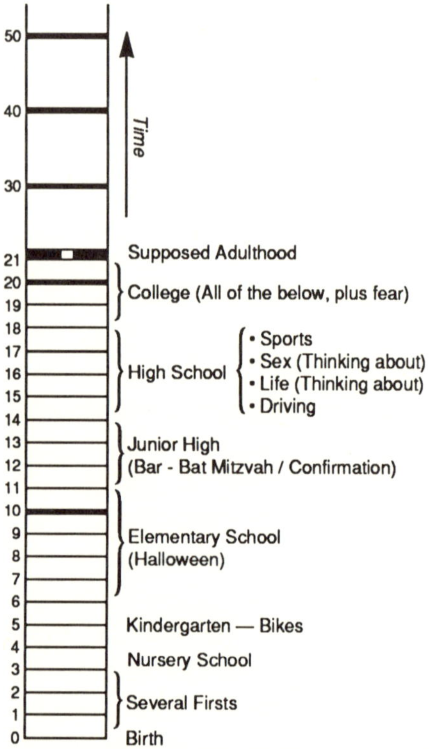

calibration almost universally breaks down is in the zero to twenty-year-old section, where, across cultures, the intensity of youth creates a kind of density of secondary demarcation lines. After twenty-five, though, decades take over, regular as a football gridiron — with, neatly, a one-decade lag. The "viewpoint" of a person's line, the place the camera aims, turns out to consistently settle ten years earlier than the person's actual age. Most people are just getting used to being thirty when they turn forty, just acclimating to forty when fifty hits.

To complicate matters, it turns out that the personal life-line doesn't operate alone; most people also visualize something you might call the "century-line." The century-line calibrates a person's march through time against the decades of his century — the historical fifties, sixties, seventies, etc. — as opposed to his life. For perverse reasons of their own, ninety percent of century lines run horizontally or at least diagonally lower right to upper left, like the week-line, or drunken Hebrew.

The anomaly is this: for most parents, children do not appear on the first graph — the personal graph — at all. On the century-line though, they appear as naturally as the multiplication tables.

A friend of mine once told me that the most profound effect the birth of his first child had on him was to "move him closer in (his) mind, to death." In synaesthetic terms, he was suggesting one of two scenarios: either a section of his life-line slid upwards when his son was born, like an extension ladder, shooting him closer to infinity — or his fatherhood simply changed the depth of focus along the line (the way a film director will with the camera to reveal the background), letting the end of himself suddenly fuse, *wham,* into a sharper reality. (Look Ma, no me!) Either way his comment was atypical. Most people will tell you that becoming parents doesn't make them feel closer to death — just the opposite in fact. Children tend to tie parental life-lines to future tributaries; they *extend* history. If they make things messier along the continuum, they also give it better connections. They make history meaningful again.

Nineteen seventy-nine, nineteen eighty-three, nineteen eighty-nine. For people born before 1960 these dates are almost impossible to accept, *viscerally,* as dates of birth. Who was born in 1983? Who could be born in 1971, for that matter, or even 1961? These were veteran years, maybe prime-time years, but never rookie years. When my sister had a baby boy in the summer of 1971 — the first member of the next generation in my family — and I happened to glance at the date at the top of the newspaper page with his birth announcement, it seemed completely unreal. *No one* was born in 1971. The forties and maybe the fifties, those were the decades of birth. People born afterward seemed robbed of the richness of all the history I knew. How could anyone be born, after all, after the Beatles, after the Cuban crisis, after glass milk bottles, the moon-walk, Woodstock, after hula hoops, Timothy Leary, the invention of the Zamboni, Ed Sullivan, even Ronald Reagan?

But of course they were being born; time was just declining to slow down enough to let us get used to it. No one can ever truly inhabit any era after his own "style" decade has passed. No amount of studying the pop charts or wearing inflatable running shoes can resurrect our feel for an era. If we do manage to convince ourselves we're still in style, it's timeliness by rote or force of numbers. Naturally we are all (literally) out of time.

Children are our anchor. In being born when they are, by redemarcating time and giving us their lives to extrapolate on the year-line, they make time graspable again. If they don't slow it down they at least let us rub shoulders with a stretch of history we thought would stay mist. Historic thieves of time, for once they give us historical breathing space instead of leaving us winded. They put flesh on future's ghost.

What, then, is our beef? And how come we're so tired? And why am I nodding my head in commiseration at a Richard Dreyfuss impersonator who's going up and down, up and down, at 5:45 in the growing twilight, when I should be racing home so I can eat supper and go out to a movie with my wife?

It's all in the nature of the deal. Parents linger because history isn't carpool, because children are real pain for metaphysical gain, and because revising a century is easy, but to have a kid is to have your time ground into little temporal flakes, amounting to nothing when you sweep them back up, but leaving you dead-tired in the process. Or leaving you paralyzed momentarily on a trampoline, with no energy to alter the course physics and the day have put you on.

Our children may let us back into history, but they exact a price for doing it.

In *Waiting for the Weekend* Witold Rybczynski lists, among others, five pastimes that have historically come to be associated with leisure: reading, sports, eating, drinking (alcohol specifically) and travelling (in particular driving). These are the staples of recreational activity in most civilized modern societies, he points out, pursuits which the evolution of the weekend has moulded, or transformed, but never replaced altogether. What he doesn't mention, maybe because it seems so obvious, is that to pursue any of these activities a person needs more than just the institution of the weekend in name. True leisure demands two prerequisites: one, that you momentarily be the centre of the world, and two, that you momentarily be completely unencumbered. To be at leisure is to have an unfettered mind. Becoming a parent means, simply, never to have that kind of mind again.

Take reading first, a kind of microcosm. If you wanted to rank the communicative arts in order of their closeness to the imagination's heartbeat, a good case could be made for this line-up: music, writing (reading), painting and sculpture, radio, movies and videos. Whatever quibbles you might have about the line-up, reading is undeniably one of the two processes, along with listening to music, that demand the greatest exercise of imagination from the "consumer." Reading is about simulation, the creation of imaginary, whole worlds; and control, the neat conceit that any world can be contained within the boundaries of two covers. This may be why under the right circumstances reading is *the* escape nonpareil, the ultimate in diversion; and why it probably requires, more than any other leisure pursuit, the most private, cocooned venue in which to operate. Ask anyone who enjoys reading, and chances are good they'll be able to describe their "ideal" reading spot for you, almost always one that originated in childhood: a bed, a couch, a stairwell, a rug, the spot under the kitchen table. As much as it requires time, that is, reading needs a space; invade either, and you compromise the process. In fact, the space-time continuum holds for all adult leisure activities. "Stealing" time to try to escape is as bad as "barricading" space. By the time you've won the battle, you've lost the war.

What parent can't find the time to relax? What writer can't find time to read? In my pre-fatherhood days I would have considered both questions rhetorical. At that point my weekend reading habits were a natural progression of my routine when I slid hijacked Harold Robbins novels under my bed in my parents' home. Now on Saturdays, instead of Chip Hilton and *A Stone for Danny Fisher,* I was reading William Styron and Larry Niven, Jorge Luis Borges and Ursula K. LeGuin. Heavy novels and surrealistic novels and sci-fi novels and lousy novels, but *novels,* stories with made-up characters and a beginning, middle and end that were finite and manageable — unlike the real world — and most satisfying when you consumed them at one sitting. Short stories at least, John O'Hara and Irwin Shaw, Hemingway and Eudora Welty, Donald Barthelme and Peter Taylor. The names breathed procrastination themselves.

It would be a lie to say I don't read any more. But I don't read on Saturday morning. Saturday morning, for all intents and purposes, has ceased to exist. Without intending it to sound anything like a complaint (because there are always compensations) here is Saturday morning now: the baby gets up at 7:00, which actually isn't that inconvenient, because I have to get Jennifer to the skating rink by 9:00. On the way home I try to buy whatever we're out of and need for breakfast — milk, bagels, etc. — then when I do get home I have to turn around and drive Ben to either a) judo, or b) drama (depending on the week). Then it's back to the rink to pick up Jennifer; and over to the dojo or theatre-school to get Ben. By the time I reach home it's 12:30, which means I get to think about doing the things I have to do around the house or with Paula. In other words, Saturday morning is pretty much like any other weekday afternoon, only sunnier.

Surveys show that adults, and particularly men, read progressively shorter things after they become parents: magazines as opposed to books, newspaper columns as opposed to magazines. Subject matter changes as well. For men fiction is the first casualty, particularly science fiction, so popular with teenage boys. This makes perfect space-time sense. To buy into sci-fi novels, mostly written in that distinctive puritanical juvenalia sci-fi style, a reader has to be patient enough to slowly steep himself in the technological mother-lode, ignoring the Tom Swiftly clunkers on the way. People short on time tend to be short on patience, too. The suspension of disbelief tends to suspend itself. Instead of science fiction, men with families, statistically, end up turning to popular "real" science books, books — like Stephen Hawking's *Brief History of Time* (the Big Bang), *Lucy* by Donald Johanson (the first human), *Chaos* by James Gleick (why Einstein was wrong), *The Flamingo's Smile* by Stephen Jay Gould (why Darwin was right) — that give us the sense that we're sorting out the *real* world now. Short on time, we don't want to expend any on theories that aren't hemmed in by fatalism, or absorbable during the consumption of half a bowl of cereal or the average visit to the can. Belatedly, my generation of fathers may even be coming to understand the allure, for *our* fathers, of *Popular Mechanics*, with its futuristic heli-cars on the cover and its Jetsons-style excitement on the inside. The average *PM* article was fantastic, brief and supposedly tied to the real world. (Meanwhile, if my wife is any indication, women go through a reverse metamorphosis; the more kids we've had the longer the books are that she's willing to read, and the lower her standards. While my suspension of disbelief contracted, hers expanded to include authors that make Jackie Collins look like Shakespeare. Like a lot of fathers, I'd love to get lost in one of my wife's "fat" books; I just can't get past the first page.)

But television is the great leveller. When I was sixteen, the one thing I swore I would never do would be to fall asleep in front of the tube the way my father did half the nights of his life, stretched out snoring on a two-piece easy chair and bathed in a blue glow, like "a patient etherized upon a table." I don't know what I thought I'd be doing instead, maybe homework or calling up girls, or even reading a book. As it turns out I've avoided the easy chair, but surrendered, on more nights than I like to admit to myself, to the vast wasteland. For one thing reading puts me to sleep lately, I find, and I don't want to be asleep so fast these days, not when I'm finally alone. And for another there's something irresistible about the passivity of watching television late at night, in a room with the lights off. Here, finally, excised whole from another era, is a slice of male time. Program offerings dwindle; sports broadcasts predominate, kick-boxing matches and badminton tournaments from Thailand joining re-runs of "The Mod Squad" and "The Bob Newhart Show," shows with the faded rose-tones of early colour TV. Half-hour commercials pitch gadgets and car-wax, big inventors with real bellies leaning over to light fires on the hoods of their gleaming muscle-cars. On the next channel over, young women in lingerie advertise 800 numbers, which you can call to hear fantasies more complex than Tom Swift's. You may not call, for the threesomes or the Carnuba wax, but it's obvious that they are all speaking to you, now that you have the time: the last man awake —barely — in the world.

Sports, the "second sex" for a whole universe of males, was the second sacrifice I made on the altar of fatherhood, and maybe the most painful. The year my first daughter was born, when I had a furnished room as an office beside a large city park, my active week went like this: every weekday I would either run in the park or play hockey in the park at noon, most nights I swam, on Tuesdays nights I played industrial league basketball, on Wednesday nights I took jazz dance lessons, on Saturday afternoons I played pick-up basketball and on Sunday nights from midnight to 2:00 a.m., just to round off the week, I played pick-up hockey. In the summer, to replace the hockey, I played baseball in a local senior county league. My schedule was probably extravagant, but it wasn't unparalleled. In fact in spite of what my wife, a non-athlete said, I had several friends who did more. For a sports addict my routine was actually modest.

All the recent cinematic and pop-psychological portraits of male-bonding have overlooked one critical fact about the games men play: they're fun. Sports may be as much fun for some men as conversation is for some women, although women generally have trouble believing it — the same way men have trouble believing in the entertainment quotient of lunch. (This may be one of the great unsung schisms between the sexes, the inability of either gender to understand the recreational appetites of the other.) But games are gratifying for more than just the body's rush; like books, they're closed systems in which the participants can, for two halves or nine innings or three periods, create order in the world. Sport is about fashioning a series of wholes that are comely and that add up to a larger beautiful whole. "Hockey," Alec Wilkinson wrote once, in a profile of the New York Ranger goalie Mike Richter, ". . . looks chaotic and formless, but it isn't. It's just fast, the fastest team sport in the world. If it were possible to freeze players in the midst of a game and trace their paths, their trails would indicate a plan as plainly as if they were steps on a ball-room dance floor." The therapeutic kick men get from games is the satisfaction of being able to briefly control space and time. It's this part of childhood, the simulative, that's the hardest for most men to give up. People may scoff at its power, but you can't go cold turkey from it without also paying a price.

Today my sports schedule goes like this: once or maybe twice a week I try to run a couple of miles around a crescent of monster homes being built just next to our street. An equal number of times I try to play squash — a solid "C" level — with accommodating partners an average ten years older and twenty-five percent more proficient than I am. Basketball is spotty — Saturday afternoons are hard (even if I can swing it logistically the guilt factor is high) — and dance and baseball are fading memories. I do play hockey every Friday night for an hour and a half, but ironically, or maybe appropriately, I play in the same rink where my daughter takes figure skating. On my way to the dressing room, hurrying over the rubber-matted floor, I can look in the glass-cased "patch" schedule and see her name pencilled in, intruding with strange familiarity even here, at midnight at a hockey rink. To make it stranger, the twenty-year-olds I play with, when they hear I have a twelve-year-old daughter are invariably more interested in her than in me — a little conflict-of-interest I could do without. On the plus side of the ledger is the prestige-edge she gives me: "You've got a twelve-year-old daughter? I don't believe it, I'm getting beat by a guy with a twelve-year-old daughter!" The trade-off rocks like an unsteady set of scales. In the dressing room I don't know whether to belt somebody, tell them to read *Lolita*, or go out for a beer with them. By the time I decide it's time to drive home anyway, so I can get up to take the Lolita in question back to the rink on Saturday morning.

Eating and drinking, third on Witold Rybczynski's list, is probably the least affected by the onset of children (other than the fact that you may have to wait fifteen years to enjoy eating in a restaurant again). But driving is something else. From Jack Kerouac to James Dean to Tracy Chapman the automobile has been depicted, accurately, as a freedom machine, a North American symbol — especially for males — of youth and escape. It's no coincidence that Henry Ford, after engineering the assembly line that made cars cheap enough for the common man to buy, pioneered the five-day work-week so that the common man would have a reason to buy it. From my own past I can recall specific "drives," drives ostensibly going somewhere, to do something, but really just about driving itself: driving home from the country one snowy New Year's Eve with a girl whose father owned a pizza restaurant and who had invented a new method of kissing; driving to the Expo '67 World's Fair in Montreal with a carload of friends, spinning the car slow-motion down the highway at seventy miles per hour and somehow coming to rest on the shoulder without dying; driving on a rainy Sunday afternoon to look for our first house, when my wife was just pregnant and her eyes were wild with a hunger for something other than real estate.

A hundred yards from our street is a main north-south drag called Bathurst Street, named after a British lord who chopped a few trees down in the area.

Approximately twenty times a week, sometimes thirty, my wife and I drive up and down Bathurst Street. She drives down it to get to work, I drive down it to do car-pool, we both drive down it to visit relatives or shop. The street is actually fascinating, famous as a kind of ethnic spawning river in the city — half the cars you see look like they're being driven by hats — but its salient feature has become the salient feature of the million trips taken by the ninety-nine percent of adults whose occupations don't change with the seasons: it is routine. And while routine may be the most important antidote to chaos in a family's life, the single most effective tactic in combating the breakdown and squandering of time, it is still routine. Routine is living proof that predestination is stultifying. Routine is knowing the future.

One Friday night about a year ago Paula and I drove the kids back up from dinner at her parents, and when we got home Lucy was still there. On a whim we asked her to stay and got back in the car, still in our good clothes, to "take a drive." We drove north on Bathurst Street, not south for once, up towards cottage country and the lakes of southern Ontario. After a few miles we opened the windows and put on a Jennifer Warnes tape: "It's the Right Time of the Night"; Paula took off her shoes and put her feet on the dashboard and started to sing. We drove until we reached Lake Simcoe, the closest body of water, making our way up a series of labyrinthine dirt roads to a long public dock beside a shuttered rock-club called The Peppermint Lounge (a place I remembered from when I was fourteen, famous for its "Seventeen-inch biceps only" admission policy). Paula got out of the car and rolled up her skirt, walking out on the little gravel ramp at the end of the dock; it was mid-June, and the wind was already warm. "I'm going in," she said. "Me, too," I said, and got out of the car, rolling up my pants as I did. We stood at the edge of the water, looking out at the diverging lights from a cottage around the curve of the bay, telling each other we were going in. But we knew we weren't. We knew that in a moment we'd get back in the car instead, with its battered car-seat in the back, missing one shoulder-cover of brown vinyl, and drive south on Bathurst Street, playing tapes and singing along now with a different kind of compulsion, testier and less wild but no less urgent. We knew it for the same reason that we knew what the first thing we had to do when an airplane landed and disgorged the two of us in Jamaica or Miami Beach for a ten-day holiday. We were sharing E.T.'s dilemma — had anyone ever considered that the aliens he was so anxious to get his intergalactic call through to might have been his children? We had to phone home.

Weekend time, according to Witold Rybczynski, is sacred time, sacred because the rituals of leisure are as engraved on our consciousness as the rituals of religion. But it is most sacred for the young. An Orthodox Jewish father might look forward intensely to the Sabbath, but he will never again look forward to it with quite the same divine intensity as his children. True sacredness is magical. Synaesthesia is, too: what else can give a colour to a trumpet's sound or a taste to a girl's name? But our magical, sense-mixing mental maps are forged when we're young, not old. That's the problem. Reluctant to relinquish the sacred, we try to use our old charts to navigate the shoals of the adult world, now too riddled with the inlets of secular deals and compromise to fit. Even if we get from A to B, it never feels quite right. We're out of sync; the times are out of joint.

But there is a way to realign our temporal maps, it turns out, and even to reclaim something like the magic of freedom. The tactics are simple. We can stop being so spoiled, for starters. We can find a new sport to play with our children. We can discover a place worth driving them to.

We can be heroes.

In the summer of 1978, a sixteen-year-old boy with severe cerebral palsy named Rick Hoyt heard that a college near his home in Holland, Massachusetts, was sponsoring a five-mile race to raise funds for a lacrosse player paralyzed in an car accident. He asked his father, Dick, who had never been very close to him — or his other two non-handicapped sons for that matter — to push him in his wheelchair during the race. His father agreed. The Hoyts finished next to last in the race, but they managed to finish. That night Rick typed on his computer, "Dad, when I'm out running, I feel like I'm not even handicapped." Shortly afterward Dick Hoyt, an aeronautics engineer, began training. By 1980 the Hoyts were entering seventy-five races a year, sometimes running three separate races on a weekend, and had entered their first Boston Marathon. By the mid-eighties Dick Hoyt had run a marathon pushing his son in two hours and forty-five minutes, an achievement Bill Rodgers, four-time winner of the Boston race, called "world-class." In 1986 the Hoyts entered and finished the Canadian Ironman Triatholon in British Columbia. To do it they had to complete a 2.4-mile swim, during which Dick towed Rick in an inflatable dinghy, a 112-mile bicycle event, when Rick was strapped into a racing "basket" mounted on the front-wheel assembly of Dick's bike, and a full 26.2-mile marathon. As staggering as Dick Hoyt's stamina was, Rick's endurance of the extreme discomfort during the twelve hours required to finish the event was probably greater.

By this time, of course, they were a racing and public-interest legend. "Chariots of Fire" was played during their races; announcers trumpeted their back-stretch runs; *People* magazine ran articles. But what was interesting was that underneath the hoopla and the hype, the obvious cliché, the real story of the Hoyts was missed. In looking to be uplifted, people missed the point.

The real point was in the plural pronoun father and son always used — "The farthest *we'd* ever run was eighteen miles," "Until *we* started running, Dad had very little to do with me," — and in what Judy Hoyt, Rick's mother, once said in exasperated response to the hero-worship: "We're not saints because we brought up this handicapped kid and make a life for him. We're not the perfect American family... We've made what could be a 'poor me' experience into a positive experience. This isn't the Brady Bunch. I have not dedicated my life to my kids. Sometimes I hate Rick." It was buried in the way Rick Hoyt broached the subject of racing to his father that first day in 1978. It was in the first words Rick typed on his computer when it was delivered, the words which everyone in his family was waiting with baited breath to see, for one thing to confirm forever that he wasn't retarded after all. Bets were in on "Hi, Mom," or "Hi, Dad." Rick was a hockey fan. He wrote "Go, Bruins."

The *ordinary* miracle was the point, not the extraordinary one. What Dick Hoyt had done was to re-create a facsimile of normality for his son, to put time back into sync. He'd straightened out a twisted map, so that his son's relationship with his father could conform to the regular timetable of any son-father relationship: dependence, ambition, Freudian one-upmanship, ascension. ("Dad's getting a little slow," Rick said at one point, "Maybe it's time for a new pusher." "No matter how fast I run," his father countered, "he always beats me by a second.") With a superhuman effort, he'd restored synaesthetic coherence to a life overwhelmed by neurological chaos. He'd found a game of catch he and his son could play together, nothing more or less. Children dream of adventure, but crave the mundane. This is what we forget. Our drudgery is their magic; our routine is their ritual. Dick Hoyt had made things normal for his son, which is the greatest gift any parent can give any child.

He had given him something to look forward to on the weekend.

8

Suppertime, Suppertime
The Showdown & the Censor

"Whatsamatta, toots — don't you like a big bang?"
Baby Herman, to a "human" prop-girl,
in *Rollercoaster Rabbit*

"I want to marry a bad man."
Rosie Teitel, age 2½

6:30 p.m.

By the time I get home with Ben and Jennifer it's past six, but Paula still isn't here. It's a point of ambivalence to me — not good because there's practically no way we'll make the early show now, but good because if she was home I wouldn't get the chance to hear her come in the door and say "Hello." For nearly all of our married life I've been the one greeting my wife coming in the door, and hearing her three-pitched sung "Hello." I may not know exactly how generations of women felt watching their husbands come over the heath on the way back from a hunting trip or up the driveway after a hard day at the office, but at least I've got the idea. Without planning to I've even developed a little theory about it. Paula thinks I'm crazy, but I figure I've got the makings of a great country-western tune: "As long as I'm glad when my wife says Hello, I know that I'm where I should be."

Paula isn't home, but Rosie is, in the den watching the famous crayon-factory segment, a classic, on "Sesame Street." At least it's not Oz, I think. She looks up when I say hello and says, "Hi, Dad, where are you going?" — as though I'm leaving, not coming, or as though we're commuters in a train-terminal. Ben starts cooing "ooh my little Rosie Bosie" and buries his head in her belly, and she starts screaming immediately, a high steady keen like a woman possessed by demons. Behind me Jennifer clumps up the stairs to her room, the loudest noises she's made since she got in the car after skating. Ben on the other hand was full of news after Skyscrapers, not about the party but about his latest concern: he's so tired he's worried he's going to fall asleep in French class tomorrow.

I look at my watch: 6:45 and still no wife. I check with Lucy to make sure she can babysit, yell at Ben that it's his turn to set the table, and go downstairs to my office. For the first time today there's no interruption when I turn on the computer, to read the last thing I wrote.

INTERIOR, JOEY'S BEDROOM, NIGHT

JOEY is sitting on his bed in his pyjamas, with his marble collection case on his lap. He's looking out the bedroom window beside him. In the backyard below, the ARMY is putting up BIVOUAC TENTS under a bank of spotlights.

SEYMOUR comes into the room; he's still wearing his striped bathrobe.

SEYMOUR

Joey. Hey, Buddy. Look, I'm really sorry about all this, I know you were looking forward to going to your mother's for the weekend. I promise, we're not going to be stuck here for seven days, no matter what the army says. As soon as they figure out that our neighbourhood real-estate lady isn't Albert Einstein, but a big phony in high heels —

JOEY

I believe her.
(A beat.)
I believe she's who she says she is. I believe she knows things.

I look up out my grass-level window, trying to think of some descriptive adjectives: over-written, confusing, hackneyed. What's the story about? A boy who's got a father who won't be a father and also doesn't believe in anything. So the person who comes into the boy's life has to be just the opposite. Not opposite gender, opposite style. A mature man who believes in miracles. That's who Einstein is. Not Auntie Mame with a great body. Charlotte should not be Charlotte.

Charlotte should be a guy.

I look out the window. Past the partial segments of tree trunks I can see the sun has almost set, and clouds are moving in. In winter I would have turned on all the lights in the house by now, running around restlessly trying to avoid that swift period between darkness and light, when night can invade your soul. "If you can get me through the twilight," Dorothy Parker once wrote, "I will make it through the night." She was talking about Manhattan, not the suburbs, but the sentiment holds.

And now above me the door opens and I hear my wife say "Hello" in three distinct syllables and pitches: "He-llo-o." From the family room Rosie answers "Hello" back in the same cadence. Paula yells "Peanut" and I hear Rosie running pell-mell to meet her. Now I feel as much as hear half of Paula's stuff — binders, notebooks — falling on the floor, as she picks Rosie up. Men come home with a briefcase, I think, women with the world. It's as though they're afraid of forgetting something, maybe a legacy of their role as prehistoric gatherers in the hunter-gatherer paradigm.

"Hello, hello, hello," my wife says. I check the synaesthetic vibes. Her voice is like bronze, and the love is not for me. But I'm still pretty glad to hear it.

"We're going out," she says when I come through the kitchen door.

"You're telling *me*?"

"No, I mean we're *really* going out. You wouldn't believe my day."

"We'll never make the early show."

"I don't care. We'll go to the late show. I'll stare at a

blank screen." She drops another bag or two on the floor. "So, where's Jenny?"

I have to think. "Upstairs, putting her skating stuff away."

"You took her skating after all?"

"Think back. You told me to decide, remember?" I remind her of school, me coming into the office, her nodding.

"It's all right, I'm not blaming you. I was on the phone, though. You can't talk to me when I'm on the phone." She squints at Rosie, who's got her mouth open in a perfect round "O" and her hands up crooked at the wrist like claws. "What is that face?"

"Mom, why did the witch put poison in the poppies?" says Rosie.

"We're going *out*," says Paula. "Let's eat, everybody! Let's go! Ben, Jennifer!"

Ben comes. Jennifer does not. We sit down to dinner.

Dinner at the Cleaver household, circa your television set, 1955, was a sedate affair, shot from June's end of the table, the camera aiming straight at Ward's vague, arch face, and his tie. "Well, Beaver, and how was *your* day today?" "Well, gee, Dad, pretty good, I guess." "You guess?" "No, well, it was good. Whitey put a frog in Brenda Wallace's desk and Brenda screamed so loud Miss Carstairs said she was taking a condition." "Not a condition, Beaver. What Miss Wallace probably said was a 'conniption.' Pass the green beans, please, dear."

Dinner at our house — tacos tonight, which I don't remember June ever making — starts off the same way, and diverges from there.

"So Ben, how was your day?" I ask. "Any tables?" (The

table is where people are sent in Ben's school when they talk too much; Ben has been there before.)

"No," he says with his mouth full of salad, "it was a *perfect* day, I swear. You would have been so proud of me, Dad." He stops, and laughs to himself through his lettuce. "Well, there was one thing. But I can't tell you."

"What was it, Ben?"

"You'll kill me. Promise me you won't kill me."

"Maybe I'll kill you. I don't know until you tell me."

"Dad, I *can't*."

"You want to tell me, Ben."

"All right, I'll tell you. We have this supply teacher we call the Duck. So we developed a new strategy for her today. Actually, I have to say it was my idea. It's called 'Operation Everybody Dance Now.' Wait — " He gets out of his chair. "The idea is, as soon as the Duck turns her back, everybody stands up and we sing 'Everybody Dance Now,' and we dance. That's the operation." In demonstration he sings "Everybody dance now" with a pulsing, Egyptian rhythm, wiggling his hips and holding up the two first fingers of each hand like a demented Richard Nixon. It's pretty good. Paula, who's supposed to be feeding Rosie, is laughing so hard not a single sound is coming out of her mouth.

"Operation Everybody Dance Now," she manages to get it out. "Ahhhh."

"Dad," he's in a groove now, "you know what we say before we go into French? 'Gentlemen, let the games begin.'"

At this point Jennifer walks into the room without any fanfare, yanks back the bench opposite Ben, and sits down hard.

"Jenny, listen," Ben tells her his story. Jennifer stares at him without cracking a smile. Paula is weeping now, wiping her eyes with a napkin. "Oh, God, I need a holiday."

"That's not really very nice, you know, Ben," Jennifer says. "She's just a substitute. I can't believe you're laughing, Mom. If I did that with my class, you'd be giving me a lecture."

"You wouldn't do it, thankfully. You've got more sense. And you're absolutely right." Paula looks at me for maybe half a second, then starts howling again.

"So can I go over to Mia's tonight? Her parents are taking her to see *Pretty Woman,*" says Jennifer, picking up a piece of cucumber out of her bowl with two fingers. This is her true opening gambit.

"It's a week night," I remind her, thinking I've been here before. "And you're sort of in trouble, remember?"

"Besides which," says Paula, "I'm not sure I want you seeing *Pretty Woman* anyway. I don't know whether it's suitable. Are you sure Mia's parents are taking her?"

"We'll see it first," I say. "Then we'll let you know."

"I don't believe you," my daughter says, dangerously now. "The whole Grade Seven has seen *Pretty Woman.* There's nothing in it. What do you think, it's going to ruin my morals? Am I supposed to become a prostitute because it's about prostitutes?"

"What's about prostitutes?" says Ben.

"The point isn't whether everyone's seen it," I say. "Everyone does lots of things."

"And," says Paula, "we haven't even discussed this morning yet. Maybe you shouldn't be going to any friend's houses for a while." She looks at me. "Okay?"

"What's a prostitute?" says Ben.

"A hooker, Ben," Jennifer says.

"I thought it was a lawyer," he says.

She says something under her breath.

"I'm not an idiot, Jennifer."

"I didn't call you an idiot, Ben."

"Yes you did. And you're not going to be a lawyer anyway, you're going to be an actor, so what are you getting so mad about anyway?"

"God," she actually laughs. "I take it back, you are an idiot, Ben."

"Maybe," I say, "but it's not for you to say. Apologize to your brother, please."

"I'm *sorry*. Now can I see *Pretty Woman*?"

"*No.*" We say it together.

"You're so strict," She's on her feet. Her expression is like her look in the car at the Skyscrapers' parking-lot; a disorienting shift to something real. "Nobody else's parents are as strict as you are. You both think I'll do things, just because you did them when you were young or something. You don't trust me at all. If I apologized about this morning you'd figure out something wrong with the apology. It's not fair." She turns, half-knocking over her chair, straightens it unconsciously, and walks out of the kitchen, down the hall, and out the front door into the evening, letting the screen slam.

The whole day might have been aiming towards this moment. My wife takes a deep breath and puts her head on the table beside Rosie's cow-jumping-over-the-moon bowl. Rosie puts her hand on her mother's hair idly, as though she's checking for grey. My son stops eating salad.

"Dad, you have to get her."

I pick up a broken taco shell, and walk outside.

The sky is clear but turning dark-blue fast, especially to the east down at the end of the crescent; the air is cold. Our crescent is a short configuration, thirty houses, with another smaller crescent of new houses being built down into a ravine across the street. Both times my daughter "ran away" before, in her younger days, I found her standing at the end of the crescent proper, in the middle of a little circle of paving stones covered with scruffy bushes that no one takes care of, but which the kids on the street ordinarily use for bicycle conclaves, like the midwestern kids in F. Scott Fitzgerald's "Basil and Josephine" stories.

I don't see any sign of her in the parkette now. I walk the fifty yards or so down to it to check behind the bushes, but she's not there either. On the way back to the house I break into a little jog, just for the exercise, I tell myself. I check the garage when I reach it; her bike is still there. Paula's waiting in the vestibule when I open the door. I tell her the bike's still there.

"That's even worse. I'd rather she was on her bike if she went anywhere. You're sure you didn't see her?"

"Don't worry, she's probably sitting on someone's front steps. I'll check the backyard."

I go around back but it's deserted; no tell-tale moving swings either. I walk back out front and look down the street. It's a relatively isolated street, one of its selling points. To get to any other developments of any size you have to cross a main regional road with no traffic lights, and very little foot-traffic. West of our street is farmland;

east is a ravine. There are large spaces between the street lights, and the cars are moving fast everywhere.

She's not on the street, and she's on no one's porch that I can make out. I go into the garage to get my bike. I could take the car, but if I see her it'll be hard to stop beside her, and if she sees me she might take off. I actually think this, at the same time thinking that of course she won't take off, that she's a solid kid with a finely developed sense of self-preservation. At the worst, at the worst, she's taken a walk to the variety store in the strip plaza three blocks away, to buy a Coffee Crisp. If she's eating a chocolate bar when I find her, I'll kill her.

The bike is a twenty-year-old racer, with toe-clips that I can't fit my bulky, 1990 sneakers into; the clips scrape the pavement rhythmically, timed to the little parents' prayer for unwanted completion. There are some questions we don't want answered. I'm nervous enough now that it overcomes my natural disinclination to causing a scene. I call my daughter's name out once, trying to make it sound bored. Then again, not quite as bored. Then one more time, not bored at all.

I hear pebbles skidding, and the word "Dad."

She's standing on the embryonic circle that will be the new crescent parkette when the street's finished, in the light of a single lightbulb slung over a hydro pole. Somehow I forgot to look there. It didn't seem like her style. Obviously my yelling embarrassed her. Either that or she wanted me to find her all along.

"Okay. You made your point. You scared everybody. Now come on back inside and we'll talk about it." She doesn't answer. "Jenny, we've been waiting to go out all week. You may have a beef, but we've got one, too. Don't pull this." This may be the wrong thing to say, but I don't care. Relief has made me too angry. "Jenny, I'll come over and carry you into the house if I have to."

This is the wrong thing to say. She just looks at me, rocking a bit back and forth. Hemmed in by my threat, I put down the bike and walk around behind her. She doesn't move. When I put my arms around her all she does is make a little noise, half-laugh, half-disbelief. I can't believe her size myself momentarily. She must have grown, what, three inches in the past year? I once dated an adult who was smaller. If I pick her up and she tries to get away, it'll be a debacle. At worst a neighbour will look out the window and yell child abuse; at best I won't be able to get her off the ground. At least not with dignity. And where's the moral high ground without dignity?

I'm standing in the middle of the road feeling like a complete jerk, "holding" my five-foot tall twelve-year-old daughter from behind. But I'm not simply holding my daughter or my own jerkiness; I'm also holding — metaphorically speaking — what might be the biggest failure of my own generation: our moral uncertainty, our skittishness around right and wrong. Our lack of ethical touch.

I have no idea what to do.

In the summer of 1976 Paramount Pictures brought out a movie called *The Bad News Bears*. On the surface *Bad News Bears* was a standard, Disney-ish kids' movie, about a dissipated ex-minor league ballplayer named Buttermaker (played by Walter Mathau), who's hired to coach a Little League team of undesirables and outcasts (including a young Tatum O'Neal). But in fact the movie created a sensation, intentionally and otherwise, primarily because of its language. It was the first Hollywood movie in which children swore. Not just swore, but swore like longshoremen, *revelled* in swearing. The innovation was so radical for its time that the film-makers felt compelled to publicly state that *Bad News Bears* wasn't a children's movie at all, but a movie for adults *about* children. The result was a ratings anomaly. In Ontario, for example, where I saw it, the *Bears* narrowly evaded a Restricted classification, and ended up rated Adult Accompaniment, which at the time barred anyone under the age of eighteen from admission to the movie unless they were accompanied by an adult. Not a lot of adults did any accompanying. I saw the movie at an old movie palace in downtown Toronto, and I can't recall seeing a single child in the audience.

In fact, to watch *Bad News Bears* today on video is to wonder what all the fuss was about. Like an old-time stag film where all the men wear black socks, the movie is still scandalous, but in a dated, close to innocent way. The innocence in this case harks from the novel idea that swearing on a movie screen, as in life, doesn't have to be totally gratuitous, that it can strive for wit, and that it can even risk being politically aware. At one point the most profane Bear, a scrappy little blonde shortstop named Tanner who looks like Dennis the Menace on speed, comments: "All we have on this team is a lot of Jews, spicks, niggers, pansies, and a booger-eatin' moron." To which the team's resident statistician and Jew, a bespectacled accountant-type (what else?) named Stein, points out that since Tanner's the only Bear who isn't a Jew, spick or nigger he better get used to it. At another point

Ahmad, a twelve-year-old who's mortified at being black and unco-ordinated, tells Matthau: "Don't bring any of your honkey bullshit into this, Buttermaker." A few minutes later, when Matthau tries to deliver a lecture about sexual precocity, Tanner yells: "Blow it out your bunghole, Buttermaker! I know an eleven-year-old girl who's already on the pill!" The lines are all awful, and the chances are slim to none that a group of eleven-year-olds would say them, but at least they have a certain moral logic, too; the Bears are engaged in a full throttle revolt against adult hypocrisy.

But in fact what was most revolutionary about *Bad News Bears* in 1976 wasn't its swearing, or even its creation of a kind of neo-quasi-swearing that involved using non-swear words in totally mean-spirited, abusive ways (Matthau told various Bears to "shut up," maybe the worst thing you can say to a child, at least thirty times during the movie.) It wasn't even unique in the moral confusion of its ending. (After losing the big game by a run but winning a bigger victory because they've finally pulled together, the Bears respond to a belated show of sportsmanship from the up-to-now arrogant winners by throwing the offered trophy back at them, calling them assholes, and vowing they'll win next year. Then Buttermaker — I'm not making this up — hands out the beers.)

No, what made *Bad News Bears* truly radical was its total dearth of adults. Sitting in the theatre watching the movie you kept waiting for a genuine grown-up to show up and, in the face of all the rotten language around, tell the kids to cease and desist — at least to display a little adult sensibility. Every time one did, though, he (or she) was notable mainly for his moral hypocrisy or dereliction of duty. The film-makers, besides wanting us to believe that this was the way kids actually spoke, also wanted to us to believe that most adults were either corrupt or absent. Given the general abandonment, what did we expect these kids to do? They weren't a squad of Dorothys in Oz, finding out the hard way, à la Salman Rushdie, that adults ultimately couldn't save them; they were an already-cynical Dirty Dozen minus three who knew they could only depend on themselves. Was it any wonder that ninety percent of the things they said or did were totally obnoxious? The film-makers didn't think they were obnoxious; they thought they were funny. It was amazing to watch.

But it was 1976. And it was only a movie.

We jump ahead now at warp-speed to the summer of 1989. I'm taking my pregnant wife and my two older kids — ten and six at this point — to another movie, an early evening movie in a suburban mall. The movie is *Parenthood,* directed by Ron Howard. This is the same Ron Howard who had started out as Opie of Mayberry (Andy Griffith's red-headed son and the apple of Aunt Bee's eye), who then played Fonzie's buddy Richie in the movie *American Graffiti* and in the TV series "Happy Days," and who had eventually directed two sweet and sentimental movies, *Splash* and *Cocoon,* which were perfect family formula movies, the kind of films you were thankful just existed once you had children of your own. Ron Howard was a parent's director; the only problem would be the popcorn line, and if Ben had to pee.

For the first ten minutes everything went as expected. There were Steve Martin and Mary Steenburgen playing parents going crazy trying to get their kids into the family wagon for an outing (*I* knew that), while they worried about their son, who was a problem because he himself worried too much (I knew that, too). And then there were Steve and Mary in the principal's office at school, worrying some more (which I knew about indirectly from my wife's viewpoint at school).

But then suddenly Steve and Mary were on their feet, embroiled in an argument over who was to blame for their son's problem that wasn't just unbelievable, it was unbelievably *rude.* Then, *wham!,* the scene switched to the home of Steve's sister (played by Dianne Wiest), whose teenaged daughter (Martha Plimpton) was having a heartfelt talk with her teenaged fiancé (Keanu Reeves). "I wouldn't live with you if the world were flooded with piss," Martha opined, "and you lived up a tree." From there the movie took us to the garage of Steve's crusty father (Jason Robards), who was showing his four-year-old grandson a beautiful cherished old roadster. "You know, the first time I got laid was in this car...," said Jason. Then it was back to Dianne Wiest's house, *pow!,* where her daughter's teenage husband — they were now married — asked his mother-in-law if she knew what a "boner" was, assured her he'd just straightened out her disturbed son by telling him it was it was all right to "slap the salami," and commented, sagely, "You know Mrs Buckman, you need a licence to buy a dog or drive a car... but they'll let any butt-reamin' asshole be a father."

Let's forget momentarily about the P.G. rating and the

semantic sloppiness ("Butt-reamin' asshole"?). By this time in the theatre what rode the air was a kind of distilled disbelief. Ron Howard, Opie, obviously not only thought what was up on the screen could pass for true parenthood, but also, that it was all right to laugh at all the little linguistic brutalities his characters were passing off as jokes. All around me people were laughing along with Ron, not just kids but adults. People I respected had recommended this movie; presumably they had laughed at it, too. I was laughing at it, too — and feeling strange all the time I did. The journey starting at *Bad News Bears* — when we were all just getting married and the intentional joke was that the children were supposed to be acting like adults — had lurched to a halt at *Parenthood* — with all of us now parents, and its unintentional joke that the world's adults all now acted like children. Something was missing in us; we were flying blind.

A couple of weeks later Paula and I went out to see another movie: *Dick Tracy* with Warren Beatty in the lead role and Madonna playing Breathless Mahoney. As an old-time-style bonus *Dick Tracy* was paired with a cartoon that played beforehand called *Rollercoaster Rabbit*. Produced by Steven Spielberg, *Rollercoaster Rabbit* started out as promisingly as *Parenthood,* with Roger Rabbit being instructed by a pair of giant matriarchal legs to take care of Baby Herman at an amusement park, and Baby Herman leading Roger blithely through a maze of near-disasters in pursuit of a red balloon. The technical high-point of the cartoon came when the rollercoaster zoomed down off the animated frame into the real-life of the film studio. Once there, Roger got chewed out by the director for his acting while Baby Herman picked up his cigar and started clumping testily off the set, followed by a solicitous real-life prop-girl. When the cartoon Baby Herman dropped his cigar, the human prop-girl stooped to pick it up. He thanked her by popping the red balloon in her face. She jumped back, and Baby Herman replied: "Whatsamatta, Toots? Don't you like a big _____?"

The ellipsis was Baby Herman's, but the missing word was crystal clear. "Don't you like a big *bang*?" is what Baby was asking the prop-girl — presumably because the writers couldn't think of a pun for "Don't you like a big fuck?" This was the tag line for a *cartoon*? I thought. What happened to "What's up, Doc?" Steven Spielberg had kids. What was he thinking? What were any of us thinking?

Kids know about censorship. They know that there are fast rules and there are leaky rules, that all rules, whether they're about the words you can use or the things you can kill, are about stretching the envelope of propriety, and that "stretching the envelope" (a phrase coined by test-pilots) is ultimately about censorship. Nature censors speed as it approaches the quickness of light; parents censor behaviour — or try to — as it approaches the realm of darkness. Confucius, a classic censor who would have refused to be called one, might have dubbed this the primacy of the appropriate. A person who would be a censor first has to decide what the parenthesis of appropriate behaviour is, whether it's a word ("butt-reamin' asshole") or a sentence spoken in the morning ("If it's time for me to get up, it's time for you to get out of here"), or refusing to rent a room to your fellow-man because he wears his hat the wrong way. Then he puts the notice of his criteria in the paper — gets it to the target public — and fines the transgressors. One thing a would-be censor doesn't do is concern himself with intent. Censors aren't judges; they shouldn't be tuned to impulse, only behaviour. Think the word, the ideal censor would say, but don't say it; dream the deed, but don't do it.

We recoil at the word censor — it sounds a bit too much like what was once Eastern Europe — but interestingly enough kids understand the job description perfectly well. You only have to spend a little time with children to realize that they have a deep-structure receptacle for the invasion of censors; their grammar is set up to understand it. But children also seem to know — they seem to *demand* — that to be a legitimate censor an adult has to have a moral "twitch," an instinctive, visceral response to a questionable act or word that's consistent and reflexive as opposed to malleable and prone to too much thought. When children talk about "fairness" (maybe the single most common word in the vocabulary of children of a certain age), this is often what they're really referring to; and when adults talk about children "testing limits" this is almost always what they're talking about. It's not simply a matter of a kid pushing the edge of the envelope to try to see the flexibility of the twitch — i.e., how far an adult will bend — it's testing to see if the twitch is even there. In fact children will use the absence or presence of the twitch as an acid test to let them know what species of adult — real or reluctant — they're dealing with.

And it's probably exactly this little reflex that we — my generation of adults — has misplaced.

My first personal experience with the waning of the twitch happened one night about a year and a half ago, when I was wrestling with Ben before he went to bed. Ben has always liked wrestling with me because of the generational comparisons: I know Bo-Bo Brazil and the Fabulous Moolah, he knows the Macho Man and the Beautiful Elizabeth. I like wrestling with Ben because it's one of the few sports he doesn't commentate. At one point on this particular night, pumped up because he'd just levelled me with a flying drop kick, he jumped on the bed, jabbed his fists waist high at me, and said, panting, "I'm gonna bust your butt!"

It was a small thing, but my automatic reaction to it was as pronounced as if it had been a lot larger. I was actually amazed; I may have even stood there with my mouth hanging open (not a good idea if you're facing a Figure-Four Grapevine or a Face Claw). "Butt" had always been a red flag kind of expression for me, along with a group of similar terms, not because of the word itself but because of how universal its use had become. Everyone was using the word "butt" lately, and it struck me that maybe not everyone should be. My son was one of them. Whether it made sense or not, coming out of my son's mouth the word "butt" seemed pristine to me with a kind of wrongness. It seemed like an aggressive, seasoned word, a word for a woman with a broken high heel selling her wedding silverware in a town in Idaho on a hot Saturday afternoon. Not for a husky moon-faced little boy who was still trying to learn how to burp.

It was only the tip of the butt iceberg. A few weeks later, during a fight with Jennifer, Ben told his sister he was going to "bite her butt." A couple of weeks after that

Jennifer, describing a female substitute teacher who had an image problem, told me that everyone in the class thought she was "butt-ugly." ("Butt-ugly" was a standard term at her school for extreme unattractiveness, she told me, with no hint that she knew she was maligning her gender, using a synonym for the slang "dog".) A month or so after that a friend of mind got a birthday card from his thirteen-year-old daughter, telling him she hoped he had a "butt-kicking good time" on his birthday. By this time it finally had dawned on me, in the proliferation of butts, that the word itself wasn't really what was bothering me; what was bugging me was a general obliviousness on the part of the kids, my kids in particular, using the word. When they said it they obviously had no clue how I would react to it; if they had they would have blushed when they said it, or run. My reaction might have been arbitrary and exaggerated and off the wall — it probably was; butt after all is only one small part of "butt-reamin' asshole" — but still, they should have known. For better or worse I circumscribed the moral solar system they inhabited at the moment, and by not knowing how that solar system would vibrate when they said what they did, they in effect had no idea what they were saying. Morally they were like people wearing leisure suits in 1990.

This isn't simple prudishness we're talking about here. I probably swear more in an average day than both my kids will in a month; I come from a generation that's always regarded profanity as a kind of unofficial birthright, that prided itself, grandiosely, on liberating language. Take the adjective "fucking," for instance. "Fucking" has become so common in cross-gender conversations for people my age that it's not unusual to hear it surfacing now in the company of strangers. But in 1969 I knew exactly what would happen if I said the word "fuck" at my parents' dinner table; I knew how much scandal or backlash it would cause. (In fact half the reason for using the word was to cause the backlash.) In order to offend my parents, I had to have an accurate sense of their sensibility, otherwise the words would have lost their intentional illicitness, which is to say their power.

Swear-words, like all moral transgressions, have to be conscious of themselves to be truly satisfying. Use "fuck" unconsciously — like a Swedish hockey player who hears it at an NHL practice and assumes it's an adjective like "lousy" — and you get to the concrete bottom of "fuck." Use it the way it's used in Spike Lee's films, as a rhythm of the real, or in a great comic split-invective like the one Julia Roberts' hooker-buddy intones in *Pretty Woman* — "Cinda-fuckin'-rella?" — and the word has truly *mysterious* power, the power of sex and helplessness, mind and body wrapped together. A swear-word conscious of itself will stay what it should be at its finest: a *deeply* dirty word, with guilty roots in the human heart. An unconscious swear-word creates a kind of moral vacuum, and leaves the swearer hanging out in limbo. This is why in a crazy way I would rather have seen Ben say "fuck" and run, than "butt" and stay.

The issue was more than language; it was moral unconsciousness. My kids were flying blind, too.

What made it extra-humbling was the fact that I'd always considered myself an ethically clear, if not exactly strict, father. Along with my wife, I had always assumed that the signals I sent out were pretty unmistakable. Our styles were diametrically opposed — mine oscillated between laid-back good-guy persuasion and crazy fits of temper, while Paula operated on a more even keel — but the intended message was supposed to be the same: there was behaviour that was acceptable and behaviour that wasn't. Kids who screamed in public places were removed from public places, and kids who wouldn't say please didn't get the first time and who wouldn't say thank-you didn't get the second. You weren't rude to people, you answered them when they asked you a question, and you didn't make arrangements to sleep at your friend's house, and then, when you got a better offer, call back and say you had strep throat. Threats were out; logical consequences were in.

And manners were paramount. As the son of a salesman I'd always had a subliminal belief in two truths: work for yourself and be polite. Good manners in the home I grew up in weren't just a prudent survival tactic, they were the beginning of civilization. One of the most well played records on the teak hi-fi in our living-room when I was eight years old was a comedy album called "The 2,001-Year-Old Man," starring Mel Brooks and Carl Reiner. In one cut Reiner, the interviewer, asked Brooks the 2,001-year-old man, about the origin of the handshake. "It originated with fear," said Brooks, in a Catskills accent. "You met a fella, you wanted to know if he had a rock or a stone in his hand, something he could stick in your eye. So the first thing you did, you gave that hand a good shake." We laughed, but my father held up a finger and said, "But you give him the benefit of the doubt that he doesn't. Otherwise you wouldn't shake at all." Those were good manners. Bad manners, on the other hand, were the first small step in dehumanizing the person you were being badly mannered towards, treating them as a little less of a human being than you yourself were. A chink, we learned, was all it took. The continuum started with a rude word, and ended with a thing called Hitler. My father knew this, and Andy of Mayberry knew this; somehow his nephew Opie failed to remember it. And so, for some reason, had we.

In the weeks after Ben said "butt" and gave me a little lesson in humility I started noticing the absence of the twitch practically everywhere I looked. Parents who had told me they were worried about what their kids were absorbing from popular culture had always struck me as alarmists — popular culture was supposed to be raw, that was what made it popular — but now, I was getting a feel for their discomfort. It wasn't just a case of witnessing what Leonard R. N. Ashley, an English professor at Brooklyn College, might have called a brand new set of the "seven dirty words." "Because the seven dirty words are in now common usage, there are different standards," the professor wrote at the time. "The new pornography is violence, often sexual violence. And the new obscenity is race. For most people, it's okay to call someone a bastard [now] but not a nigger or a kike." It wasn't just profanity I was seeing, but something blunter and more general in all kinds of "public" behaviour. I saw it on TV in the obvious places, on shows like "Married with Children," and in less obvious ones too, on re-runs of "The Cosby Show," where even the paragon Claire Huxtable could be heard telling her kids to "Shut up." I saw it in newspaper columns trying to decide if comics like Andrew Dice Clay were racist or just "raunchy," and I kept seeing it, like the obligatory cleavage in horror films, in almost every "family" movie we went to. And all the time I was seeing it, the mystery of its origins loomed larger. No matter how arbitrary the walls of propriety were in our parents' homes in 1962, the walls were solid and they were there. How had we managed to come up with such an open-concept morality?

It wasn't until I took my son to McDonald's one afternoon last spring after a judo class that an answer suggested itself. A bit after we sat down with our food a father came in with three of his kids, a boy a little younger than Ben and two small girls. The boy had his hair shorn short in front like a marine, but with a stumpy pigtail in back. His father was by contrast dumpy and not stylish at all. As soon as they sat down they started to yell at each other, the son on the edge of hysteria, the father with a big, sick, cheerful, desperate grin on his face. Apparently the boy didn't want to eat something he'd ordered, something his father had warned him he wouldn't like. The boy was incredibly abusive; rude was too polite a word. He kept calling his father a "jerk" over and over again, screaming that he wouldn't eat the food, and he was going to tell his mother on him, or kill him. The father, other than the odd time he'd flash his sick grin at an adult close to him, seemed to have no idea how much he was embarrassing himself and making everyone in the restaurant uncomfortable. "Now come on, Jason," he kept saying, "I knew this would happen, I knew this would happen when I left, I told you this would happen. I'm gonna take you out of here, Jason, we're going to go." "Don't touch me, you jerk," Jason said, "I'll kill you." The parents were probably divorced, but who could tell? This might have been a cogent family unit.

At this point my own son said: "He's scared."

I wasn't sure who he was talking about at first. But then I realized he meant the son; and of course he was right. The boy, Jason, was afraid — not of his father, but of how *helpless* his father was. It was an awful thing to watch: a kid in trouble who had no way of telling the person who could help him about it other than by making more trouble. Jason wanted his father to do what we in the restaurant were praying he would, to grab him and take him outside. He wanted someone to do a little censoring, to clothe him in morally stylish clothes and so protect him. In the absence of that protection the world must have felt as out of control and bottomless as a hurricane.

But fear isn't exclusive. Jason's father was obviously afraid too; he just had no idea what to do. There's a perverse logic in the old warning "You're looking for a smack." The father knew his son was looking for something, but he didn't know what it was or how to supply it. So the two of them were caught in a terrible status quo. Not only did the dad not know what to do to get his kid to stop, he was afraid of not knowing what to do. He was afraid of his own helplessness as much as he was afraid of his own son.

And maybe this was what all of us, parents of a certain generation, were afraid of, too. Maybe, because of our own protracted adolescence, or the sheer volume of crummy external values pelting down on our kids every day, we had no confidence left in our moral efficiency either. And because helplessness is a terrible thing to acknowledge, maybe we'd decided that we better join them if we couldn't beat them. And so we ended up doing nothing at all.

And this, I think, is where we made our big mistake.

One of the worst things you can do is try to give advice to another parent; your words always come back to haunt you. And standing in the middle of a half-built crescent in the suburbs, trying to figure out how to get my pre-teen daughter into the house in time to go to a movie, I might not seem like the obvious candidate to dispense advice to anyone. But I will give it a shot. If I had the chance to say one thing to Jason's father it would be this: Helplessness is nothing to be afraid of, it's something to be looked past. It's the camouflage hiding the one place where parents will never be helpless, no matter how much bad press it gets. Not the world of action, but the world of guilt.

The fact is all our children will eventually be big enough to do what they want to do, to break away from us, to humiliate us or beat us up or laugh in our faces. As far as forcibly affecting our kids' behaviour goes, we have the most limited time imaginable to use the tactic, whether the force originates in the body or the mind. So that if we try to regard discipline as a way of actually controlling someone's behaviour — a mistake fathers make more than mothers — then we're doomed to repeat history. Discipline never works when it tries to amend behaviour — only when it transmits prejudice. This is why *public* censorship is bound to fail, and *private* censorship can't help but work.

The critic George Steiner, talking about the anti-semitic misanthropic French novelist-genius Céline, once wrote: "The liberal case against all censorship is often cant. If . . . the arts can educate sensibility, exalt our perceptions, refine our moral discrimination, they can, by exactly the same token, deprave, cheapen, and make bestial our imaginings and mimetic impulses."

This of course is the argument against pornography, and for, by corollary, public censorship. I have a twelve-year-old daughter, and I'm as paranoid as anyone about the spectral loner lurking in the rented room with his skin-mags and his videos—but I still don't buy the argument. Depravity doesn't exist in a vacuum. I can't think, in fact, of a single piece of literature or art, a movie or a music video, that could deprave or harm someone on its own. What could ultimately harm him, though, would be the absence of a moral response attached to the obnoxious event. Of all the things I can't say with certainty about being a parent, this is the one I'm less uncertain of than anything else. Assuming the medium is parental, the message is all-important.

Will my daughter become a hooker after watching *Pretty Woman*, because the movie makes the oldest profession seem like cheerleading in hip-boots? Will my son turn into Al Bundy because he watches "Married with Children"? I don't know for sure. I hope not, because they'll both see these things and more, at friends' houses, in variety stores, in someone's basement. But what I'm pretty sure of is that not knowing how I feel about these things has a good chance of leaving them morally messed up. This is the real power of parents, for good or bad, to create, in large part, Gandhis and Hitlers. If someone tells a racist joke in your living-room and you do the equivalent of slapping him down, chances are your child will not be a racist, no matter what he hears on the street. If there's a different response, or no response, anything can happen. The joke isn't the problem, the laughter is. The bias gets noticed more than the content.

If this leads to certain contradictions, I don't think there's anything we can do about it. The trick when you're a parent is probably to be contradictory with conviction. And so it is that my son won't find *Playboys* lying on the kitchen table in our house — not because they won't be in the house, necessarily, but because I don't want him to think I think it's okay for a father to leave *Playboys* lying on the kitchen table for anyone to find. But he will find them in the house of at least one of his friends — this is an inevitable male law of nature — and that's somehow all right with me, too. It's not simply that I poured over *Playboys* in Louis Pollock's basement when I was nine and I wouldn't want to deprive him of the pleasure. It's that for some reason it's perfectly all right with me if he thinks Louis Pollock's father endorses leaving *Playboys* around for his kid to read; it's just not all right if he thinks *I* do. If this is addled, maybe so is the road to civilization.

One Friday night we were in the car on the way to dinner at my in-laws when a radio program came on the air that included a panel discussion of Canada's new abortion bill. In ten seconds everyone was talking. Ben was totally against abortion, even in cases of rape or incest, once he understood the words. He couldn't handle the killing of a baby; there was no question of anthropomorphism for him; the baby was a baby, and he would never have an abortion if he was a woman, he said. Would he want a law to force all women not to have abortions, just because he wouldn't have one? "Well I wouldn't *want* them to have one," he said. And how did he even know it was killing, Paula said. A lot of people thought ending a pregnancy before a baby had a chance to live on its own wasn't killing at all, at least not killing a person. I stuck my nose in from behind the wheel and said there was no question in my mind that abortion was killing, but that it was the kind of killing women had the right to do, because they were landlords of their bodies. "That doesn't make sense," Jennifer said, speaking for the first time. "Ben makes more sense. Either killing's right or killing's wrong. If I'm a woman and I'm against the death penalty, how can I just decide to kill my baby? Just because I'm the boss doesn't change the rules." So was she against abortion? No, she was for it, but not for that reason. What reason? She'd have to figure one out, she said.

And I knew she would. It would nag at her, bothering her the way she'd been bothered for a month at school one year when she'd been mean to a classmate, and couldn't figure out how to apologize, and then apologized, but knew it wasn't enough. It would bother her the way the fate of the world's population bothered Ben. Without my being able to claim any of the credit, the twitch was twitching.

A few weeks after the conversation in the car, I had to go to New York on board-game business. Coming back from a meeting the first evening, traffic was heavy and I had the taxi drop me at the corner of 42nd Street and

Eighth Avenue, across from the Port Authority, so I could walk back to my hotel. On the corner was a decrepit parking lot that was home to New York's usual set of contradictions: drug transactions going on in the rear of the lot, a would-be Louis Farrakhan preaching a fiery anti-white sermon closer to the street. Just as I walked past, a beefy shirtless black man standing in the lot maybe five yards from the sidewalk unzipped his fly, took out his penis, and staring at the passing crowds, urinated leisurely on the pavement in front of him. There was nothing furtive or drunken about it, and nothing political either — it was just totally brazen, an act of aggression not against the status quo, or white people *per se*, but sensitivity itself.

Men in business clothing, women pushing children in strollers, a multi-coloured world was passing by — virtually everyone saw what was happening, but no one said a word. I didn't say anything, either; the man was big and it wasn't my town. But in the space of time it took him to shake himself off and zip up again, something happened to the quality of the air on the street. Things seemed to glaze over and to lose focus. The ground itself seemed less secure, the way it must have seemed to the out-of-control little boy Jason in McDonald's. Gertrude Stein might have said there was less "here" here. I had the feeling the people around me were no longer as sure as they'd been five seconds ago exactly where they were. It was only a physical act that had occurred, but in a world where a physical act, any act, loses its ethical meaning, the subtlety starts draining out of all our moral distinctions. If we don't know what to be shocked at any more, we don't know what to appreciate either. We come to rely on the super-real, the dead hand of the photographic. Imagination dies slowly, and our spirits do as well.

I crossed the street and walked up Eighth Avenue towards my hotel, thinking it was a good thing my kids weren't there with me — and then thinking that I wished they were.

Of Professor Ashley's seven dirty words, I can only think of six. They're the six that a camper named Marvin Fell used to say in his sleep one summer when I worked as a counsellor at a camp north of the city. Marvin wasn't in my cabin, but in the cabin of a friend of mine in the same unit. A ten-year-old who loved to make announcements over the camp P.A. system, Marvin displayed no symptoms of repression or jadedness during the day; he swam, and played with his food like any other kid; he was only wild at night. My friend would collect me from the counsellors' lounge at one a.m., and take me into his cabin, where we'd sit on the edge of his cot, waiting for Marvin to turn over and swallow a couple of times and blurt out, pell-mell, his taboo masterpiece: "*Fuck-shit-cunt-tit-ass-bugger*!" Afterwards he always rolled over and went back to sleep. If he ever said the seventh word, we never heard it.

Just before this school year started, Jennifer, scouting possible musicals for a school show, rented the video of the movie version of *West Side Story*. Watching the movie in the den with her, it was almost impossible to believe that when it first reached the screen in 1961, it was as controversial as the play it was based on, not just for its subject matter but for its language. In fact from its inception there wasn't a single unvarnished swear-word, not from

Professor Ashley's or Marvin Fell's list, in *West Side Story*. What there was instead was a subset of profane euphemisms that at the time spawned a whole theatrical pseudo-curse-list. "Fuck" was "fug"; "fucking" was "fugging"; "Fuck you" became "Krup you" in the Jets' famous ode to authority, "Officer Krupke." Initials were paramount — at one point the wistful tomboy Anybody (one of the greater nicknames ever) told fellow gang-member Axle: "You bet your sweet A." And that was about as tough as it got. "Butt-reamin' asshole" was as distant as Mars.

But the thing was, the movie still *worked*, on the big screen and in our living-room, in spite of the arty rumbles and Natalie Wood's dancing. It worked at conveying the anger under the "swear" words and the integral fear of the violence behind them, the innocent power in proscribed language and the terror that in committing a single irrevocable deed you could shatter the universe. It worked precisely because the moral codes the movie launched itself against were scalpel-clear, to the audience and to every character in the story: the hypocritical code of Officer Krupke, and below it the deeper, truer code Officer Krupke couldn't touch. Whether it was fear of the censors or not, the makers of *West Side Story* somehow ended up knowing what Opie should never have forgotten. They knew what was shocking; they knew when they were being shocking, and when they weren't; they had a feel for what they were saying. The Sharks and the Jets did, too, which is why they were so cool. The movie twitched.

But today the protective arch of that moral twitch crumbles a little more with every passing minute. This is why the battle is worth waging, because the message we have to give to our children is critical: the notion that the danger is never the word or the image, the danger lies in not knowing how the particular room we're in will vibrate when we speak a certain word or cast a certain image. The danger lies not in a father taking his son's heart, but in not knowing what taking that heart signifies. Knowledge is everything. Bow to the queen or piss on 42nd Street, I want to tell my kids, the choice is yours.

But *know* the difference.

At the far end of the street, about a hundred yards from where Jennifer and I are standing, a car's headlights swing into view. It's my next-door neighbour, coming home from work.

The twitch is one thing; embarrassment is another. Seeing the car, my daughter takes the opportunity to shake loose of my arms with a kind of impatient disdain, walk across the road, go into the house and up to her room, where she closes the door immediately.

She's still there when Paula and I leave for the movies fifteen minutes later.

9

The Movies
Enemies, A Love Story

". . . Sophie's dilemma itself is too specific to be universally moving or cathartic . . ."

Pauline Kael, reviewing *Sophie's Choice* in *The New Yorker*

"Auschwitz. I think of Auschwitz."

Paula Friedman

9:15 p.m.

How can we leave like this, with our daughter cloaked in bitterness, sheathed in iron, sealed in her room? Easy. She's safe, she'll be too embarrassed to make a scene now that she's alone with Lucy, and we're going out. We have to go out. We've reached the point in the day where if we had to wait till midnight to get away from the house, we'd figure out a way to do that, too. I lock the doors, close the blinds, and slip outside into the car with my wife, both of us looking to escape in our own ways, heading, we think, for a movie and *freedom*.

But not so easy after all. The night is clear and cold, with a big moon hanging over the road. The movie multiplex we're headed for is a maximum nine-minute drive on a four-lane road. This is one advantage of the suburbs; on the frontier's edge flight is quicker. Paula takes her loafers off and puts both feet up on the dashboard.

"You think she'll be all right?" she says.

"I don't think I want to talk about her; I don't want to talk about any of them," I say.

"I don't know. I'm worried about her."

We drive. If there are any cops around I'm in trouble, but this far north the police tend to disappear from the roads at night, maybe a tribute to the suburban lack of imagination.

"How did Rosie's appointment go?" Paula says suddenly. "I can't believe I forgot."

"I thought we weren't going to talk about them."

"This doesn't count. Come on, what did he say?"

I relay the doctor's answers to her, at least the ones I can remember. This isn't too many, because I wasn't really listening at the time; I just assumed Rosie was fine, and the answers would be positive. When I finish, I think, my wife will probably tell me she's going to have to go with Rosie herself next time.

"That's all?" she says when I'm finished. "Next time I'm going to have to take her myself. How about Benny? How's he doing?"

"He's worried he's going to fall asleep in French class. Narcolepsy is on his mind."

"Great. One's got anxiety attacks, one's running away, and the other one wants to go to Oz to murder witches. Our lives are falling apart." She looks over at me. "How was your day, by the way?"

"I have to change Charlotte into a guy. How was yours?"

"Don't ask." She looks back out the window. After a while she says, "Who's Charlotte?"

The multiplex theatre we pull up in front of is part of a larger industrial-park complex that includes four or five office towers, half a dozen restaurants, and several surrounding unit strips containing lawn-furniture dealers, foam-rubber outlets and roller-blade warehouses. By day the complex has the look of a gargantuan sci-fi architectural set from the fifties blown up with Lex Luthor's "increasing ray" and stuck whole in the centre of a flat piece of rural Southern Ontario veldt. By night it looks like an alien space casino that set down for fuel in our quadrant just after the ship in *Close Encounters of the Third Kind* took off.

It's half-price night; we forgot. A huge line of people, mostly teenagers, already extends outside the door. The boys are wearing baseball caps, the girls pants and sweaters whose fullness pulls them towards the centre of the earth like adolescent earth-mothers. Everyone looks wider than they do tall.

I drop Paula off to get into line, and park the car. When I get back she's looking up at the marquee listings behind a boy in a Chicago Bulls jacket. *Pretty Woman* is playing in two of the theatres; half the line is headed there, the other half to *Predators*, with Arnold Schwarzenegger.

"We'll never get in," Paula says, talking about *Pretty Woman*. "I don't feel right about going to see it, anyway. It's like rubbing her nose in it."

"So let's see *Predators.* A good Arnie flick."

"Get real."

The other movies playing are *Enemies, A Love Story* with Ron Silver and Lena Olin, and *Don't Tell Mom the Babysitter's Dead,* with no one over eighteen I've ever heard of. I read *Enemies,* the Isaac Bashevis Singer novel the movie is based on, a long time ago. I don't remember the story that well, but I think I liked it.

"Is it depressing?" Paula says, suspicious.

"I don't think so. It's sexy. You know, in that I.B. Singer way. Like catching Jackie Mason with his clothes off."

"Yechh."

"No, I'm kidding. It's supposed to be a great story: mistaken identities, crazy coincidences, in New York. I read a review somewhere. And everyone says the acting's great."

We have no trouble at all getting a ticket; the theatre where *Enemies* is being shown is only a quarter occupied when we come in, and doesn't look like it's getting any fuller. This is a good sign, because with the sparse crowd the chances we'll have to tell anyone to be quiet are slimmer. It could be creeping old age, but every movie I go to lately seems to contain at least half a dozen couples in the audience, with the woman explaining the action on the screen to her male partner in a careful, pedantic non-whisper. Why is it always the women who are explaining, and the men who have the learning disabilities? Maybe for the same reason that it's usually my wife and not me who ends up telling the transgressors to quiet down. Men approaching their imaginations can be as paralytic as men approaching love. Either that or as cowardly.

Tonight the natives seem quiet. My wife puts her hand on my arm, and we lean back into our jackets, a couple of (can it be?) middle-aged human beings looking for oblivion. The lights come down.

When I was seventeen years old I rode the rides one afternoon on the midway at the Canadian National Exhibition with a friend of mine whose nickname was "Space." Space — his given name was Marshall — was famous for liking things that shattered the bonds of gravity and let him reach up and "touch the face of God." If bungee-jumping had been around at the time, Space would have been bobbing up and down in the air on big elastic bands every day. As it was, he had to content himself with smoking marijuana and riding rollercoasters; Space would ride anything. Aware of it, I'd made a point of telling him I wouldn't ride anything that went upside down; I had a thing about vertical equilibrium. For most of the afternoon Space behaved, dragging me on fast but upright rides like "The Wild Mouse" and "The Caterpillar." Just before we went home, though, he convinced me to try a ride called "Rocket Star." At rest the Rocket Star resembled a huge bicycle wheel lying horizontally on the ground, while someone fixed a flat; but it had that upside-down potential look to me. "You sure it doesn't go upside down?" I asked Space. "It doesn't go upside down, look at it, it's a sister ride." "It looks like it goes upside down." "It doesn't go upside down, trust me." So I climbed with him into the Rocket Star, which started to spin in centrifugal circles, slinging the basket we were in laterally off the ground, and then, of course, slowly stood on a huge axle to a perfect ninety degrees, so that not only were we going upside down in the larger circle, but also in the tighter internal gyroscopic circle of our own basket, which Space, who was laughing now like someone with dementia tremens, was spinning at about a hundred miles an hour. I lost all my change, and, pressed against the wire mesh like Isaac Newton's sacrificial pullet, most of my faith in my own gut instinct. But if someone had asked me halfway through the ride if I wanted to get off early, I also would have said no; I was hooked enough to want to see the limits of my endurance. There was still a little space left for the ride to make me feel even lousier.

Up on the screen now, *Enemies, A Love Story* is unfolding. I'm starting to remember the story a little more clearly at this point, with its crazy turns. Herman Broder (Ron Silver), a Polish Jew who escaped the Nazis but lost his family in the process, is living in postwar New York City, married to the Catholic servant girl, Yadwiga, who saved him in Poland. At the same time, Herman is carrying on an affair with a sultry fellow camp-survivor named Masha (Lena Olin, looking *extremely* sultry). The scenes between Herman, a deadpan adulterer, and Masha's mother, a Jewish mother Mrs Portnoy could have taken lessons from, are hilarious; the scenes between Herman and Masha are European-steamy (it helps that it's summer). Now into this mix comes the big twist, Herman's *first* and supposedly *dead* wife, Tamara (Anjelica Huston), who by all accounts was supposedly killed in Poland. Tamara gets in touch with Herman through an intermediary, without Yadwiga or Masha knowing, and

Herman goes to visit her at an apartment in Brooklyn. To this point the action on the screen has the feel of a sex farce directed by Brueghel. Herman decides to stay over at the apartment, using the living-room couch, but when he has trouble sleeping Tamara, looking beautiful, invites him to join her in the bedroom, albeit just to sleep. The conversation they have starts out predictably enough:

> "I want to ask you something," says Herman. "Don't be mad at me. During all those years, you never had a single man?"
> "Suppose I did?" says Tamara.
> "I'm just curious. You can be perfectly honest with me."
> "Then why are you shaking?"
> "I'm not shaking."
> "Yes. There was someone. In Russia."
> "Who was it?"
> "A man, not a woman."
> "One? Several? You told me this much. You might as well tell me everything."
> "Three."
> "Three? Three men?"
> "I just did what I assumed you were doing."
> "Well, then you're a whore."
> "Didn't I tell you?"

And then of course they fall into bed together. So far, so good. The movie and the night are still intact.

But then their love-making is over, after the classic cutaway. And the two of them, Herman and Tamara, are sitting back against the headboard, having a cigarette. And in the audience at least one middle-aged human is starting to remember this scene dimly, like the slow, inevitable raising to the vertical of a ride on the midway.

Because now Tamara is saying: "Herman, there was no one. Not three men. Not half a man . . . Over there women gave themselves to men they hardly knew. But whenever anyone tried to get close to me, I always saw . . ." — and by now Anjelica Huston is weeping and I'm hoping that maybe the director changed the line, or Anjelica did it herself — "the faces of our children before me. Oh God, oh God, oh God, Herman . . ."

She says "Herman" with a wail, but it's overkill. Paula's hand tightens on mine. The fun is over.

We're lost.

Because, of course, parents are not free to go see a movie — not most movies, maybe not any movie — the way they once did. For parents, "cultural" freedom, the licence to react to stories with anything close to objectivity, is an illusion. If stories are the exoskeleton of dreams, then parents are permanently reverie-impaired. The emotional baggage we bring to any medium that relates stories — movies, books, a fifteen second TV commercial — changes the medium and the stories forever. Because all stories either include children, or don't. If they don't, as parents we watch them with the sneaking feeling, no matter how faint, that they're not totally true. And if they are about children, the fictional world as much as the real becomes a field of landmines.

When I was in my first year of university I fell, like a tree, in love with a girl who felt lukewarm about me, a week before spring exams started. I decided to go up to a farm owned by the parents of a friend of mine to study, I thought the distance would help, but I ended up calling her long distance at least three times a day. During one call I told her that from where I was sitting I could hear cows lowing in a field and children playing in a school yard. "I don't like kids," she said. "Tell me about the cows." As of 1988 this girl had four children, wanted a fifth, and cried exclusively at Nestlé Quik commercials — in particular one commercial the chocolate milk giant was pushing that year.

If you're a parent you may know it. A little boy comes into a dim, still kitchen with his head down after playing his hockey game. His mother asks him, "Did you win?" The boy shakes his head. His mother says, "Did you play your best?"; the boy says yes; his mother says, "Well then, that's all that matters," and gives him a cup of hot Quik, while gentle music plays and the gloom becomes even more moony and womblike. The commercial was a jamboree of sentimentality; Rod McKuen could have taken notes. But for the girl who once liked cows more than kids, it worked like a charm. What the Nestlé people had a firm handle on was the difference between the public and private capacity for the maudlin in their target audience. It isn't that parents don't cringe with the rest of the world at commercials like this (parents know how manipulative this stuff is). It's that they cringe and while they do, they feel deep in the core of them something turning slowly and perversely, that giant corkscrew that operates the muscles of their hearts and their faces. Even while we're being put through a midway-sized wringer of sentiment that Space would have loved, we know that something fundamentally true is going on. We haven't changed; the soul of the story itself has. All clichés are profound the first time you hear them; becoming a parent lets you slip back into them at a time when they still owned their original sheen.

A year after the Nestlé ad hit the airwaves Michelin, the tire company, brought out a commercial that became another immediate underground classic, but for different reasons. The Michelin ad was simplicity itself: against a white background the viewer saw a baby crawling around and through a tire, while off camera we heard a man's voice, obviously its father, trying to rationalize to a woman, its mother, buying cheaper tires for her car. "After all," the male voice said, "you don't use the car much, just a little grocery shopping once in a while, going around the corner to your mother's, taking Janey for a drive . . ." — there was a pause — ". . . We'll get the Michelins."

In football terms the Michelin ad was an end-run as opposed to the fullback plunge of the Nestlé commercial — it made the issue (parental concern) bigger by skirting it; as a bonus, where in the chocolate milk ad we saw the parent, in the tire ad we were the parent. But the critical difference was in the stories: the Nestlé tale was about a mother nursing her son, who had a minor wound, back to a smile; the Michelin story was about a father and mother taking steps to protect an innocent child from possible disaster. One was about cure, the other prevention. In the parental lexicon there was no contest.

The Michelin ad appeared to be the ultimate stop along the continuum of classy manipulation — until Volvo came out with a print ad a year later that established a new standard. The Michelin spot had cast a six-month, maybe seven-month-old baby, in the title role; the Volvo ad featured an ultrasound of a baby in utero, complete with centimetre calibrations and medical shorthand; the mother was identified as "Pt: Mitchell, M., 11:09 AM, 27-July." The caption at the bottom of the ultrasound ran: "Is something inside telling you to buy a Volvo?"

The story in the Volvo ad narrowed its beam even further and zeroed in on an unfailing target: fear. And not simply fear, but the fear all parents have of that single moment that could change their lives.

One Saturday night about a month ago Paula and I couldn't get a baby-sitter, so we took the kids with us to visit some friends downtown. Another couple was over with their two-year-old boy, and when we all left together, at around ten o'clock, the second couple walked across the road to where their car was parked. We were parked on the near side, but Rosie, either thinking we were across the road, too, or wanting to see her new friend, starting running down the walk, heading across the sidewalk before anyone knew what was happening, in front of a parked car and onto the street. The street was a fairly busy one, with half the cars that turned onto it coming off a main road and travelling fast around a blind curve as they approached our friends' house. As Rosie ran off the curb, a car's headlights swung onto the curve, so that the two of them, the little bobbing figure in a red wool coat and the dim rectangle of the car, were moving like the converging vectors on the sonar screen of a submarine.

It was like a movie. I had the same feeling over the ten seconds that followed that I'd had in the delivery room when Rosie was born, not so much that it was happening to someone else, but that someone else was watching it happen behind or above me, waiting to see what I'd do. What I did was shout — scream actually — my daughter's name, and then the word "No." Then her name again, and the word "Stop." All in a voice, a timbre, that I would never have believed I was capable of producing, that came from somewhere deep and old in me, maybe from the ground under my feet. "Rosie, no. Rosie, stop." On the stop she did stop, recoiling jerkily like a marionette on a string. The car stopped too, with a squeal. Both of them had about a foot left to go before the vectors met. Paula ran down and picked up Rosie, who, ordinarily tough as nails, cried and cried, and then said she was going to "kill the car." Knocked out from the shout, I made a kind of feeble wave to the driver of the car, who looked ashen and not pleased with me. It was only in our car, driving home later, that I said it, because my wife wouldn't.

"It makes you think," I said.

"Don't say it," she said.

"One inch either way, and that was it. One second, and it would have been over."

"Don't say it," she said.

Movies — a famous director and not particularly distinguished linguist once said — are called movies because they're supposed to "move" people. The fear of the transforming moment, the terrible moment, moves us in the movies we make in our lives, and ultimately invades the ones we see on the screen. The result is the transformation of the celluloid movies, and books and TV ads, into art forms that no longer say what the man in the crane had in mind. Instead they become the raw material of the audience's paranoia.

A year or so after I was married, the movie *Porky's* was released, and quickly became one of the most financially successful films in history. It was the first in a long line of party-animal movies, filled with drunken teenagers and neanderthal feuds; the feud in *Porky's* being between the patrons of an infamous roadhouse across the "state-line" somewhere in the South, and a group of high-school boys who wanted to drink and lose their virginity there. The first time I saw the movie I thought it was idiotic but harmless; it even had a couple of decent laughs. The second time I saw it was just after my first child was born. Not only did it no longer have any laughs, but it made me nervous, and more than a little pissed off. *Porky's* wasn't about teenagers having a dumb, good time any more — at least it wasn't only about that — now it was also about teenagers who got into cars drunk. There was a piece of me that couldn't afford to have a sense of humour about good times like these any more, a place where I had to be a drag whether I wanted to or not. Now that I was a father, my mind was on *Porky's* alert. Teenagers I was starting to see as a sort of natural enemy, temporarily insane aliens who matched in unfocused passion what I had in focused spades. And *Porky's,* in one stubborn fold of my mind, was now the movie in which my daughter would not be alive.

But *Porky's* was small potatoes. *Porky's* I could still watch. When I was Porky's age myself, in high-school, you could say "*Fanny Hill*, page 17" to a group of your friends and elicit a common idiot flush. Parents are less picky about page numbers; but if they weren't you could probably amend the shorthand to "*The World According to Garp*, page 214," and hit on the same sort of communal recognition. This is the famous page of John Irving's novel which a large percentage of parents — mothers and fathers — do not get past: the page where the crazy car accident occurs on Garp's driveway, where — not necessarily in this order — Garp's wife inadvertently bites off most of the penis of her lover, one of his sons is blinded, and the other, the younger, sweeter son, Walt, is killed. ("The bodies of some wrestlers' children are stronger than others.") Described out loud the scene sounds like the last page of "Hamlet" staged by "Saturday Night Live"; when you read it it doesn't sound that way at all; it unfolds with a lyrical inevitability. Everything leading up to falling away from the scene is real; only the outcome, the single moment everyone wants back, is crazy. The accident, like all accidents, is about omission — all the things Garp and his wife could have done or not done to prevent it from happening. Coming up to the driveway his kids ask him to turn off the lights and coast down the hill, because they love the feeling; he agrees, but he could have said no. The knob on the Volvo's stickshift is missing; he could have had it replaced, but he put it off. His wife is sitting in a dark car at the bottom of the driveway with the lights off, performing fellatio on one of her college students, because she couldn't figure out a better way to tell him that their affair was over; she could have tried harder. The accident itself, which in a way is no more outlandish than the Raleigh father-son heart-transplant story, is an accumulation of "stupid" oversights, a parents' second-guessed nightmare. For all its picaresque overtones, it seems even more real than Garp's strategy earlier in the book of planning to ambush a car that's been racing dangerously fast every night through his neighbourhood (possibly driven by one of the teenagers in *Porky's*).

Garp, which appeared in 1983, was the first book or movie that "got" to me for specifically "parental" reasons — professional pride kept me going to the end as much as curiosity — but it wasn't the last. As the size of my family grew, the number of stories on my "hit list" multiplied exponentially. And as they did, I started to find out I wasn't alone. All around me parents were compiling unspoken lists of their own, stories that either took a toll for them to finish, or were abandoned halfway, or couldn't even be started. It was a game and a pastime; there were legions of us, outwardly normal people walking around with invisible Achilles' heels, trying to avoid having them pierced by the wrong kind of tale at the wrong kind of time.

A Top Ten list might run this way:

10. *The World According to Garp* — John Irving's novel, in which the hero Garp loses one son in a car accident, which also costs his second son an eye (see above).

9. *Terms of Endearment* — the movie adapted from Larry McMurtry's novel, which might as well be about a minute and a half long, the length of time it takes Shirley MacLaine to get a vapid nurse to give her dying daughter

(Debra Winger) morphine. (In reviewing the pop group Wilson-Phillips, music critic Elizabeth Wurtzel wrote, "...for a moment, if you're the sort of person who cries at weddings and at movies like *Terms of Endearment* you really will feel sorry for them," proving either that she has no children herself or she's a fool.)

8. *Something Happened* — a novel by Joseph Heller, in which a father suffocates his son to death while hugging him in relief, after the son narrowly escapes being killed in a car accident.

7. "The Story of Adam" and its imitators — TV dramas about children kidnapped by strangers and never found.

6. "Sole Custody" — a short story by Lynna Williams about a bereaved woman who decides to fly to Chicago to kidnap her ex-husband's new baby, because her ex-husband has written a story in the newspaper about his belief that his new baby is actually the reincarnation of his (and the heroine's) first daughter, who died of cancer...

5. "The Shawl" — a two-page story about a Holocaust mother who kills her baby daughter rather than have her die in the gas chamber (possibly the worst single thing I've ever read).

4. *In Cold Blood* — the movie version of Truman Capote's docu-novel, in which two escaped convicts terrorize and eventually murder an entire farm family.

3. "Everyone Is Wearing a Hat" — a short story by Janet Desaulniers, about a woman grieving for an eight-year-old "pale" son "Natty" killed by a car nine months before (the period of gestation).

2. *Let Him Have It* — a British movie based on a "real-life" miscarriage of justice in the fifties, in which a nineteen-year-old epileptic boy with the mental age of eleven is erroneously sentenced to die by hanging.

1. *Sophie's Choice.*

Of course, *Sophie's Choice.* If there is a single story, high-art or low, that personifies the agony of a parent, William Styron's novel about a Polish Catholic Holocaust survivor who's forced to choose which of her children, her son or daughter, will survive the gas chamber at Auschwitz, is it. The thing that always amazed me most about *Sophie's Choice* was the fact that William Styron, a parent, was able to write it at all. That and the fact that none of the critics who subsequently reviewed it seemed to know what the book was about. For a year after the novel was first published you could read columns and newsmagazine articles telling you that *Sophie's Choice* was about man's inhumanity to man, about Hannah Arendt, about frigidity, about the tragic flaw in the

German soul, about everything but Sophie's *choice.* About everything, that is, but a parent who has ten seconds to choose which of her two small children will live, and which will die alone.

That *Sophie's Choice* was a story set, like *Enemies, A Love Story,* in the context of the Holocaust might have been part of the reason. "The characters are not only Nazi victims but victims of their own personalities and fates," I.B. Singer wrote in the foreword to *Enemies.* "If they fit into the general picture, it is because the exception is rooted in the rule." The Holocaust itself has become a Satanic myth for parents — and not just Jewish parents — the nightmare story against which we measure all other bad dreams. When my wife wants to put a bad personal experience in perspective, she literally says to herself: "Auschwitz." If the Holocaust is the given, parents can be seen as machines invented for suffering. What William Styron did was excruciatingly simple: he tried to think of the worst thing you could do to a human being — then he went one step deeper. In terms of human pain, there is no below, below Sophie's choice.

After the movie version of *Sophie's Choice* came out, starring Meryl Streep and Kevin Kline, I had a conversation about it with my older sister, whose two sons were in their mid-teens at the time. She had read the book twice *and* seen the movie, but she still she couldn't remember, she told me, who Sophie actually chose to save that day at Auschwitz: her son or her daughter. It just wouldn't register. Thinking about what she'd said later, it occurred to me that most of the critics who reviewed the book were parents too; maybe they were practising the same kind of repression, an unintentional conspiracy of silence. It was weird enough to be true: parental de-construction. If you can pretend a story is about larger issues that hurt everybody, you can avoid thinking about the "smaller" issue that can shatter your heart.

That smaller issue is a question: "What if?" "What if," a parent asks, "it happened to me?" Or "What if I knew it was going to happen? What would I do?" Parents play the "What if?" game all the time, with hypotheses ranging from the banal to the unmentionable. "What if she comes home with someone I don't like?" What if the amnio shows the fetus has Down's Syndrome?" "What if he calls us up one day and tell us he's gay?" "What if something happens . . . ?" But there are certain stories that force us to play the "What if?" game at the most difficult level, even when we're not in the mood.

And at the core of these stories, when all the euphemisms for pain are peeled away, is wonder. We live behind our children's eyes. We wonder what they saw, and how they felt. This is why Sophie knows she's died the moment she makes her choice, even though she lives a decade longer, because she'll live forever behind the eyes of the child she didn't choose — her daughter — in the last moments of her life. "Will it hurt, Mum?" the slow-witted nineteen-year-old asks his mother in *Let Him Have It* before his hanging. "I know, I'll ask Dad. Dad'll know." In "Everyone Is Wearing a Hat," Janet Desaulniers' narrator remembers her eight-year-old, killed crossing the street, this way:

> I think of Natty, of my pale child, of his face, still smooth and credulous, as he glanced up to

> see . . . what? The silver grille of a burgundy truck? A license plate that began EXK or JXK or J8E? There wouldn't have been time for his mind to name it — only the dark roar of mystery, and him there, poised, one eye wider than the other, openmouthed and alone, a moment just shy of the blow that would end all he'd known for certain."

If these are the stories we can't abide, what about the ones we can? What about the ones we use for recreation?

The rules for parental escapism turn out to be simple: if you want the story to soothe the soul, forget about kids.

i.e., forget about the truth.

This is a law that directors of Hollywood romantic comedies and writers of detective and espionage fiction have known, it seems, forever. If you put a child into a story, the story will be about that child. This isn't simply because children are cute, like pets, it's because children carry a portable value system with them, an indestructible valence of significance when it comes to life on the planet. The camera doesn't "go" to children, in movie-maxim-parlance, just because they're photogenic, it goes to them because the people looking through the camera's eye, the audience, instinctively acknowledge that the well-being of a child is more important than practically any adult crisis imaginable. The fact that they might not want to acknowledge it is irrelevant; the prejudice is there, clouding the frame.

If you want to make up stories about romantic love where the romantic lovers are the most important people in the universe, or a mystery story where the identity of the murderer is the most important thing in the universe, leave out the kids. The level of levity is irrelevant: *Elvira Madigan* would have been just as impossible to pull off with a six-year-old running around as *Pretty Woman* would have been. Mike Hammer and Sam Spade and James Bond don't resort to midget sidekicks for a reason; if Dick Tracy and Indiana Jones do, it's because the story *is* about the sidekicks. And the sidekicks are *theirs*. This is a secondary imperative: the only way to defuse a kid in a story is to adopt it, to become a parent yourself. If V.I. (Vic) Warshawski is going to solve a murder that a fifteen-year-old runaway's father is suspected of committing, she better adopt the fifteen-year-old runaway, at least for the duration of the movie. She better get the kid safe, fast. People can watch that.

When Woody Allen became embroiled in a convoluted domestic debacle involving, among other things, the nineteen- (twenty-one?) year-old adopted daughter of his ex-lover, then went on television to say "The heart wants what it wants," fans everywhere expressed amazement that he could be so lacking in insight when it came to the place of adults and children in the world. What's interesting is that none of Woody's movies before the incident contained any similar insight either. They didn't have to, because they didn't contain any children. This was perfect for his younger, funnier films; they were romantic comedies. Who couldn't love Woody when he was discussing Spinoza with Louise Lasser in Central Park or yelling "Slide!" in bed with Diane Keaton? He was prime evidence of the fact that art doesn't imitate life, it imitates life the way people think it ought to be. Woody was the ideal escape artist — not only did we get to laugh at his stories, we got to convince ourselves he was showing us relationships between men and women as they really were. We knew deep down that half of the dark magic in that relationship — posterity — was missing, but that was okay, it was part of the deal. Besides, we assumed Woody *knew* it was missing; we assumed he knew he was a retarded adolescent, too. This was Woody Allen, who revelled in his fallibility — how could he not know?

It was only when Woody started getting more sure of himself and less funny, when he started to insist that he was an adult in his movies, that things began to fall apart. If you're going to be an adult you have to lug all the baggage of adult men and women — including children — onstage. But for some reason Woody couldn't bring children into his stories, maybe because he resented being upstaged on the one hand and because he so obviously had no clue what being a parent meant on the other. His stories about adults in love ended up being fifty percent bull's-eye and fifty percent bull. They were stories about superannuated adolescents in love. The movie he brought out while his heart wanted what it wanted, *Husbands and Wives*, was a kind of apotheosis, a grim view of marriage that dispensed with the next generation in the phrase, "Your children are grown." How could anyone tell an embittered story about the fates of middle-aged husbands and wives without acknowledging the shared creation that just might justify those fates? How could you *not* end up being bitter about the ultimate course of romantic love if you didn't consider the wild card of children? (It's hard to fuck with the kids in the house? Lock the doors. Go without. Be a man.) Philip

Roth, another late father, went through this same sort of cranky teenaged routine in his book *The Professor of Desire,* but at least by *Zuckerman Unbound* he had come to know what he didn't know. Lie all you want if you're going to leave us laughing — but if you want us to cry, or even muse, you better grow up and tell the complicated truth. You better include the family.

They'll include themselves if you don't. This is why Pat Conroy had to have Tom Wingo travel to New York in *The Prince of Tides,* far enough away from his kids that we could sympathize with him while he went through his tormented self-analysis with Lowenstein the siren shrink. (Who has time to have a nervous breakdown when his kids are around? Who likes a guy who does?) This is why the script-writers had to "kill" Ronald Coleman's baby in the classic 1942 movie melodrama *Random Harvest,* after Ronald walks out of the house one day during the blitz, gets hit by a brick, suffers total amnesia, builds a new life, and re-meets his old wife in the guise of his secretary (really, where would the kid fit?). This is why in a television series ostensibly *about* families, "thirtysomething," the children had to stay in the background, little more than ornaments to their parents' yuppie angst (How did Michael and Hope get to spend all that time on the porch, anyway?) This way Edward Albee made such a dead-on choice in his play *Who's Afraid of Virginia Woolf* for the real reason underlying George and Martha's existential angst — the fact that they couldn't have children. Thwarted parenthood is one of the few scenerios that could convince us to care so deeply about a middle-aged married couple's pain.

This may also be why European movies always seem more elusively mature than their Hollywood counterparts, and also less perfect as escapist fare. Kids are always getting in through the cracks. In the *The Icicle Thief*, an Italian take-off on the classic *Bicycle Thief*, one recurring image dominates the black-and-white old-time segments: a plump toddler, the benignly neglected baby of the family, crawling through a minefield of potential disasters. Now we see the infant navigating pieces of broken glass under a chair, now picking up a knife under someone's foot, now examining the frayed edges of an electrical cord. The movie isn't about the baby, but the baby informs everything. When his parents make love he's there, climbing out of his cradle in the next room, possibly fine, possibly courting catastrophe. This is the way life works. We reach for each other never knowing how much of the future hangs by a thread in the balance.

In a review she wrote of *Sophie's Choice* when the movie first appeared in the theatres in 1982, Pauline Kael commented: "Eventually we get to the mystery — to Sophie's choice — and discover that the incident is garish rather than illuminating, and too particular to demonstrate anything general."

If she thought Sophie's choice was too particular, what would she have made of the father in Raleigh, debating over his son's heart? What about Herman Broder's choice, up on the screen now in front of us in *Enemies, A Love Story*, between three women and life on the lam?

In the half-empty theatre the quiet has taken on suspended proportions. Whatever certainty is holding the other people in the audience, I'm only sure of one. There hasn't been a single mention since the bedroom scene of the children who didn't survive, but it's half of what the movie is about now as we watch it run its course, the whisper of parenthood bereft. Masha commits suicide because, it turns out, she can't have children, a souvenir of the war. Herman can't live with his wife, Tamara, because she alone knows what they've lost; he leaves to wander America. Ironically Tamara *can* live because of a child — she stays with Yadwiga to help her bear and raise her baby. The last scene is of the two of them bathing a curly headed blond child in a basin on the kitchen table. I.B. Singer flips a coin, and the story ends with hope. And the credits come up.

It isn't exactly escapism, though. In the car afterward Paula sits with her hand on her cheek. "We should have seen *Pretty Woman*," she says after a while. "What a sad story. Oh, what a sad story." We drive the ten minutes home and into the garage without speaking.

And then we open the front door and we see, standing at the top of the staircase in the semi-dark, where she might have been waiting for a long time, our daughter, Jennifer. She's wearing her mother's flannel nightgown with the small, leaping deer, and my Moose-head beer T-shirt over it. Something old, something new.

"Mom, Dad," she says in a clear, quiet voice, new herself. "I'm sorry."

10

A Father's Dreams

"Dad, I don't want to get married."
"How come?"
"I don't want to have to sex [sic] with a girl."
A pause.
"So get married."

a conversation with Ben Teitel, 1991

"It's a game of inches."

Casey Stengel, more than once

1:05 a.m.

We'd planned to make love, but first we had to make a different kind of love, with our daughter, in her bedroom.

I'm not even sure now what we said, or what she said when we did. After she mentioned she was sorry, Paula and I mounted the steps with a kind of ceremonial gingerliness, and escorted her, like a princess in flannel, into her room, each of us with a hand on her back. Then we sat down on her bed, with her between us, and listened. She talked about her day, school, unfair teachers, friends, skating, with a candid breeziness that was familiar, but not completely familiar. She seemed to be herself again, at the same time as it felt as though she hadn't quite come all the way back. Who knew where she'd been? Who cared, really? Her mother, for one. Paula tried to ask her more than once, sidling up on the question the way you'd round a blind corner in a car, but she would only say, "It was nothing, really." And it was nothing — nothing we were going to find out about, anyway. Despite all the talk, the conversation we were having with her was more tactile than wordy; she seemed happy to be just hanging out with us, like a cat after a hard day at the office. Over her head her mother and I kept up a running exchange of looks, but she didn't seem to mind that, either, for once. And when she said, fairly suddenly, "Mom, I need new fancy shoes. Mine are way too small," it didn't seem sudden but necessary, the only place this little *kaffee-klatsch* could go to. "Let me see what's in your cupboard," my wife said, and they got up to check it out. A kind of breeze went with them. From behind I was surprised again at how tall my daughter was; they were two good-looking women instead of one now, doing business. And then the younger of the two good-looking women lifted her arm and placed it almost without consciousness on her mother's waist, and her mother's arm came up, just as naturally, to rest on hers.

But *something* had changed: the girl holding up loafers for her mother to look at had entered the world of irretrievable actions. She had done it with just a tiny step, but one day, I knew, her stride would be larger. When I was eighteen years old my only remaining grandparent, my mother's mother, died, and I refused to go to her funeral. I had my reasons at the time, but none of them was sufficient to justify the crime. It was probably the worst single thing I ever did, worse because I would never have it back again. Grandmothers only die once. I sat on my bed at the time, listening to my parents' entreaties, feeling myself slip like a stubborn rock down a gradual incline into the pool of irrevocable things. It's the same pool that my daughter is just testing now with her toe. The little ripples she set off today have been intercepted with a minimum of damage. The bigger ones to come won't be as co-operative.

"Let me ask everybody a question," I say now. And leaning back on my elbows on the bed, I tell them the story of the Raleigh father. What, I say when I have finished, would they have done in his place?

"Who even wants to think about that?" my wife says. "Especially after that movie you took me to see."

"Was it bad? *Pretty Woman*?" Jennifer says.

"We didn't see *Pretty Woman*. We *should* have seen *Pretty Woman*."

"What did you see?"

"*Enemies, A Love Story*," I say. "It was great."

"It was depressing," says Paula. "And it was your father's choice."

"It wasn't depressing, it was thought-provoking."

"That's the movie with Lena Olin, right?" says Jennifer. "The one about the Holocaust, from that I.B. Singer book?"

We both look at her. "Yes, it is," Paula says.

"Do you think I'd like it?"

Paula looks at me. "Yes, you would. For sure you would."

"Can I go see it?"

Paula doesn't even pretend to look at me this time. "Yes, you can," she says, and brushes the hair out of her daughter's eyes again.

"What about *Pretty Woman*?"

Since when did she set people up? Since when did she get droll?

"Good-night, Jennifer," I say. I tell Paula I'll meet her in the bedroom and walk down the hall to Ben's room.

Once there I take the book off his chest and turn off his light. Other than the fact that he has the covers pulled up tightly to his neck, like an old lady in a deck chair on an ocean cruise, his sleeping pose is fairly conventional. Maybe he's losing his touch for bizarre unconsciousness, I think, something falling out, like a prenatal tooth. Maybe he's losing his hold on the world before birth, where sleeping with your arm up in the air is perfectly natural, the cosmic equivalent of hanging onto a subway strap at rush hour. Maybe he's becoming simply human. But that would mean he's growing up, and a few days ago he asked me to tell him a "Ben and Sven" story before he went to bed.

I was amazed. I hadn't told him a "Ben and Sven" story for at least three years. The whole idea originally sprang from his confusion, when he was little, over the fact that everyone else called him Ben, but I called him Sven, a name his mother said make him sound like a character in a Bergman movie. He liked having two names, but he didn't like the tension. In the one single act of domestic creativity I've ever committed, I invented Ben and Sven, two robots whose mission in life was to vie for their master's favour and get him to choose their name as his own.

The only story I could come up with when Ben asked me for one this time, though, had the kids on the street apparently ganging up secretly to plot against him, with Ben and Sven — uneasy co-existors now — threatening to blow all of them up, along with their houses, if they didn't stop. The Ben in the story dissuaded them, luckily, because it turned out the kids were actually planning a big surprise party for him. In his bedroom listening Ben wasn't really impressed by the story; it wasn't too realistic, he said. It wasn't one of his favourites. Then, maybe thinking I was crushed, he told me a story of his own. That weekend he'd been at his cousin's house, playing with his "scanner," a futuristic vacuum-cleaner that could reproduce any photograph on a computer screen. His cousin had taken a snapshot of our family, and started drawing moustaches and beards on all the faces, taking enough comic licence that Ben — he admitted — had almost started to cry. In the end they'd reached a truce: "You can do it with everyone else's face," Ben made his cousin promise, "but don't do it to my dad."

I look down at him for a few more seconds. Then I go down the hall to Rosie's room.

She's on her back in her crib, with her bunny blanket kicked off in a corner. There's not much leg-room left for her any more; soon she'll be in a bed, and the crib will be back in the loft in the garage, maybe permanently. The outline of her diaper against her pyjamas lends a deceptive heft to her. She's on the cusp between diapers and underwear. Last weekend Paula came into her room after she'd woken up from a nap and found her dressed in a different sweatsuit, on all fours on the carpet, trying to rub out a damp spot with a washcloth. She'd peed in her sleep, changed her clothes by herself, and decided, out of fear or duty, to clean up.

I pull the blanket up over her chest now, and head down the hallway towards our bedroom. The light in Jennifer's room is off, and the light in ours is on. It's a good thing, I think, because sex isn't easy with kids in the house at the best of times, let alone when they're awake. What you have to be careful with children is where you slot them temporally in your love-life. Like jazz, children are post-coital music; you talk about them afterwards, not before. Beforehand the thought of procreation can be exciting, but not the result. On our last anniversary we came back to our bedroom at night to find candles burning on our night-tables and champagne flutes all ready for the champagne — it turned out to be Jennifer's work; she wanted to help us set the mood. It was a nice gesture, but the wrong mood-setter. The last person whose sanction I need to greet the wild half of myself is my daughter.

But tonight the air is unencumbered; the interlopers are all unconscious. Through the half-open door to our bedroom I can smell a mixture of soap and my wife's perfume.

I open the door. The TV's on — Arsenio Hall interviewing Maria Shriver — and my wife, efficient as ever, is already in her nightgown, lying with her head at the foot of the bed so she can better catch Arsenio's next deathless question. She looks great. She's fast asleep.

Downstairs I close the living-room blinds, turn off the vestibule lights and turn on the porch lights. I lock the garage and side doors, and check to make sure the stove's off and the kettle's unplugged in the kitchen, then open the basement door and go halfway downstairs to make sure nothing's still running in my office. Then I go into the den and pull the easy chair within five feet of the TV — a secret, no one in my family knows I do this — and in the dark I turn on "The Tonight Show."

Thirty years ago my father did the same thing. The only difference was the chair and the host. Jay Leno is on tonight, guest-hosting for Johnny. Word is that Carson will announce his retirement in the next few months, and Leno will take over for good. A comic is going through his routine on the show now, a crazy-looking guy with hyperthyroid eyes and a habit of licking his lips like a lizard after every punchline. He looks like William F. Buckley on LSD. What if I make Charlotte into a character like that, I think, a fabulous apparition. But no, I'm doing the same thing again. I need a folksy godfather, someone who's serene, not frantic. A big, older guy who looks like a deposed Russian hockey coach, maybe, or someone's Greek uncle who used to be a hit man, the kind who commiserated with his victims before he bumped them off.

I watch the comic, trying to decide if I should see what else is on, trying at the same time to remember the last time I made love with my wife with no one around. Trying to remember the last time we made love at all. Lust is the first casualty, I think. No, not Lust, Time. Parents dream first about Time. Time to do your work, to polish your nails, to sleep in. To feel Lust you have to *have* Time. But then I'm thinking about the Raleigh father, a man not folksy or fabulous, and I'm realizing that we don't dream first of Lust or Time, but Luck.

I press the little spongy lozenge on the remote, cancelling the wild-eyed comic, and press it again. The channels flip by like filing cards. Here's a program to help you quit smoking cigarettes. Here's a hand-held blender from Switzerland. Here's a truck with large wheels crushing automobiles. Here's a child the width of a sign-post lying comatose in the dust in Africa. Here's a war. Here's George Burns and Gracie Allen. Here is mortality everywhere, I think, and the only thing that separates us from it is luck. Luck controls whether a car will hit your son and render him brain dead while his heart lives on; luck determines whether a twelve-year-old girl's mysterious angst will emerge as an apology from the angels or incipient suicide. Our dreams on the one hand are nightmares, filled with "What if something happens," and on the other hand a kind of wilfully blind "It can't." We cope with the disaster we have to imagine by making it unimaginable. We are the amazing Kreskins of fatality. Maybe this is why my father has left every family celebration I can remember early, because with so much happiness in the air he doesn't want to tempt the fates. Maybe this is why my father's son sits in his chair now, secretly convinced that he's holding the house and his family together with his crazy, bricklike stillness, half-sure that if he moves their luck will disintegrate to dust.

I move. Nothing happens. I click off the TV and go back into the kitchen, to check the stove one last time and the security bar on the sliding glass door, which I forgot about before. I go back into the hallway and stand at the bottom of the stairs, listening. The only sounds I can hear are the hum of the refrigerator, which is getting old, and the pulse of the high-efficiency furnace, which I keep telling Paula has already paid for itself three times over. This is pure father hyperbole; I'm actually not sure if it's paid for itself once. From where I'm standing I can see the doorways to all three of my children's rooms: Jennifer's closed, Rosie's half-open, Ben's open all the way, like a chance comment on the accessibility of their spirits.

A few weeks ago there was an article in the opinion section of the newspaper, written by a thirty-five-year-old Vancouver man who with his wife had decided not to have children. The couple's decision had apparently been an exhaustive, objective one, based on their preferred life-style and their feelings towards children in particular and the state of the world in general — what had amazed them both had been the antipathy they'd encountered from their community of friends who did have children. According to the husband, they'd been greeted with a brand of disbelief that bordered on hostility, a stigma he'd never felt before.

Standing at the foot of the stairs, I wonder now if the man who'd written the story hadn't mistaken something else for disapproval, something like the frustration of people who were frustrated not with him, but with their own inability to convey what they were trying to say — the frustration of people who felt totally inadequate to explain what they meant. When they said, "How could you decide that?" they may not have been directing the question to the man and his wife, but in a way at themselves. What they were asking was: "How can this be a decision?" Because the notion of a decision was such a foreign proposition to them. It wasn't that they didn't have doubts every day about what their lives were, or that they never regretted it, or never wished to be somewhere else with someone else — it was that this is where they were, in this job that bestowed no prestige on themselves in its proper acquittal, only a potential lifetime of problems for every wrong step. In the beginning was the experience; there were just no words for it.

There are no words. If I had to describe to the Vancouver man, for example, how satisfying, how soul lightening, this moment is, standing on the stairs knowing my kids are safely asleep, each in the capsule of his or her room, I couldn't do it. What could I say? Only this. That at the end of the day, I'm a fool after all. That the question was never whether or not to take the son's heart, but whether or not to take the son, knowing that doom lurked around every corner. That precariousness is probably no grounds for cancellation. That peace of mind and weekends may not be too much to pay. That it's probably all worth it.

I stand on the stairs. Soon I'll move. When I figure out what kind of guy Charlotte should be. When my wrist stops hurting from clicking the channel-changer. Soon. In six hours I have to get up and make breakfast. Soon.

I move. Luck holds.

We have made it through another day.